. . . AND SO THEY WENT OUT

. . . AND SO THEY WENT OUT

The Lives of Adam and Eve as Cultural Transformative Story

DAPHNA ARBEL, J.R.C. COUSLAND
AND DIETMAR NEUFELD

t&t clark

Published by T&T Clark International
A Continuum Imprint
The Tower Building, 11 York Road, London SE1 7NX
80 Maiden Lane, Suite 704, New York, NY 10038

www.continuumbooks.com

British Library Cataloguing-in-Publication Data
A catalogue record for this book is available from the British Library

ISBN: 978-0-567-02679-8 (Hardback)

Typeset by Pindar NZ, Auckland, New Zealand

CONTENTS

Dedicated to our parents:

Hanna and Micha

Irene and Alastair

Frieda and Isaac

CONTRIBUTORS

Daphna Arbel, Ph.D. (1997) in Religious Studies, Hebrew University of Jerusalem, is Associate Professor of Biblical and Early Jewish Literature at the University of British Columbia (Vancouver, BC, Canada). Her publications span the Hekhalot and Merkavah literature, Myth and Mysticism, and Women in Biblical Traditions including *Beholders of Divine Secrets: Mysticism and Myth in the Hekhalot and Merkavah Literature* (2003, SUNY).

J.R.C. Cousland, Ph.D. (1991) in New Testament, University of St Andrews, is Associate Professor of Christian Scriptures and Classical Religion and Mythology at the University of British Columbia (Vancouver, BC, Canada). He has written widely on the Pseudepigrapha and is the author of *The Crowds in the Gospel of Matthew* (2002, Brill), and co-editor (with James R. Hume) of *The Play of Texts and Fragments* (2009, Brill).

Dietmar Neufeld, Ph.D. (1991) in Religious Studies, McGill University, is Associate Professor of Christian Origins at the University of British Columbia (Vancouver, BC, Canada). His interests span language theory and its application to the Epistle of 1 John and the use of the social sciences in interpreting texts of the New Testament. His publications include *Reconceiving Texts as Speech Acts: An Analysis of 1 John* (1994, Brill) and *The Social Sciences and Biblical Translation* (2008, Brill/SBL).

PREFACE

This volume is the second in the UBC Studies in Religion series (the first being *Jesus in Twentieth Century Literature, Art and Movies*). This book, with its focus on the lives of Adam and Eve, is designed to present different methodological approaches to established traditions of their lives.

The authors would particularly like to express their gratitude to the UBC Hampton Foundation for their generous funding of this project. We are also grateful to the editors of Continuum who have worked with us to bring this volume to fruition.

Daphna Vita Arbel
J.R.C. Cousland
Dietmar Neufeld

ABBREVIATIONS

AB   Anchor Bible
ABD   *Anchor Bible Dictionary*
AGJU   Arbeiten zur Geschichte des antiken Judentums and des
          Urchristentums
AJA   *American Journal of Archaeology*
AJP   *American Journal of Philology*
ANRW   *Aufstieg und Niedergang der Römischen Welt: Geschichte*
          und Kultur Roms im Spiegel der neueren Forschung
          [H. Temporini, and W. Haase (eds). 1972– . Berlin.]
AQ   *Anthropological Quarterly*
BA   *Biblical Archaeologist*
BASOR   *Bulletin of the American Schools of Oriental Research*
BDAG   *A Greek-English Lexicon of the New Testament and other Early*
          Christian Literature [F.W. Danker (ed.)]
BETL   Bibliotheca ephemeridum theologicarum lovaniensium
Bib   *Biblica*
BibOr   Biblica et orientalia
BRev   *Bible Review*
BTB   *Biblical Theological Bulletin*
CBET   Contributions to Biblical Exegesis and Theology
CBQ   *Catholic Biblical Quarterly*
CJ   *Classical Journal*
CQ   *Classical Quarterly*
CRINT   Compendia rerum iudaicarum ad Novum Testamentum
GLAE   *Greek Life of Adam and Eve*
HT   *History Today*
HTR   *Harvard Theological Review*
HUCA   *Hebrew Union College Annual*
IDB   *The Interpreter's Dictionary of the Bible* [G.A. Buttrick (ed.).
          1962. 5 vols. Nashville.]

JAAR	*Journal of the American Academy of Religion*
JBL	*Journal of Biblical Literature*
JECS	*Journal of Early Christian Studies*
JFSR	*Journal of Feminist Studies in Religion*
JJS	*Journal of Jewish Studies*
JQR	*Jewish Quarterly Review*
JSJ	*Journal for the Study of Judaism in the Persian, Hellenistic, and Roman Periods*
JSJ Sup	Journal for the Study of Judaism Supplements
JSNT	*Journal for the Study of the New Testament*
JSOT	*Journal for the Study of the Old Testament*
JSOT Sup	Journal for the Study of the Old Testament: Supplement Series
JTS	*Journal of Theological Studies*
LCL	Loeb Classical Library
LIMC	*Lexicon iconographicum mythologiae classicae*
LLAE	*Latin Life of Adam and Eve*
LSJ	*A Greek-English Lexicon* [H.G. Liddell, R. Scott, and H.S. Jones (eds)]
MH	*Museum Helveticum*
NovT Sup	Novum Testamentum Supplements
NTS	*New Testament Studies*
OTP	*Old Testament Pseudepigrapha* [J.H. Charlesworth (ed.). 1983. 2 vols. New York.]
PVTG	Pseudepigrapha Veteris Testamenti Graece
RevQ	*Revue de Qumran*
SBLDS	Society of Biblical Literature Dissertation Series
SBLEJL	Society of Biblical Literature, Early Judaism and Its Literature
SNTSMS	Society for the New Testament Monograph Series
SVTP	Studia in Veteris Testamenti Pseudepigrapha
TDNT	*Theological Dictionary of the New Testament*
TPI	Trinity Press International
TSAJ	Texte und Studien zum antiken Judentum
WBC	Word Biblical Commentary
WUNT	Wissenschaftliche Untersuchungem zum Alten und Neuen Testament
ZNW	*Zeitschrift für die neutestamentliche Wissenschaft und die*

the story thus far

so they went out
clay and morning star
following the bright back
of the woman

as she walked past
the cherubim
turning their fiery swords
past the winged gate

into the unborn world
chaos fell away
before her like a cloud
and everywhere seemed light

seemed glorious
seemed very eden

Lucille Clifton (1991)

INTRODUCTION

'... and so they went out'

The poet Lucille Clifton uses the simple but pregnant phrase 'and so they went out' to describe the momentous departure of Adam and Eve from the Garden of Eden. Yet the phrase just as aptly describes the diaspora of the books of Adam and Eve — the many versions of the stories of Adam and Eve that began to circulate in the ancient world about the turn of the Common Era. They too 'went out' in a multitude of versions and languages, and include such works as the Greek *Apocalypse of Moses*, the Latin *Vita Adae et Evae*, the Armenian *Penitence of Adam*, the Georgian *Book of Adam*, and the Slavonic *Life of Adam and Eve*.

This remarkable diaspora attests both to their widespread popularity and to their perennial appeal to the world of antiquity, since they continued to be consulted and venerated at least until the time of the Renaissance. Nor let it be said that their appeal was simply confined to antiquity and the Middle Ages: Milton likely relied upon the Adam and Eve literature. And though they are less well known today, these stories continue to fascinate and, happily, the various versions of these Apocryphal books of Adam and Eve have been increasingly investigated by the scholarly world.

Not the least of the fascinations of these works are the multiple text forms, manuscripts and translations in which the 'books' occur. For much of the past century, these variant accounts have spurred on investigation of text forms and the establishment of sound stemmata. If, initially, the scholarly focus was on the Greek and Latin versions, in recent years it has been expanded to include the Armenian, Georgian, Coptic, and Slavonic versions.

Nevertheless, among scholars there has been a marked tendency to concentrate on the Greek version (*Apocalypse of Moses = Greek Life of Adam and Eve* [*GLAE*]) because it was thought to be the oldest.

Consequently, much effort was expended to secure a single stemmatic prototype of the manuscripts. This endeavor has recently borne fruit in the welcome edition of Johannes Tromp (*Life of Adam and Eve in Greek*), who has come to recognize 'that all the available manuscripts contain a number of certainly secondary readings which show that a single copy of the Greek life of Adam and Eve is at the fountainhead of the entire manuscript tradition' (2005: 71).

In his identification of three major subtypes, Tromp acknowledges that the *Life of Adam and Eve* in all its versions contains inconsistencies, curious transitions, and other literary imperfections. The *Life of Adam and Eve* was never 'accomplished' in the literary sense, not when it was first written, not in its last revision (2005: 70): it is a work in constant flux. In other words, he suggests that all the 'Lives' underwent a *process* of reshaping and transformation as they came to be appropriated and adapted by various persons and groups for their own purposes.

Accordingly, we suggest that the 'Lives' should be regarded as *transformative* stories, whose main characters — God, Satan, Eve, and Adam — were repeatedly reconfigured to reflect the changing needs and self-understandings of the societies that invoked them. In these stories, Adam and Eve have been continually re-created, re-designed, reconstructed — they have assumed new and different lives to reflect their new social contexts.

This recognition has informed the methodological approaches adopted here. We draw upon our respective areas of expertize to investigate the Adam and Eve literature, particularly the Greek life. Adapting literary feminist criticism methods of 'reading against the grain,' Daphna Arbel demonstrates the multivocality of the narratives in the *GLAE* and their diverse representations of the emblematic Eve. Dietmar Neufeld draws on a methodology adapted from the social sciences to demonstrate the strong social hierarchies underlying the Adam and Eve stories. Finally, J.R.C. Cousland uses genre theory to explore the literary forms of both the Greek and Latin 'Lives' of Adam and Eve.

These very different approaches are quite deliberate, and are designed to mesh with the multivalent character of the narratives. As these stories have rarely been approached in such a fashion, we hope that our discussions will reveal more of the central fabric of these puzzling and protean narratives.

PART ONE

Daphna Arbel

Introduction

The intriguing Apocryphal work known as the *Greek Life of Adam and Eve* (*GLAE*), written somewhere in the period 100–300 CE, includes one of the earliest and more significant narratives about Adam and Eve after the Hebrew Bible. Drawing on Genesis 2–4, among other sources, the *GLAE* elaborates on the story of Adam and Eve's transgression and their expulsion from the Garden of Eden. Accordingly, many studies of the *GLAE* have treated its depiction of the emblematic Eve first and foremost in relation to the well-known tradition of the first human sin. In the following two chapters, I seek to demonstrate that the *GLAE* reveals an interest in Eve that is not limited to the role she plays in the transgression in Eden. Rather, it contains an intriguing array of multi-faceted and at times contradictory traditions of Eve, both dominant and marginal, that echo in several of its narrative scenes in varying degrees of clarity.[1] Drawing on feminist literary criticism and its reading strategy of 'reading against the grain,' I aim to point out features that are often obscured within the *GLAE* and its traditional condemnation of Eve, and thus to identify several of these traditions. I will then consider the cultural setting in which these traditions seem to have emerged, and discuss their possible cultural ideological significance in the complete *GLAE* narrative.[2]

In approaching the *GLAE*'s Eve traditions in his manner I take into consideration imperative observations, suggested recently by several scholars, that shed light on the fluid and plural nature the *GLAE* in antiquity. For example, after discussing key concerns that seem to have motivated this narrative, John Levison has posited that the *GLAE*

3

is inspired not only by a specific theology, but also by everyday-life concerns related to human realities. As he has stated: 'this narrative is driven not only by theological concerns but equally, perhaps even more so, by the basic realities that drive human beings to the brink of their experience.'[3] Discussing the *GLAE* composition, Johannes Tromp has similarly emphasized both the everyday-life setting in which it emerged, and its fluid, hybrid interests: 'the *GLAE* is a compilation of stories and mini-stories, which may have had their original context in everyday discourse,' reflecting 'a living oral narrative tradition shared by Jews and Christians.'[4] Examining the role that oral tradition may have played in the origin and development of the *GLAE*, Tromp has further noted its tendency to escape theological classification, as well as to incorporate general issues, traditions, and convictions rather than more official subjects. In Tromp's words:

> If the Greek *Life of Adam and Eve* is understood against the background of a living and continuing tradition of storytelling, it also becomes evident that no theological finesses may be expected. Biblical exegesis, dogmatic expositions, anthropological and theological analysis are not the subjects of these brief stories. Instead of a systematic and consistent exposition, one should expect a rather diffuse compound of general and possibly some individual convictions and associations. (Tromp, 2004: 220)

These observations raise questions about the specific features that characterize a 'living and continuing tradition of storytelling,' as well as about their implications for our reading of the *GLAE*. In her work on everyday-life narratives, Galit Hasan-Rokem has articulated several methodological observations that shed light on these issues.

As she has amply elucidated, everyday-life narrative discourse, in common with folk literature, is conceptualized as collective: 'its authors and perfumers generate it through a persistent link with the community that creates this literature together with them. It is traditional, and transmitted from one generation to another. Its main and original mode of existence is oral' (Hasan-Rokem, 2000: 7). Drawing on Michel de Certeau's theoretical and methodological writings, Hasan-Rokem has further suggested that 'everyday life is a primary cultural category . . . from which follows a research strategy designed to encompass varied expressive modes . . . which constitute the fabric of everyday life as experienced and as recorded' (Hasan-Rokem, 2003: 11). Tromp's observations regarding the *GLAE* seem to emphasize similar features: 'It can safely be assumed that the traditions about Adam and Eve were primarily transmitted orally.' As he has further elucidated, every culture, or subculture, has its founding stories, known in their main outlines to members of the culture. 'In this function, a founding story may attract details added to the main outlines, representing additional truths that are sufficiently qualified for being included into one of a culture's basic stories.'[5] These details eventually form the subject of brief, self-contained tales that may not require a more specific context than that of everyday conversation.

These observations, regarding the nature of the *GLAE*, in particular, and of everyday-life narratives, in general, allow us to consider the *GLAE* as a unique source that bears a collective, non-official hallmark. Unlike more dogmatic and authorized documents, in which views were typically assessed and formulated to express a coherent message of dominant Jewish or Christian theologians, the *GLAE* was not compiled within the official establishments. Rather, it was shaped in everyday-life situations and fluid communication between living people where, characteristically, diverse theological-ideological notions are continuously expressed and renegotiated. In other words, the complete, redacted *GLAE* does not seem to be completely controlled by any specific group or ideology. Rather, its overall discourse appears to juxtapose a number of overlapping and, at times, conflicting possibilities. These include well-known traditions about a blameworthy Eve, as well as alternative traditions about a praiseworthy Eve, that may have circulated in the cultural world in which the *GLAE* emerged.

In my examination, together with several feminist critical scholars, I am also inspired by the work of the Russian philosopher and cultural theorist Mikhail Bakhtin, for whom the concept of *heteroglossia* (and its accompanying term *dialogic*) is imperative.[6] *Heteroglossia*, as used by Bakhtin, describes the dynamic interaction of a number of voices, ideologies, and positions, both traditional and subversive within the same text, by which it constructs its meaning.[7] From Bakhtin's perspective, a text does not speak in one voice. Rather, different discourses, embedded in every text, may be 'juxtaposed to one another, mutually supplement one another, contradict one another and be interrelated dialogically' and thus create a tapestry of all voices (Bakhtin,

1981: 262–63). To be clear, I do not deem Bakhtin's views 'feminist.'[8] Yet, I found Bakhtin's assertions significant, for they shed light on the co-existence of multiple dissimilar traditions, counter-traditions, socio-ideological positions, viewpoints and voices, both loud and soft, that exist simultaneously in the context of every textual discourse.[9] For this discussion of the *GLAE* and its diverse traditions of Eve, this view is particularly important.

Accordingly, in the following chapters I treat the figure of Eve as a culturally constructed and performed representation of woman, and seek to identify and bring to the service diverse traditions of Eve that seem to have been integrated into the *GLAE*'s framework. These include conventional representations of a sinful Eve, which correspond to prevalent Jewish and Christian portrayals rooted in exegetical sources from antiquity, as well as representations of a virtuous Eve, which seem to be potentially subversive, given that they challenge and invert her dominant formulaic image.[10] In addition, I consider the ideological stances, which these representations seem to reveal, as well as the multivocal nature of the complete *GLAE* narrative, which does not seem to be homogeneous but rather contains a complex discourse that integrates a number of overlapping traditions and counter-traditions of Eve.

Chapter 1

TRADITIONS OF SIN AND VIRTUE — COMPETING REPRESENTATIONS OF EVE IN THE GLAE

'. . . all those who have sinned will curse me, saying:
"Eve has not kept the commandment of God."'

(*GLAE* 10.2)

'. . . and do guard yourselves from transgressing against the good.'

(*GLAE* 30.1)

INTRODUCTION

A number of *GLAE* narrative scenes associate the figure of Eve with acts of wrongdoing.[1] In these scenes Eve is characterized as a wicked figure who transgresses God's way; as Adam's deceitful wife; and as an errant woman, attracted to the sins of the flesh. These depictions correspond to prevalent exegetical views, rooted in diverse Hellenistic-Jewish, Rabbinic-Jewish, and Christian sources from antiquity, which typically associate Eve with notions that are considered theologically and socially blameworthy — transgression, temptation, deception, and sinful sexuality. But Eve is not presented in essentially the same way throughout the *GLAE*. Instead, I contend that the *GLAE* reveals more than one conceptualization of Eve. Side by side with depictions of a sinner Eve, several narrative scenes surprisingly characterize her as an ethical and moral figure; as Adam's devoted and dutiful wife; and as a figure

7

who beholds divine visions that are typically reserved only for worthy
and righteous figures in a variety of contemporaneous Qumranic,
Pseudepigraphic, and Merkavah sources. Moreover, I further suggest
that these uncommon representations of Eve seem to be potentially
subversive in nature. They invert dominant characterizations of Eve
as an innate sinner, introduce alternative views, and associate her with
notions that are considered theologically and socially honorable and
praiseworthy.

In the following discussion, I will further examine these suggestions
in four sections. After a brief introduction of the *GLAE*'s thematic
development in section one, the second section will examine depictions
of Eve as associated with several acts of wrongdoing. The third section
will then explore parallel, prevalent, conceptualizations of Eve, found
in diverse Jewish-Hellenistic, early Jewish, and Christian exegetic works.
The fourth section will examine a cluster of *GLAE*'s depictions of Eve,
as associated with notions that are culturally considered estimable, and
further discuss them as counter-narratives that seem to resist dominant
discourses. Finally, the last section will conclude the discussion by rais-
ing questions concerning these diverse representations of Eve, their
cultural-ideological significance, and the nature of the *GLAE* complete
narrative, which seems to integrate into its framework several discourses
of Eve, both conventional and more subversive.[2]

THEMATIC DEVELOPMENT

Before I develop my examination further, it is useful to present a brief
outline of the thematic progression of the text. The *GLAE*, like other
versions of the books of Adam and Eve, draws on the Genesis account
of Adam and Eve as well as on other traditions. It expands the account
of the first couple's transgression, and develops additional traditions around their lives after the expulsion from Paradise. These are
described in several sections: introduction, the murder of Abel by Cain,
the birth of Seth (1.1–5.1); Adam's illness (5.1–6.3); Adam's account
of the transgression (7.1–8.2); Eve and Seth's failed quest for the healing oil of life (9.1–14.2); Eve's account of the transgression (14.3–30);
Adam's death and burial, Eve's visions, Eve's death and burial (31–43).

As this brief summary demonstrates, the *GLAE*, in accordance with
its tendency to draw on and juxtapose different traditions, does not

include a single consistent and unified account of the first human sin.[3] Rather, it contains two accounts of the transgression, each of which presents the figure of Eve and her acts from a different perspective: the short textual unit in *GLAE* 7–8, commonly referred to as 'Adam's account' of the transgression, and a more extended account in *GLAE* 15–30, known as 'Eve's account' of the sin.[4] As John Levison has amply contended, Adam's account has typically been thought to present Eve as the primary agent of the transgression. In contrast, several *GLAE* text-forms of Eve's account contain different views, which reflect attempts to explain Eve's specific circumstances, dilemmas, and struggles in an effort to win the empathy of the audience and exonerate her to some degree.[5] Parallel to these competing theological stances, that both denigrate and exonerate the figure of Eve, it is possible to identify additional contradictory representations of Eve in other narrative scenes. These include competing portrayals of her as both a sinful and a virtuous figure, as will be demonstrated below.

Eve and Her Sins — *GLAE*

'O wicked woman! What have you done to us? You have deprived me of the glory of God' (21.6). This accusation, presented by Adam's narrative voice, is not isolated. Rather, several acts of wrongdoing are particularly associated with Eve in the *GLAE*, including transgression of God's path, deception of Adam, and illicit sexuality. Mentions of these charges are not confined to one distinct narrative scene. Rather, they re-echo, with differing degrees of clarity, in a number of scenes throughout the *GLAE*.

Transgressor of God's Way

The weightiest sin with which Eve is repeatedly accused is her transgression of God's path. This allegation is expressed through the narrative voice of several key characters in a number of scenes. As quoted by Eve's voice, God's indictment leaves no room for doubt: 'And the Lord turned to me and said: "Since you have hearkened to the serpent, and transgressed my commandment, you shall suffer torments and intolerable pains."' (25.1).[6] Adam's narrative voice, noted above, makes clear that Eve's grave transgression of God's command not only jeopardized the relationship between humanity and the divine, but also bereft him of

God's glory: 'And to me he [Adam] said, "O wicked woman! What have you done to us? You have deprived me of the glory of God."' (21.6).[7]

Eve herself is represented as repeatedly confessing and admitting her culpability in different reports. For instance, in *GLAE* 10.2 Eve states: '. . . all those who have sinned will curse me, saying: "Eve has not kept the commandment of God."' In *GLAE* 27.2 she similarly affirms: 'For I alone have sinned.' Later, in *GLAE* 32.2, Eve is made to pronounce an extensive declaration of guilt: 'I have sinned against You [God]. I have sinned against your elect angels. I have sinned against the Cherubim. I have sinned against Your unshakable Throne. I have sinned, O Lord, I have greatly sinned, I have sinned before You and all sin has begun through my doing in the creation.' During her and Seth's quest for the healing oil, the wild beast is made to reproach Eve and explain that the lack of human rule, as well as the enmity between humans and animals, resulted directly from her offense against God's order: '. . . for (it is) from you [Eve] that the rule of the beasts has arisen. How was your mouth opened to eat of the tree concerning which God commanded you not to eat of it? On this account, our nature also has been transformed' (11.1-2).

Eve's role as God's transgressor seems to be further amplified in several scenes that associate her with the ultimate opponent of God, the Devil. While this condemning association is not explicit, it is insinuated implicitly in several striking descriptions that portray Eve, parallel to the serpent, as the Devil's vessel, agent, or even as his manifestation.[8] For instance, *GLAE* 16.4 includes a description of the Devil beseeching the serpent: 'Fear not, only be my vessel and I *will speak through your mouth* words to deceive them.'[9] In the same manner, a scene in *GLAE* 21.3 presents the Devil turning Eve into his vessel and his spokesperson, as she is made to attest: 'For when he came, *I opened my mouth and the Devil was speaking . . .*' The matching style and wording that are utilized and repeated in these parallel passages manifestly amplify the fusion between the Devil, the serpent, and Eve. Not only is the serpent conflated with the Devil, but Eve herself is also implicitly seen as comparable to God's ultimate transgressor for whom she becomes a vessel.[10]

Adam's Deceptive Wife

Eve's acts of wrongdoing include more than her transgression of God's path. Several *GLAE* scenes also highlight Eve's sinful conduct in the familial sphere. As has often been demonstrated, the Genesis account, on which the *GLAE* partly draws, does not portray Eve as tempting or deceiving Adam; she neither betrays him nor coerces him into eating the forbidden fruit.[11] In contrast, several scenes in the *GLAE* construct Eve as a deceptive wife who tricks her husband into violating God's command, using manipulative acts and seductive words. A short description in *GLAE* 21.1-5 vividly illustrates both Eve's treachery and her betrayal of Adam:

> And I cried out in that very hour, 'Adam, Adam, where are you? Rise up, come to me and I will show you a great mystery.' But when your father came, I spoke to him words of transgression which have brought us down from our great glory . . . and I began to exhort him and said, 'Come hither, my lord Adam, hearken to me and eat of the fruit of the tree of which God told us not to eat of it, and you shall be as a God.' And your father answered and said, 'I fear lest God be angry with me.' And I said to him, 'Fear not, for as soon as you have eaten you shall know good and evil.' And speedily I persuaded him, and he ate and his eyes were opened and he too knew his nakedness.

In this presentation Eve is already aware of the grave consequences of her disobedience, as she mourns the loss of the glory with which she was clothed.[12] Nonetheless, rather than obeying God's command, she keeps her oath to the serpent/Devil. Consequently, Eve conceals the truth, betrays Adam and, with her false promises of divine status and knowledge, deceives him into eating of the fruit.[13]

Eve's Sins of the Flesh

Another offense for which Eve is blamed is her attraction to the sins of the flesh. Here too it is important to note that in Genesis 3 Eve's sin is not associated with illicit sexuality or sexual temptation.[14] Yet, as Levison, among others, has observed, several details in the *GLAE* present the transgression as sexual in nature, albeit not directly.[15]

One notable example is the extensive modification of Genesis 3 in *GLAE* 19.3. This episode describes how the satanic serpent places its 'poison of wickedness' in the fruit that Eve ate, and further identifies this poison of wickedness as desire — ἐπιθυμία — which is ultimately declared as the origin of every sin:

> And when he had received the oath from me, he came and entered and placed
> upon the fruit the poison of his wickedness — which is (the sense of) desire, for
> it is the beginning of every sin — and he bent the branch on the earth and I took
> of the fruit and I ate.

This short passage not only alters the nature of the first human transgression from disobedience to lust, but also depicts Eve's role in this event in a far more complicit and condemning manner than in Genesis 3. Implicitly, Eve is not only cast as a disobedient figure, but is also associated with illicit desire and lust, as her act of eating the fruit acquires sexual connotations. According to this scene, Eve not only ingests the Devil's/serpent's poison of wickedness, but also becomes responsible for introducing unlawful desire — presented here as the beginning of every sin — into the world. The carnal aspects of Eve's sin are further insinuated in God's accusing sentence in *GLAE* 25.3:

> But you shall confess and say: 'Lord, Lord, save me, and I will turn no more to
> the sin of the flesh.' But even another time you shall so turn.

Here, Eve's transgression as well as her accountability for being intrinsically and repeatedly attracted to the 'sin of the flesh' are both assumed and condemned. Although the two statements do not overtly refer to Eve's unlawful sexuality, they nonetheless seem to eroticize her transgression by emphasizing lust, desire, and carnal sins.

EVE AND HER SINS — PREVALENT DISCOURSES

Evidently, the *GLAE* is not the only source that represents the figure of Eve in this manner. Rather, diverse Hellenistic-Jewish, Rabbinic-Jewish, and Christian exegetical traditions convey a similar ideological-theological perception, ascribing to Eve similar acts of wrongdoing. A few references from the period of c. 200 BCE to the fourth century CE will here suffice to demonstrate these prevalent representations of Eve.

Transgressor of God's Way

Ben Sira's statement, 'From a woman sin had its beginning and because of her we all die,' is often cited as the first mention of Eve's transgression.[16] *1 Timothy* 2.14 makes this accusation explicit: 'Adam was not deceived, but the woman was deceived.' In the second century, Theophilus characterizes Eve as the 'author of sin.'[17] A few years later, Tertullian presents Eve to his male and female listeners as the first 'deserter of the divine law.'[18] Similar constructions of Eve's role as the primary transgressor are found in Ambrose's *On Paradise* (c. 375 CE): 'the woman . . . instigated the crime, originated the deceit.'[19]

Traditions about an innate affinity between Eve and the ultimate transgressor, the serpent or Satan, can be discerned in several sources. For instance, rabbinical texts such as Genesis Rabbah 17.6 state: 'As soon as she [Eve] was created, Satan was created with her.' Genesis Rabbah 20.11 correlates the Hebrew name Eve (*Hawwah*) with the Aramaic snake (*Hiwiah*), and asserts: 'the snake was your [Eve's] snake and you were the snake for man.'[20] In a similar vein, Tertullian characterizes Eve as the 'Devil's gateway,' and John Chrysostom (347–407 CE) presents Eve as the Devil's vessel: 'She got involved in conversation with the serpent and through him, as through an instrument she took the Devil's deadly words.'[21]

Adam's Deceptive Wife

Focusing on Eve's wifely conduct, several sources include traditions about her betrayal, deception, and dishonesty. Rabbinic views, found for example in Genesis Rabbah 22.11, claim: 'She was given to him [Adam] as an adviser, but she played the eavesdropper like the serpent . . ..' In a similar vein, Genesis Rabbah 22.2 states: 'He [Adam] knew how he had been robbed of his tranquility; he knew what his serpent [Eve] had done to him.' Patristic interpretations convey similar patterns. For instance, in Tertullian's reading of Genesis, Eve 'persuaded' Adam to eat of the fruit. Similarly, according to Ambrose's reading of Genesis, Eve misled her husband and betrayed his trust: 'Although Adam believed that he would have his wife as a helper, he fell because of her'[22] . . . 'she should not have invited her husband to share in her sin.'[23] Likewise, in the fourth century Gregory Nazianzen declared that Eve 'beguiled her husband by pleasures' and 'proved to be an enemy rather than a helpmate.'[24]

Eve's Carnal Nature and Sins of the Flesh

A variety of Jewish Hellenistic, early Jewish, and Christian exegetic works emphasize Eve's sins of the flesh and construct her primarily as

a sexual temptress. Moreover, a number of sources link these features
with Eve's carnal nature and in turn, in accordance with the Platonic
distinction between body and soul, associate Eve with the corporal and
sensual, in contrast to Adam as associated with the mind, spirit, and
the transcendent. Arguments concerning the innate carnality of Eve
have often been evoked in these sources in order to justify her inability
to access or participate in realms that are considered divine or lofty.

For instance, Philo of Alexandria (c. 20 BCE – c. 50 CE), who was thoroughly rooted in both early Jewish and Hellenistic cultures, develops
his allegorical reading of Genesis in which he interprets Adam as the
mind and Eve as the senses. In Philo's reading, Genesis 1 depicts the
creation of a purely spiritual and incorporeal being. Genesis 2 describes
the creation of a corporeal Adam — who corresponds to mind — for
whom Eve — who corresponds to sense perception — was created. She
in turn introduced bodily pleasure, which results in sin, violation of
God's law (*Opif.* 151–52, 165–66), and ultimately death (*QG* I: 37, cf. 43,
45)."[25] Rabbinic literature does not typically project Eve's sin as sexual
in nature, as Daniel Boyarin has amply demonstrated.[26] Nonetheless,
several sources underscore the notion of lust and sinful sexuality,
and further associate them with Eve. This is evident, for example, in
Yebamoth 103b, which includes the following tradition about Eve and the
serpent: 'For R. Johanan stated: When the serpent copulated with Eve,
he infused her with lust, the lust that the Israelite who stood at Sinai
came to an end, the lust of the idolaters who did not stand at Mount
Sinai did not come to an end . . ..'[27] In its eroticizing of Eve's sin, this
tradition seems to speak about a sexual encounter between Eve and the
serpent during which the serpent not only implanted his lust in her but
also, through her, polluted her and her descendents.

Treating Eve as part of a broader theology of Creation and the Fall,
early Christian representations likewise often eroticize the primary
human transgression and link it to Eve's sexual temptation. Moreover,
diverse sources promote traditions concerning Eve's innate carnality in
order to justify her exclusion from spiritual and elevated pursuits. For
instance, in his allegorical discussion of Genesis in Homily 1 (c. 240
CE), Origen suggests that each human is both male/spirit and female/
soul. Yet, in his view, the female soul is often attracted to carnal matters and inferior pursuits. 'Defiled by the adultery of the body,' such
a soul turns to 'bodily pleasures and turn[s] back its inclinations to

the delight of the flesh and at one time yield[s] to carnal vices . . . .'[28]
Equating Eve with materiality, Ambrose evokes a similar tradition:
'The woman stands for our senses and the man for our mind, pleasure
stirs the senses, which, in turn, have their effect on the mind. Pleasure
therefore is the primary source of sin. For this reason do not wonder
at the fact that by God's judgment the serpent was first condemned,
then the woman, and finally the man.'[29] In his *Literal Commentary on
Genesis*, Augustine similarly interprets the transgression in Eden with
references to traditions about the carnality of Eve that prevent her from
accessing superior realms. In his view, Eve was 'of small intelligence,
and who perhaps still lives more in accordance with the promptings of
the inferior flesh than by the superior reason.'[30]

To summarize, this brief survey does not strive to promote a false
assumption of uniformity among idiosyncratic early Jewish and
Christian traditions of Eve. Rather, it intends to demonstrate the
prevalence of several dominant Jewish and Christian interpretations
of Genesis 2–4, which contain formulaic traditions and depictions of a
deprecated Eve.

Similarly to her representations in the *GLAE*, Eve is often associated
with three sinful notions and is characterized as a transgressor of God's
path, as Adam's deceptive wife, and as bound to the flesh and to sinful
sexuality.

Eve and Her Virtues — *GLAE*

Surprisingly, in addition to these prevalent common traditions that
the *GLAE* incorporates, it also embraces alternative perspectives and
conceptualizations of Eve. This is evident in several narrative scenes
that abandon the typical portrayal of a defamed Eve and associate her
instead with notions that are considered honorable and praiseworthy,
both theologically and socially. Moreover, such *GLAE* representations
of a valued Eve seem to be potentially subversive in nature. In contrast
to prevalent characterizations of Eve, they endorse conceptualizations
of a worthy Eve, and thereby undermine and conceptually contradict
dominant portrayals of her as an innate sinner. To be clear, these
alternative portrayals of Eve are not always made explicit, nor are
they presented in a developed fashion in direct polemical arguments.
Nonetheless, ultimately they seem to upset formulaic configurations

of a sinful Eve, disrupt the *GLAE* dominant representation of a wicked Eve, and cast her in the following contrasting roles.

Eve, Instructor of the Right Path

In contrast to repetitive depictions of Eve as a transgressor of God's way, noted above, several *GLAE* scenes remarkably underscore her commitment to God's path. Accordingly, she is characterized not only as a reliable figure but also as one who exercises her authority and teaches her children the value of submitting to God's right course. *GLAE* 14.3, for instance, presents Adam assigning the didactic role of parental teaching to Eve: 'Call all our children and the children of our children and tell them the manner of our transgression.' In a later scene, Eve is indeed made to tell the story of the sin, in order to educate her offspring and instruct them how to guard themselves from deception and consequent transgression. Moreover, Eve's message is made to contain more than details about the sin in Eden and how one is deceived into disobedience. In her address to her children, Eve seems to be represented as a wise instructor, who urges her descendants to avoid evil and faithfully proclaims the good way of God:

> Now, then, my children, I have shown you the way in which we were deceived; and do guard yourselves from transgressing against the good. (*GLAE* 30.1)

Here, Eve's words seem to claim an authority, validity, and universality that are greater than her individual voice and experience. Her message includes broad ethical and theological implications regarding the necessary commitment to God's truthful way of the good. It is also noteworthy that this message of righteousness is not isolated. Instead, as Michael Eldridge has amply noted, this *GLAE* scene presents Eve's concerns with additional moral and ethical issues. Accordingly, she warns against obeying the voice of someone other than God (17.2, 21.5), succumbing to flattery (16.2-3, 18.1), being enticed by outward appearances (17.1, 18.5), and allowing an initial fear of offending God to be overcome (16.4a, 18.2, 21.4).[31]

This depiction of Eve as a moral instructor of the true path evidently contradicts her characterization as the primary deserter of God's way. Moreover, I suggest that this representation resonates with several key features that are associated with the personified figure of Wisdom in several wisdom traditions, and thus further emphasizes the characterization of Eve as an ethical figure. While the scope of this chapter does not allow an extensive examination, the following brief examples from Proverbs and the book of Ben Sira will illustrate this observation.[32] The book of Proverbs typically presents Wisdom as a personified feminine being in three major pericopes, including 1.20-33, 8.1-36, and 9.1-6, 10–12. In one of her roles, this figure is cast as a wise teacher who publicly addresses her children with authority and teaches them about God's upright path.

Depicted as the embodiment of virtue, the feminized Wisdom educates her offspring about the credible way of righteousness, and gives distinct instructions about 'what is right,' 'noble,' and 'true.' For example, in Proverbs 8.6-8 she states, 'Hear, for I will speak noble things, and from my lips will come what is right for my mouth will utter truth; wickedness is an abomination to my lips.' In a similar vein in Proverbs 7.24-27, Wisdom calls upon her sons to avoid options and paths other than God's way, which are represented especially by the personified 'Strange Woman': 'And now, my sons, listen to me, and be attentive to the words of my mouth. Let not your heart turn aside to her ways, do not stray into her paths.'

Drawing on Proverbs, Ben Sira's writings, dated to the first quarter of the second century BCE, similarly present Wisdom as a pious and reverent personified female figure, whose way exemplifies God's path (1.1-20, 4.11-19, 6.18-37, 14.20-27, 15.1-10). Comparable to Proverbs, Ben Sira 4.11-14, for example, portrays Wisdom as a wise instructor who urges her children to cling to God and avoid other options and paths: 'Wisdom teaches her children and gives help to those who seek her . . . Whoever holds her fast inherits glory, and the Lord blesses the place she enters. Those who serve her minister to the Holy One; the Lord loves those who love her.' To be clear, I am not suggesting that Eve functions as wisdom figure in the *GLAE*. However, depictions of Eve's ethical public plea to her children and of her universal moral message seem to resonate with typical descriptions of the personified feminine Wisdom found in both Proverbs and the book of Ben Sira.

This resonance, in turn, seems to supplement the *GLAE* portrayal of Eve with associative connotations that indirectly characterize her as a wise instructor of righteousness. While this representation is not overly developed, it nonetheless conveys a notable view of a worthy, ethical

Eve. Furthermore, this depiction of Eve appears to include subversive elements. It undermines conventional and dominant depictions of Eve as an innate sinner and the transgressor of God's way, constructs a contradictory representation of her, and thus underscores Eve's standing as a virtuous instructor of God's course.

Eve, Adam's Dutiful Wife

A similar subversive tendency seems to be suggested in the manner in which the *GLAE* remarkably represents Eve as Adam's dutiful wife. In contrast to her portrayal as Adam's deceptive and dishonest spouse, several scenes cast Eve as a respectful and devoted wife who is trustworthy and loyal. As Eldridge has contended, it is as a good wife that Eve is made to address Adam as 'My Lord Adam' (9.2), to silently accept his reproach (14.3), to obey Adam's commands (14.3), as well as to offer to bear half of his sickness when he becomes ill (9.2).[33]

Cast as a devoted and loving wife, Eve is also depicted as being eager to die with Adam and be buried in the same grave (31.2, 42.5-7). Eldridge has shown that the expression of a desire to be buried with one's beloved is a *topos* found at high points in the Greek Classic texts and romances.[34] In my view, this depiction also resonates with other references to the right conduct of traditional wives found in several sources. In the Apocryphal book of Judith, for instance, the protagonist Judith is buried in the cave of her husband, Manasses (Jdt 16.23). The book of Tobit, as well, suggests that a husband and wife should be buried together (Tob. 14.12). An analogous view is found in a Talmudic rule, in *Tractate Mourning*, which quotes a statement by Rabbi Judah ha-Nasi: 'Whomsoever a person may sleep with when he is living he may be buried with when he is dead' (*Semahot* 13.8).[35] In a similar vein, Tractate Mourning states that a woman would be buried in her husband's tomb if she had male children (*Semahot* 14.5-7).[36] The *GLAE*'s presentation of Eve's anguished grievance to Adam, 'How is it that you die and I live?' (31.2), as well as her painful appeal, 'God of all virtue, do not alienate me from the body of Adam' (42.5), seems to resonate with these traditions and thus to characterize her, indirectly, as Adam's caring and devoted wife, who resembles other recognizable loyal women.

Once again, the several descriptions of Eve discussed in this section do not include any overt polemical argument. Nonetheless, these depictions do not seem value-free. Rather, their representations of

Eve as a trusted and loyal wife seem to contain a subversive tone that sequentially undermines dominant constructions of Eve as Adam's deceptive and misleading wife.

Eve and Divine Visions

Our last example is the unique depiction of Eve in *GLAE* 33.2-3. Unlike common depictions of a carnal, material Eve, this passage unexpectedly associates Eve with divine visions and with realms that are typically considered unearthly, transcendent, and typically accessible only to several worthy 'ideal figures,' as a variety of Qumranic, Pseudepigraphic, and Merkavah sources evince. The concise description of Eve's vision in *GLAE* 33.2-3 forms part of a broader account of Adam's death in *GLAE* 31–46 that describes how, after Adam's death, Eve confesses her sins and prays to God in order to intercede for her husband's soul in heaven.[37] The angel of humanity then directs her to behold the assumption of Adam's spirit (31–32.4) and Eve sees a chariot of light borne by four bright eagles descending to the place where Adam is lying (33.2-3):

> And she gazed steadfastly into heaven, and beheld a chariot of light, borne by four bright eagles, (and) it was impossible for any man born of woman to tell the glory of them or behold their face; and when they came to the place where your father Adam was, the chariot halted and the Seraphim were between the father and the chariot.[38]

Scholars have interpreted this scene in diverse manners. For instance, Michael Eldridge has suggested that the chariot that bore Adam's soul on his upward journey points to a familiar Hellenistic Greek tradition, which envisions the transportation of the soul to heaven by such means as winds, wind-gods, eagles, phoenixes, winged horses, as well as by the chariots of the sun.[39] Similarly, Anne Marie Sweet has argued that the chariot is a psychopompic device that carries Adam's soul to heaven after his death. Sweet has also treated this theme in the context of Eve's repentance, suggesting that Eve's vision of the chariot emphasizes that her penitence was indeed accepted.[40] Timo Eskola, too, has emphasized the idea of repentance, albeit in a larger communal sense, and claimed: 'here the scene is evidently cultic. It is right and proper that the sins of the righteous Jews were confessed before the throne, where the atonement was made for them.'[41] From a different perspective, I suggest that this short description of Eve's visions resonates with typical formulaic tradition of the chariot-throne vision, that is often ascribed to a variety of 'ideal figures,' such as esteemed patriarchs, seers, priests, and scribes in a variety of traditions from the late Second Temple period onwards. Moreover, by alluding to this formulaic tradition, the *GLAE* implicitly casts Eve as one of these ideal figures and associates her with their virtues.

The prophet Ezekiel's poignant vision of the chariot-throne carried by four four-faced creatures provides the core model for later traditions that came to be technically known as 'visions of the chariot-throne' (Hebrew: מרכבה, Greek: ἅρμα).[42] Although this term was not explicitly mentioned in Ezekiel's account of his vision, it was employed later, in the second century BCE, by the priest and author Yeshua Ben Sira to recount about this vision, and consequently by other writers from the late Second Temple period to late antiquity. The enigmatic vision of the chariot-throne has been the subject of broad and diverse exegetical interpretations, visionary accounts, and mystical speculations, as a variety of sources attest. Images and themes related to the chariot-throne vision are found, for example, in Qumran fragments of Enoch (4Q204); the Aramaic Testament of Levi (4Q213), and *Pseudo-Ezekiel* (4Q385); the the Watchers; the *Testament of Levi*; the Similitudes of Enoch; the Exagoge of Ezekiel the Dramatist (frag. 6, lines 8–10); the *Apocalypse of Abraham* (18.3, 12–13); the *Ladder of Jacob* (2.7-18); the Latin *Vita* of Adam and Eve (25.2-3); the *Testament of Abraham* (10:1; 11:4); the *Testament of Isaac* (6.4-5); *4 Ezra* (8.20-25); the *Testament of Job* (33.9, 52.4-7); and the late Hekhalot and Merkavah literature.[43] No doubt, these sources attest to a wide spectrum of variations in the employment of the chariot-throne vision, and evidently reflect diverse circumstances, and ideologies.[44] Yet, in their portrayals of both the chariot-throne and its recipients a variety of sources often include several shared features that are significant for our discussion of Eve.

For example, the Hebrew and Greek terms מרכבה and ἅρμα are typically employed to describe God's chariot-throne; the latter is often envisioned as both God's lofty throne in the heavenly sanctuary as well as his luminous mode of transportation that is carried by four-faced creatures, each possessing the face of a human, a lion, an ox and an eagle. Parallel depictions emphasize the glorious radiant appearance of the chariot-throne, as well as its angelic convoy; many sources employ verbs related to the acts of seeing, beholding, or gazing to describe how one perceives the chariot-throne. These visions are typically ascribed to esteemed figures, be they patriarchs, priests, scribes, prophets, seers, or members of pious communities — historical or pseudepigraphical. These figures are routinely characterized by their respective communities as worthy, exemplary, and credible 'ideal figures,' able to see, observe, and behold such overwhelming visions.[45]

GLAE 33.2-3's depiction of Eve's vision seems to resonate with several of these formulaic hallmarks of the chariot-throne vision traditions. For instance, analogous to standard terminology, *GLAE* 33.2 utilizes the term ἅρμα for God's chariot-throne. Likewise it employs the verb 'to behold,' ἰδού, to recount Eve's spectacle: 'And she [Eve] gazed steadfastly into heaven, and beheld a chariot of light, borne by four bright eagles, (and) it was impossible for any man born of woman to tell the glory of them or behold their face; and angels going before the chariot.' The description also points to the quality of light associated with the chariot-throne, and further refers to its angelic convoy and to the four eagles that carry it.[46] Although these four eagles are different from Ezekiel's four creatures with their multiple faces, the depiction seems reminiscent of this formulaic image. Like other traditions that often alter the imagery of the creatures, it also seems to modify it, depicting not only one eagle-faced creature but four such creatures that carry the chariot-throne.[47]

Evidently, this short account in *GLAE* 33–34 does not overtly present Eve as an elevated figure. Yet, her portrayal as the exclusive recipient of a typical lofty vision of the chariot-throne does not seem to be accidental. Rather, by evoking this well-known formulaic trope, the *GLAE* 33–34 appears to associate Eve implicitly with a long line of righteous male 'ideal figures' and their virtues, and thus deliberately to represent her as an esteemed individual, worthy of beholding sublime visions that are normally accessible only to worthy and chosen figures. Moreover, by associating Eve with experiences and realms that are considered unearthly, transcendent, and lofty, this terse *GLAE* account may convey an ideological position. Indirectly it disrupts dominant interpretations, mentioned earlier, that associate Eve exclusively with materiality, carnality, and illicit sexuality and make a subtle case for a privileged worthy Eve, a figure of superior status, prophetic abilities, and elevated spiritual standing.

CONCLUSION — THE *GLAE* AND EVE TRADITIONS

Several *GLAE* scenes, paralleling prevalent Jewish and Christian interpretations of Genesis, present Eve as an errant figure who transgresses
God's way, as Adam's deceiving wife, and as one drawn to materiality
and the sins of the flesh. At the same time, other *GLAE* scenes include
a cluster of alternative conceptualizations, characterizing Eve as an
instructor of the right path, as Adam's dutiful wife, and as a figure who
is privy to superior transcendent visions of God and his chariot-throne. I
have suggested that these latter representations do not seem value-free.
Rather, through constructing an esteemed figure of Eve, they seem to
subvert more prevalent depictions of a sinful Eve found in the *GLAE*
and in parallel cultural discourses. One can disregard the significance
of any single one of these representations. But that they are cumulative does not seem accidental. Collectively, they appear to represent
traditions and conceptualizations that assert an ideological stance
concerning the high status of Eve, in the context of other dominant
ideological-theological views.

But how can the presence of these contradictory constructions of Eve
within the framework of the complete *GLAE* narrative be explained?
Levison and Tromp, among other scholars, have demonstrated that
the *GLAE* has not come to us as a single literary tradition.[48] Instead, it
is built up from separate blocks of material that were later integrated
into the *GLAE* narrative in an attempt to create a coherent whole.
Accordingly, it is possible that diverse traditions of Eve emerged separately in the context of independent tradition and sources. But this
suggestion cannot detract from the fact that, in its final redacted form,
the *GLAE* represents a complete narrative that does not amount to the
sum of the points made in the separate accounts. As Tromp has rightly
cautioned, the *GLAE* is a purposely composed text, which desires and
deserves to be comprehended as a unity.

> Therefore the interpretation of the *Greek Life of Adam and Eve*, even if an under-
> standing of the way in which it originated and developed is useful, should
> still begin from the fact that this is writing with a beginning and an ending, a
> structure, an intention, and a meaning as a whole . . ..[49]

It thus seems significant that the complete, redacted *GLAE* narrative
juxtaposes contradictory representations of Eve. This integration, in

my view, can be elucidated by the nature of the *GLAE*. As Tromp also has noted, the *GLAE* represents a living oral and written storytelling tradition shared by Jews and Christians:

> Storytelling is flexible, variable, but not random or indifferent with regard to content. It is variable because of its being situated in real life, being performed as part of communication between living people, and it is conservative for the same reasons. There appears to be a widespread network of closely interlocking traditions in which contents that could be used for interpreting the facts of life were created, transmitted, lost, but above all preserved.[50]

In light of these observations, it seems necessary to suggest that, akin to a folk-narrative, the redacted *GLAE* bears a collective, non-official hallmark. Unlike more dogmatic and authorized documents, in which views typically were assessed and formulated to express a coherent message of dominant Jewish or Christian theologians, the *GLAE* was not compiled within the official establishments. Rather, it was shaped in everyday-life situations and fluid communication between living people, both men and woman, where, characteristically, competing stories, diverse theological, ideological, and social notions are continuously expressed and renegotiated.[51] In turn, the *GLAE* seems to reveal the rich inherent multivocality of the 'Eve traditions' that circulated in the world of antiquity, adding additional everyday voices to the conventionally acknowledged theological view, and thus replacing assumptions about a static, homogenous discourse of Eve.

In other words, the complete, redacted *GLAE* does not seem to be controlled by any specific group or ideology. Rather, its overall discourse appears to juxtapose a number of overlapping and, at times, conflicting sociological, ideological, and theological positions. These include both dominant and more subversive traditions about a blameworthy and a praiseworthy Eve, which may have circulated in the cultural world in which the *GLAE* emerged, and in turn were integrated into its framework. Mikhail Bakhtin has contended that, at any moment, texts are multi-vocal. They convey opposing stances, plural value systems, and diverse ideological positions, all coexisting side by side.[52] This *heteroglossia* breaks down official dogmatic views, exposes alternative discourses, and reflects competing voices. The complete, multi-layered *GLAE* seems to do just that. It appears to reflect the coexistence of multiple

Eve traditions, to mark the fluidity of plural conceptualizations of her, and juxtapose narratives and counter-narratives about Eve's sins and virtues.

Chapter 2

EVE, FUNERARY PRACTICES,
AND ADAM'S DEATH

But when I die, anoint me,

and let no man touch me

till the angel shall says something concerning me

(*GLAE* 31.3)

O Eve, What have you done to us?

You have brought great wrath upon us

which is death which will rule over our entire race

(*GLAE* 14.2)

INTRODUCTION

The culpability of Eve for Adam's death is explicitly stated through Adam's narrative voice in *GLAE* 14.2, and this charge is far from isolated. Rather, several of *GLAE*'s narrative units convey a similar view regarding Eve's accountability for Adam's death, and for introducing death into the world. Moreover, analogous condemnations are found often in a variety of Jewish and Christian exegetical sources. In light of such indictments of Eve and her exclusive culpability for inflicting death on Adam and all humanity, it is somewhat surprising that the short account of Adam's death in *GLAE* 31–42 does not indict Eve with a similar charge. Moreover, a nuanced reading reveals that this passage tells about Eve's beneficial and valuable involvement in Adam's death, as she cares for his body, mourns his decease, pleads for his soul, and

25

witnesses his final ascent to heaven. This chapter treats this exceptional portrayal of Eve and its salience. In particular, it seeks to consider the manner in which the figure of Eve is constructed in *GLAE* 31–42, and how this representation functions in the context of the complete *GLAE* narrative.

Adapting feminist critical methodologies of 'reading against the grain,' I seek to direct attention to gaps in the *GLAE* dominant ideological coherence, and to consider subtle themes that it may contain. Accordingly, I first attempt to bring to the surface implicit themes and traditions that seem to be embedded in this short account, and to show how the account associates Eve with several death-related beliefs and practices directed to care for Adam's body and soul. I then consider the extent to which these literary depictions of Eve resonate with a set of valued funerary practices and norms, primarily associated with women's realms of responsibility, that were well established in the multicultural Greco-Roman world of the *GLAE*'s narrators and audience. Finally, I suggest that by associating Eve with these funerary practices and the cultural values attached to them, the account in *GLAE* 31–42 subtly conveys views about the positive role of Eve in Adam's death. These views counter other stances in the *GLAE* about Eve's liability, and thus reveal, once again, the multivocal nature of this narrative and its multiplicity of perspectives and ideological conceptualization of the emblematic Eve.

EVE AND FUNERARY PRACTICES: *GLAE* 31–42

The complex account of Adam's death and burial found in *GLAE* 31–42 is riddled with confusing and conflicting details. Johannes Tromp's studies help to elucidate the literary process that led to these inconsistencies.[1] As Tromp has convincingly shown, the existing *GLAE* 31–42 is combined from two separate original stories. The first story, presently included in *GLAE* 31–37, describes Adam's heavenly afterlife and his assumption into the heavenly Paradise. The second story, now found in *GLAE* 38–42, describes the burial of Adam's body near the earthly paradise, and the promise of his eschatological resurrection. As Tromp has concluded, both stories introduce related subject matter, but were clumsily unified into one narrative, probably in an earlier 'authentic' form of the *GLAE*. The authors of the *GLAE* probably adapted various views of the afterlife and put them together in a story, 'not bothered by literary aspirations, and logical consistency.'[2] Instead, their main objective was to emphasize the central concerns of everyday life, such as the unavoidable reality of illness, the necessity of death, as well as the prospect of life after death.

I suggest that, alongside these concerns, the account of Adam's death and burial also associates Eve with specific funerary customs and norms that were prevalent in the cultural world of the *GLAE*'s authors and audience. In their discussion of the *GLAE*, Marinus de Jonge and Johannes Tromp have doubted that the *GLAE* references to funerary norms reflect actual norms and rites that were practiced in reality, for the reason that 'only when Eve has been buried as well, the archangel Michael instructs Seth to bury every man and woman who died "in the same way"' (43.2).[3] It is plausible, however, that even what appears to be a prescriptive account of the ceremony may have been shaped by the rhetorical purposes of the specific text in which it is embedded. Thus there is no apparent reason to prioritize this narrative voice attributed here to the angel Michael as the only authentic representation of the *GLAE*'s norms. Rather, it is likely that the present account of Adam's death includes implicit and explicit echoes of a wide array of beliefs and practices concerning death, mourning, and burial that are all equally relevant. To be clear, I do not assume direct referential relationships between literary descriptions and the realities in which they were formed. Yet, it seems that the meanings associated with several literary descriptions of Eve in the account of Adam's death can be elucidated in light of funerary practices and norms which were well known in the cultural context of the *GLAE*.

GLAE 31–37 opens with a picture of the dying Adam. Awaiting his inevitable demise, Adam plans his end by issuing a variety of instructions regarding distinct procedures that he expects Eve to undertake during and after his death:

> But when I die, anoint me and let no man touch me till the angel shall says something concerning me . . . Now, arise, and pray to God until I give up my soul, which he gave me, into His hands. For we know not how we are to meet our Maker, whether He will be angry with us, or will turn to show mercy on us. And Eve rose up and went outside and fell on the ground and said: 'I have sinned, O God I have sinned, O Father of All . . . .' (31.3–32.1)[4]

Although this abbreviated description does not present a detailed and elaborate picture of funerary practices, it nonetheless contains significant references to several key customs. First, Eve is appointed to anoint Adam's body after his death. Second, she is required to guard Adam's body and prevent people from touching it, possibly until his soul reaches heaven. Third, Eve is asked to pray to God for Adam's sake when his soul departs from his body and faces God's judgment.

This description evidently associates Eve's prayer with her atonement for her sins. Yet, it also associates her prayers with Adam's destiny after death, and with Eve's ability to intercede on Adam's behalf in heaven when he faces God's unknown anger or mercy. This presentation, evidently, draws on a specific idea of the afterlife. In contrast to the view of the dead, frequently found in the Hebrew Bible, which shows them in *Sheol*, barely existing and never to return, here Adam's soul is assumed to have some kind of existence after death and is expected to face God's judgment, a view that accords with beliefs about the resurrection of the body and immortality of the soul that were prevalent in the Graeco-Roman world of the early centuries CE.[5] In this context, Eve seems to be called to pray to God for Adam's sake, possibly in order to exculpate him and prevent him from facing God's harsh sentence.

The next episode draws an interesting link between Eve's repentance and prayer and her ability to see visions. It depicts the angel of humanity who immediately directs Eve to witness the ascent of Adam's soul to heaven:

> Rise up, Eve, from your penitence, for behold, Adam your husband has gone out of his body. Rise up and behold his spirit borne aloft to meet his Maker. (32.4)

Eve then beholds a vision of a chariot of light descending to the place where Adam was lying: 'And she gazed steadfastly into heaven, and beheld a chariot of light . . .' (33.2).

The second account of Adam's death, *GLAE* 38–42, provides additional details about his obsequies. Following God's promise of resurrection (39.1-3), the angels Michael, Gabriel, and Uriel prepare Adam's body for his burial, cover his body with these shrouds, and pour sweet-smelling oils upon him (40.1–40.2). The next episode presents a brief picture of Eve, who mourns Adam and weeps at his death: 'But while she was living, she wept bitterly about Adam's falling asleep for she knew not where Adam was laid . . .' (42.3). It is important to note that the reason given here, 'for she knew not where Adam was laid,' is not a common feature in all *GLAE* text versions. Instead, as John Levison has noted, several text versions link Eve's bitter weeping to her feelings of pain, sorrow, and grief. For example, the text form identified as NIK describes the first woman who does 'not know in great grief, and was weeping much about his [Adam's] death.'[6]

Moreover, this tradition further intensifies the emotional aspects of Eve's grief by providing a vivid description of her tears, soaked face, and swollen eyes: 'Eve cast her hand upon her face, and wiped it off, for it was soaked from many tears. And her eyes were puffed up' (31.1).[7] The reasons that motivate the disparate depictions are not altogether clear. However, as I will demonstrate later on, it seems plausible to suggest that the 'rational' justifications of Eve's weeping in several *GLAE* versions — because she does not know where Adam was buried — may reflect concerns over women's mourning and weeping, which were frequently considered excessive, overly emotional, and unwarranted. By minimizing the dramatic emotional picture of Eve's grief, and by providing a logical reason for her weeping, certain versions of the *GLAE* may have aimed to characterize Eve as behaving in a more controlled manner, and thereby evoking a high level of empathy of or approval of Eve and her demeanor. Next, Eve prays to God and pleads to be buried in the same grave with Adam when she dies:

> And Eve prayed while weeping that she might be buried in the place where her husband Adam was. And after she had finished her prayer, she said: 'Lord, Master, God of all virtue, do not alienate me from the body of Adam, from whose members you made me.' (42.4–42.5)

It is notable that the references to funerary practices embedded in the accounts of Adam's death are brief and laconic. They are not presented in an organized, orderly fashion, as though they were standard practices of a particular ritual. Nor do they seem to bear marks of a distinct Jewish or Christian theological tradition. Rather, the accounts of death-related notions and practices appear terse, inconsistent, and transitory. Nonetheless, all of these references consistently present Eve as a key performer of funerary practices, and further emphasize her

grieving voice, expressive mourning, and the celestial vision it seems
to have invoked. These roles that Eve is cast to play in Adam's death
are evidently not recorded in the biblical story of Genesis 2–4 on which
the *GLAE* draws.[8] Nor do they accord with the widespread Jewish and
Christian exegetical interpretations, which frequently highlight Eve's
sin and the death it brought upon humanity and Adam.[9]

Moreover, as noted above, diverse statements included in other
GLAE text forms convey contrasting traditions regarding Eve's liability
for Adam's death. For instance, Adam's story of the fall unequivocally
condemns Eve for inflicting death on Adam and all humanity: 'When
God made us, me and your mother, through whom also I die . . .' (7.1).
Adam's allegation in *GLAE* 14.2 likewise underscores this view: 'O Eve,
What have you done to us? You have brought great wrath upon us which
is death which will rule over our entire race.' Furthermore, this claim
that charges Eve with death's gaining mastery over the entire human
race is also associated with a parallel indictment making her responsible for the estrangement of Adam, Eve herself, and all humanity
from the glory of God. This indictment is found in several references,
such as Eve's statement in *GLAE* 21.2: 'But when your father came,
I spoke to him illicit words, which caused us to descend (κατήγαγον)
from enormous glory.' As Levison has elucidated, 'the verb κατάγειν
was adopted in antiquity to express various descents . . . the verb was
most typically associated, however, with a descent to death, the grave,
and *Sheol*.'[10] Accordingly, this passage also makes clear that Eve's illicit
words caused her and Adam to exchange the enormous glory of God
for death, and descend from immortality in Paradise to the place
of death.

Evidently, the brief depiction of Eve in the account of Adam's death
in *GLAE* 31–42 represents a notable departure from these traditions.
Not only does it ignore Eve's liability for inflicting death on Adam and
all humanity, but it also portrays her as playing valuable roles in Adam's
death, both in the earthly and the more transcendent realms. Here, in
this short depiction, Eve anoints Adam's dead body, prevents people
from touching it, and weeps and laments his death. Eve also prays for
Adam's soul as he stands before God, and witnesses his spirit's ascent
to the celestial sphere.

WOMEN AND FUNERARY PRACTICES AND NORMS — CULTURAL CONTEXT

This juxtaposition of two differing views regarding Eve's role in Adam's death is puzzling. How does a favorable representation of a mourning, compassionate Eve function in the framework of a composition that is preoccupied with her liability of introducing death? What kind of meanings and connotations does this representation convey? The significance of this literary presentation of Eve, I suggest, can be considered in light of cultural perceptions and norms embedded in the world of antiquity from which the *GLAE* emerged. More specifically, I propose to understand the succinct depiction of Eve in *GLAE* 31–42 within the specific cultural systems that seem to afford its meaning and sense. In the following discussion, therefore, I will explore prominent cultural conventions about women's roles in funerary practices, and consider the degree to which they shed light on the *GLAE*'s representation of Eve as a practitioner of death-related practices, and who comforts and assists Adam, rather than causes his demise.

Before exploring this suggestion, however, it is necessary to clarify the relationship between literary descriptions and the cultural realities to which they are related. It has been widely recognized that rhetorical strategies and literary conventions often affect the shaping of literary narrations. Thus, in general, a direct relationship between literary descriptions and the realities to which they refer cannot be assumed. The combined *GLAE* account of Adam's death, too, may have been shaped by literary conventions or by other rhetorical purposes. Nonetheless, the distinct nature of this account, which reflects interest, knowledge and concern with an array of cultural and everyday-life issues, allows for the possibility that its descriptions convey contextualized meanings, rooted in the cultural world from which it emerged, including the cultural perceptions and realities of women.

As we have already noted, both Levison and Tromp have convincingly inferred that the *GLAE* has a preoccupation with everyday life and culture. For instance, Levison has discerned that beneath the *GLAE*'s concern with theological themes there is a fundamental interest in the inevitability of pain and disease, that is reflected in each of *GLAE*'s narrative segment: 'The narrative is driven not only by theological concerns but equally, perhaps even more so, by the basic realities that drive human beings to the brink of their experience.'[11] Reflecting on the nature of the separate accounts from which the *GLAE* was shaped, Tromp has further contended: 'no theological finesse may be expected. Biblical exegesis, dogmatic expositions, anthropological and theological analysis are not the subjects of these brief stories.'[12] Instead, these stories may have originated in everyday discourse, as part of communication between living people, and can be seen as 'a culture's founding stories . . . which parents (perhaps mothers and grandmothers in particular) tell their children,' that convey their beliefs, truths, concerns, and traditions.[13] Both Levison's and Tromp's insights reinforce the possibility that, as part of a living storytelling tradition, the *GLAE* account of Adam's death incorporates cultural notions into its literary framework, and thus the meaning of its particular representations can be considered in light of contemporaneous everyday-life practices, norms, and conventions.

Attempting to substantiate such a possibility, the following discussion will situate the cluster of literary descriptions that associate Eve with funerary customs and norms within a broader context of everyday life. It will show that Eve's roles in the account of Adam's death resonate with a set of cultural conventions associated with women's realms of responsibilities that were rooted in the broad Greco-Roman cultural world of antiquity, and which the *GLAE* narrators/redactors and audience seem to have shared. As Peter Brown has emphasized, burial customs have remained among the most stable cultural features of the ancient Mediterranean world.[14]

Accordingly, the following sets of examples will illustrate cultural perceptions of three areas in which women typically play key roles, including caring for dead bodies, weeping and lamenting the dead, and caring for souls. Intended as a brief illustration rather than a comprehensive exhaustive overview, these examples, as we shall see, are rooted in a range of 'pagan,' 'Jewish', and 'Christian' textual and social traditions. Furthermore, the following examples of norms and practices relate to ancient women who were evidently not an undifferentiated group but individuals from different cultural/religious groups, distinguished by many criteria. Nonetheless, these examples convey perceptions regarding women's agency and their pivotal functions in funerary practices that were prevalent in the *GLAE*'s hybrid cultural world.[15]

In general, conventional cultural associations between women and death could be understood against the widespread view of life as a circle between birth and death, a mother and a mourner, in which life begins and ends through women. Karel Van Der Toorn's observations, which focus on Mesopotamian women, nonetheless shed light on general cultural perceptions of women and notions of death: 'In many respects the link between the dead, the living, and the coming generation was effected through the woman. As a mother she was familiar, in a special manner, with the mysterious interdependency between life and death.'[16] Ruth Padel's observation of Greek traditions advances a similar view:

> Greek societies, male-ordered, generally assigned to women ritual presidency over transitional experiences, dying or birth, which are perceived as passages into and out of darkness. Dying is going into the dark being born is coming into the light, an image often doing double service for the body's emergence from the womb and passage into the grave and for the soul's passage into whatever obscurity imagined to perceived life.[17]

Barbara Goff has shown that in ancient Greece women played a conspicuous part in assisting in childbirth and funerals, without much differentiation between these events that carry diametrically opposite significance. In her view, women had a particular association with the polluting aspects of the human body (emergence from dark at birth, departure into dark at death), which gave them 'uncanny' status in the eyes of men and a propensity for contact with the 'uncanny' spirit world, which was exploited in certain religious contexts.[18] These explanations present various views regarding the essential, innate link between women and death in distinct cultures. Yet, as was indicated above, they all highlight a common, cross-cultural view that was generally held in antiquity, one that recognized the central role of women in funerary practices and their responsibility to care for, and lament for the dead. Several funerary practices are especially relevant for this examination of Eve in the *GLAE*: caring for the bodies, lamenting the dead, and caring for the souls.

Caring for Dead Bodies

Treating the dead body immediately after death — including washing, anointing, and dressing it with shrouds — was one of the tasks that were typically performed by women in the ancient world. For instance, in ancient Greece, women customarily closed the eyes and mouth of the deceased, possibly to secure the release of the psyche from the body, as some sources suggest.[19] Women also normally washed, anointed and dressed the corpse before laying it out to be mourned by relatives, during the first stage of an elaborate Greek burial ritual entitled the 'laying out of the body' (*prothesis*).[20] In Roman burial customs, women performed similar practices of taking care of dead bodies. The deceased's eyes and mouth were usually closed by a close relative, typically a woman; a coin was placed in the mouth to pay the fare for Charon's ferry; dead bodies were washed and anointed; a wreath was placed around the head; and perfumes were sprinkled on the body.[21]

Women also played a central role in washing and anointing the dead body in Jewish funerary practices in the first century CE and later periods, as several passages in the Gospels, as well as in Rabbinic sources demonstrate.[22] For example, according to Rabbinic sources, although men are allowed to prepare men's bodies for burial, women were responsible for taking care of the corpses of both sexes. Mark's depiction of the unnamed woman who anointed Jesus in 14.3-9 illustrates the involvement of women in such practices, as Kathleen Corley has shown.[23] Evidently, the *GLAE*'s account of Adam's death does not assign to Eve the full scope of practices mentioned above. Nonetheless, its presentation of Eve's role as anointing Adam's body resonates with these women's traditional tasks of caring for the body.

Weeping and Lamenting for the Dead

The practices of weeping, mourning, and lamenting the dead were associated with women throughout the ancient world.[24] In Greek vase representations, for instance, women form the majority of those participating in mourning processions and lamenting. They are often depicted with gestures of mourning, such as putting both hands to their heads and tearing their hair.[25] Once at the tomb, women continued their lamentation and calling to the dead, and accompanied them with various offerings and libations.[26] Roman women, as well, were key participants in mourning practices. Accordingly, in addition to literary evidence, various artistic representations frequently depict women beating their breasts or stretching out their arms towards the deceased, giving expression to their grief by gestures as well as lamentations.[27]

Corresponding representations of weeping lamenting women are found in biblical sources.[28] The prophet Jeremiah, for example, utilizes the typical image of a weeping woman, and evokes the image of the matriarch Rachel weeping over the loss of Israel, even in his lament over exile of the northern tribes (Jer. 31.5). Judges 11.40 describes women's ritual lamentations for the death of Jephthah's daughter.[29] This perception continues in later Jewish texts, such as 2 *Esdras* 9.26–10.54, where a weeping woman represents Zion in a vision. In Josephus's *Antiquities*, a first-century Jewish text, Jephthah's daughter, re-named Seila, utters a full dramatic lament.[30]

In a similar vein, the Gospel of Peter refers to women who came to lament over Jesus (13.55-57), and John 20.11 mentions Mary Magdalene, who wept for Jesus outside the tomb.[31] Several Aramaic laments, attributed to women, are preserved in Rabbinic literature.[32] Material images of mourning women are found on the end panels of a tenth-century BCE sarcophagus of Ahiram.[33] Much later, after the fall of Jerusalem in 70 CE, the defeated Israel was still personified and portrayed as a typical weeping woman, who laments the destruction of Jerusalem, on the 'Judaea Capta' coins struck by the Romans.[34] In Rabbinic times, as Judith Baskin has noted, public lamentation had become an exclusively female role and one that was deemed essential to appropriate mourning.[35] Furthermore, Tal Ilan has observed 'all verbs concerned with bewailing the dead appear in the feminine in rabbinic sources.'[36]

In diverse cultures, traditional women's roles of weeping and lamenting were associated not only with humans but also with the gods. For example, the death of the youthful shepherd god Tammuz/Dumuzi was mourned by women in lamentation rituals which spread from Mesopotamia and survived in Syria, Palestine, and Greece well into Christian times.[37] The book of Ezekiel, for instance, describes ancient Israelite women participating in the lamentation for Tammuz and weeping for him in the temple precincts (Ezek. 8.14).[38] In its Greek form, the young god Adonis replaced Tammuz, and was mourned, exclusively by Athenian women at the yearly festival Adonia, which survived until the fourth century CE.[39] Women's laments were also a central component in the Isis traditions that spread from Egypt throughout the Greek world to Asia Minor and Rome. Here women re-enacted the mourning of the goddess Isis over the death of her husband Osiris.[40]

But what are the cultural connotations that are associated with these practices? And how are they significant to this discussion of Eve? Several studies have related women's participation in funerary practices to notions of pollution. These studies have often evoked ancient perceptions according to which birth, like death, was regarded as a source of pollution. They further suggested that women's capacity to give birth deemed them as both polluted and polluting, and thus suitable for dealing with the pollution of death.[41] In contrast, other studies have linked the extensive involvement of women in funerary practices to the essential cultural roles that women played, as well as to women's social control and authority in various contexts. For instance, in her examination of Greek rituals Gail Holst-Warhaft has contended that the practice of lamentation enabled women to play a dominant role in the rituals of death, and thus associated them with certain power, control, and authority.[42] Karen Stears has similarly emphasized that the participation of women in funerary practices fulfilled a number of valued social functions.[43] Through these practices women demonstrated 'correct' female behavior and thus enhanced both their status and that of their kin group. Likewise, they crossed the divide between public and private and thereby affected the public standing of their kinship group and the relations between this group and the public. In addition, women's participation in funerary rituals may have helped to legitimate claims on estates, to underpin a family's ritual health, and to act as a tool for the construction and promotion of family history.

To be sure, the *GLAE* does not present an elaborate picture of Eve's mourning and lamenting Adam. Yet, as mentioned earlier, some versions refer to her grief, expression of loss, and emotional weeping and soaked eyes. This representation resonates suggestively with cultural traditions of female mourning and the positive connotations associated with them. In turn, this representation aligns the figure of Eve with a widespread and ongoing multicultural tradition of women's mourning, and thus seems to characterize her, implicitly, as the one who performs a significant and esteemed cultural role in the event of Adam's death.

In addition to this model of expressive grief, in which women were expected to express feeling with some emotional intensity, a number of ancient sources describe a more limited model of controlled female grief that seems relevant to this discussion of Eve. As several Greek sources demonstrate, for example, in diverse contexts women's mourning was considered 'uncontrolled' and 'unmanly,' whereas the noble grief of males was characterized by restraint and praise for the dead.

Accordingly women's excessive mourning was restricted in Greek legislation in a number of places in the Greek world, from the seventh century BCE onwards.[44] Although such restrictions varied from place to place, they nonetheless reveal standard features intended, among other objectives, to control women's emotional expression. Several Roman sources likewise reveal attempts to limit women's emotional grief. For instance, Cicero, writing about 70 BCE, explains that the Athenian sixth-century Solonic restrictions on funerals were written into Roman law. Hence similar restrictions on the grief expressed by women were found in the Roman Twelve Tables of law.[45] This conception of women's excessive grief seems to have persisted, since Lucian continued to parody women mourners in the second century CE, arguing that the deceased received no benefit from such behavior.[46] Several Hellenistic-Jewish texts seem to reflect similar ideals.[47] One example is the martyrdom account of the mother and her seven sons found in *4 Maccabees*, especially her two speeches in chapter 16.[48] The first speech describes what the mother would have said if she were weak. For instance, she would have wept and mourned for the death of her children (16.5-11). Emphasizing the merits of controlled grieving, the narrator affirms that the mother did not give this speech, but rather a second speech in which, instead of weeping and mourning, she encouraged her sons to die on behalf of their people (16.16-23).

Some versions of the accounts of Adam's death in the *GLAE* 31–42 seem to resonate with these cultural conceptions of controlled women's mourning. As discussed earlier, these versions minimize the dramatic emotional image of Eve's weeping and mourning and characterize her in a more 'rational' manner. This depiction of Eve appears to resonate with the cultural model of controlled female grief and to present a favorable picture of Eve's response to the event of Adam's death.

Caring for Souls

Instances of women's capacity for witnessing the soul's ascent to heaven, an experience that Eve undergoes in *GLAE*, may be associated with cultural views of women as linked to the realm of the spirits. For example, Holst-Warhaft has directed attention to numerous portrayals in Greek tragedy of women who invoked and communicated with the spirits the dead. In her examination of Jewish women's funerary practices in Graeco-Roman Palestine, Léonie Archer has suggested that because women were recurrently perceived as representing the world of nature, they were also seen as being closer to the 'shadowy world of spirits.' Similarly, Susan Sered has emphasized cross-cultural views regarding the role of women as ritual experts and communicators with the spirits of the dead.[49]

Several sources include more specific references to women and their spiritual visions. One example is implied in the Gnostic *Gospel of Mary*, especially in Mary's speech about visions and the ascent of the soul (*Gos. Mary* 9.2–17.9/15).[50] The *Testament of Job* presents an even clearer picture. It describes the magical cords that Job's daughters inherited from him, which enabled them to understand, communicate, and behold heavenly things, as well as 'to see those who are coming for [their father's] soul' (47.11). Thus, when Job dies, his three daughters gain insight into the transcendent heavenly reality; they behold the ascent of his soul and see how it is taken up and brought to heaven by the angel in a chariot:

> . . . they saw the gleaming chariots which had come for his soul. And they blessed and glorified God each one in her own distinctive dialect. After these things the one who sat in the great chariot got off and greeted Job, as his three daughters and their father looked on, though certain others did not see. And taking the soul he flew up, embracing it and mounted the chariot and set off for the east. But his body, prepared for burial, was borne to the tomb as the three daughters went ahead girded about and singing hymns to God (*T. Job* 52.7-12).

Discussing this passage, Pieter van der Horst has insightfully observed: 'It seems clear that what is being said here is that women can move in the spiritual realm better than men do. Job's daughters have insight (literally and metaphorically) into the heavenly world . . .'[51] The *GLAE*'s depiction of Eve, who beholds the ascent of Adam's soul, resonates with cultural conceptions of women's spiritual abilities and visionary experiences. In accordance with these conceptions, Eve transcends the natural human limits, demonstrates elevated spiritual abilities, and can witness the ascent of Adam's soul to the divine realm at the event of his death.

In sum, the *GLAE* account of Adam's death, which associated Eve with funerary practices, presents a concise description of Eve's actions. Yet, the brief examples cited above demonstrate that these distinct death-related notions resonate with a set of death-related practices and beliefs, primarily associated with women's realms of responsibilities in the broad Greco-Roman cultural world of the *GLAE*'s narrators and audience.[52] Particularly notable are three realms of experience — caring for the body, weeping and mourning the dead, caring for the soul — where women were perceived as acting with authority in the public sphere. They gave voice to their experiences and griefs, employed their skills of consolation, and revealed their spiritual virtues in the transcendent realm. By associating Eve with these cultural conceptions and norms, the account of Adam's death develops suggestive connotations that link her not only with the gender roles of caring for the dead, but also with the esteemed cultural value that was attached to these roles. In so doing it subtly disrupts the coherence of the text and its depiction of Eve's culpability in Adam's death, and communicates a different perception of her role in this event.

Conclusion — The *GLAE* and Eve Traditions

While it is certainly important to identify and examine this *GLAE*'s unusual portrayal of Eve, it remains vital to ask what kind of an ideological stance this subtle depiction might convey. As noted earlier, various *GLAE* 31–42 depictions, in accordance with prevalent early Jewish and Christian exegetical traditions, depict Eve as being responsible for inflicting death on Adam and all humanity. It is evident that in *GLAE* 31–42, Eve is not portrayed as the bane of Adam, the root of all evil, and the source of death. Instead, its depiction both distances her from culpability, and associates her instead with a realm where women occupy socially sanctioned funerary roles.

The contrast between these contradictory *GLAE* depictions of Eve is striking. The portrayal of Eve in *GLAE* 31–42 departs from the dominant and widespread theological trope of a sinful and culpable Eve. Moreover, by depicting Eve as a beneficial figure in the drama of Adam's death, the *GLAE* 31–42 seems to offer a counter-tradition to Jewish and Christian traditions emphasizing the fault of Eve, and thus provides indications of a rich, multifaceted cultural discourse, which includes conventional as well as alternative traditions about Eve's role and standing.

It is possible that these diverse traditions of Eve emerged separately in the context of independent everyday-life accounts that variously

represented Eve as sinful or virtuous. But these various representations cannot detract from the fact that, in its final redacted form, the
GLAE represents a coherent narrative. In the previous chapter we have
already noted Tromp's important observation regarding the coherent
nature of the complete *GLAE*. In light of this present discussion of Eve,
it seems possible to suggest that, at least on one level, the complete
GLAE constructs its meaning by appealing simultaneously to various
competing traditions. What characterizes the complete text is not
its fixed and homogenous message but rather its multiplicity. In its
juxtaposition of diverse cultural traditions, positions, and conceptualizations, it seems to oscillate between several attitudes and points of
view, all collectively in dialogue, conveying parallel contemporaneous
traditions, and constructing various models of the emblematic Eve.

PART TWO

Dietmar Neufeld

INTRODUCTION

The *GLAE* recounts that both Eve and Adam came to an awkward awareness of their nakedness and, Eve in particular, quickly covered their nakedness. It is my contention that when the narrator of the *GLAE* divested Adam and Eve of their garments of glory and reinvested them with the mundane clothing of post-Paradise existence, he intended to signal new and suitable social identities, commensurate with their loss of status. In this connection, it will be instructive to examine theories of bodies as social entities upon which are written the cultural codes of society. My supposition is that bodies encapsulate social rules that differ for men and women — this will help to explain the multivalent characterizations of Eve and Adam in the *GLAE*.

In Chapter 3, 'Body, Clothing, and Identity: Clay Cunningly Compounded,' I explore the *GLAE*'s description of both Eve's and Adam's nakedness and their subsequent attire. By elucidating ancient attitudes to *body* and *clothing*, I argue that, as in modern times, so too in the ancient world, the human body was a cultural costume decorated from birth to death by diverse cultural traditions and was, therefore, at all times a medium of cultural communication. The *GLAE* utilized the body surfaces of Eve and Adam to mark rank and relationship between females and males, to authenticate their identities, to define power personally and socially, and to keep their desires in check. Discourse about the body and adornment was critical to regulating the body's dangerous potential to disrupt social relations and organization. The author of the *GLAE* was aware that the bodies of Adam and Eve were most dangerous in moments of ambiguity and permeability, because in such states breaches in wholeness threatened undesired social changes,

43

both between males and females and between humans and God. Thus, in the author's narration of the failure of the first humans, bodies, nakedness, and clothing were integral features of the story to help with the elucidation of the complex relationships that were envisioned to exist between women, men, and God.

Chapter 4, 'The Exoneration of Eve in the Key of Honor and Shame' focuses its attention upon Eve's monologue. I apply the cultural codes and values of honor and shame and their social repercussions in order to explain why Eve's account of what went wrong in Paradise differs from Adam's. The honor–shame values were ubiquitous in ancient societies and helped to establish social roles and hierarchies between women and men. These values and the role that they played in establishing how women and men were evaluated will be fully explored in this chapter. Society provides the matrix in which these culturally shaped values operate and, significantly, these values operate differently for males and females. Males tend to be more vulnerable to societal opprobrium than women are. This insight is fundamental for assessing the behavior of the protoplasts in the Greek life.

I contend that when Eve's monologue is taken to reflect conflicting notions of honor and shame, each played out in the dissimilar courts of reputation that both Adam and Eve represented, a different understanding of Eve emerges which, at the same time, also makes sense of her desire for exoneration. Taking into account the work of Levison and his conclusion that Eve's first-person confessions 'tend, if not to exonerate her entirely, at least to win the affection and empathy of her audience' (2000a: 40–41), I investigate why it appears that the author of the text was obligated to absolve Eve of wrongdoing. I argue that the confessions of Eve and Adam function as discourse offered from two different perspectives. One is generated by views peculiar to the world of males, with the propensity to denigrate Eve, and the other from the world of females, with the inclination to exonerate her. In order to make clear these two perspectives, I argue that the societal values of honor and shame operated differently in their treatment of male and female infidelity. Eve's female court of reputation would have measured and evaluated her betrayal in terms quite different from those applicable to Adam. I am not suggesting that these courts of reputation are in evident display in the text under consideration, but it seems quite likely that the monologue of Eve would have been driven by the cultural values of shame and honor in a collectivist society — embedded and actualized in a social context concerned to win honor and mitigate shame — often defined in gender stereotypical ways.

I argue that in the world of women, Eve's disloyalty/betrayal would have been of marginal concern because she was still possessed of traits (shame, sorrow, generosity) that rendered her an honorable person. Her confession was not an admission of her failures and frailties, but rather a reflection of her desire to set right the wrong precipitated by her behavior. Actuated by her fear of disgrace, a sense of responsibility as a mother to set an example, and a deep-running concern for the good reputation of Adam, her children, and children's children, her confession softened any accusation directed against her and cleared her from blame. So while her honor in Adam's view was utterly disgraced, in her estimation it was still intact. Eve declared herself free from shame with rhetorical flourishes calculated to magnify her status as an honorable person and to furnish the grounds of her exculpation. Thus, after Eve's 'seduction' by Satan, she and Adam each respond in a socially conditioned manner, but the consequences are more severe and far reaching for Adam. He is unable to recover his lost honor, and his resultant suffering and death are emblematic of this loss. Eve is both more resilient and repentant, and the unusual depth to her monologue gives expression to both of these features.

Chapter 3

BODY, CLOTHING AND IDENTITY — CLAY CUNNINGLY COMPOUNDED

What says Zeus? Epictetus, had it been possible, I should have made this paltry body, this small estate of thine, free and unhampered. But, as it is — let it not escape thee — this body is not thine own, but it is clay cunningly compounded.

(Epictetus, *Discourses* I.I.II)

QUESTION AND HYPOTHESIS

That both Adam and Eve came to an awkward awareness of their nakedness and what that *awareness* meant have been repeatedly investigated.[1] Moreover, that they both quickly covered up their nakedness and the meaning of that *covering up* have been equally and frequently discussed. As this chapter intends to show, when the narrator of the *GLAE* divested Adam and Eve of their garments of glory and reinvested them with the mundane clothing of post-Paradise existence, he intended to furnish them with suitable social identities commensurate with their loss of status. Moreover, by having them come to an awareness of their nakedness, the narrator marked the bodies of Adam and Eve with religious, political, and social distinctions and other forms of embodied social meaning that were essential to maintaining and regulating relationships between women, men, and God (Esler, 2001: 26–30; Satlow, 1997: 429–32). In the *GLAE*, the imagery associated with the bodies of Eve and Adam, their initial nakedness, and the subsequent clothing of their bodies is integral to erecting and conceptualizing the boundaries between women, men, and God.

As will be shown below, however, female nakedness as understood

47

and interpreted by females was different from female nakedness as understood and interpreted by males. Attitudes to male and female nakedness were context dependent, which once determined will help to explain why in the *GLAE* it is Eve only who initiates a hunt for something with which to cover herself while Adam does not engage in any such hunt. In the eyes of the writer, because Eve's nakedness was more dangerous than Adam's, covering her body was necessary. While Adam eventually covered his body, he would have done so for reasons different from those applicable to Eve. It is in this connection that we need to explore how the body is utilized to display the values and attitudes of the narrator in areas such as knowledge, desire, and sexuality. Thus, before beginning with an analysis of the *GLAE*, it is essential to consider the various theoretical constructs of the body. This will help us to understand how the narrator used the storyline of the *GLAE* to manipulate the bodies of Eve and Adam to inscribe and reproduce power and hierarchy that was befitting males and females. Their bodies, so to speak, put them where they belonged in the social order of things.

I suggest that as these stories about Eve and Adam went out and were taken up by groups and their cultures for a variety of reasons, nakedness and clothing came to be associated with sensuality, sexuality, and temptation, especially with regard to Eve. The naked or clothed female body became a screen on which a group's fears and fantasies of sin, sexuality, and evil were projected (Ross, 1991: 293). Michael J. Satlow avers that 'by understanding how a group addresses questions of shame and nakedness . . . we can gain insight into how that group and its culture understand what it means to be naked. This understanding, in turn, can provide a window into how a culture constructs and reproduces power and hierarchical relationships' (1997: 429). He goes on, 'nakedness, like clothing, is culturally complex. On some level, we are all aware of the polysemous messages transmitted by clothing and adornment. Within any given sociocultural context, clothing can function to suggest the behaviors (roles) expected of people . . . and can, therefore, distinguish the powerful from the weak, the rich from the poor, the hero from the outcast, the conformer from the non-conformer, the religious from the irreligious, the leader from the follower, *male from female*' (1997: 430, emphasis mine). The same can be said of nakedness: 'Nakedness is not merely being without clothing;

it also can carry sociocultural and theological meaning . . . Nakedness can also convey ritual meaning' (Satlow, 1997: 431). As much as societies make assumptions that permit clothing to convey meaning, so also societies make assumptions that permit nakedness to convey meaning.

THE GRAMMAR OF THE BODY

The display of *bodies* in both society and popular culture has become the focus of active investigation. In an amazing display of interest in the body, books and articles on the topic abound — from interest in the laboring body to the desiring body — the body is pampered, primped, tanned, pierced, tattooed, exercised, downsized, starved, surgically enhanced, for the central purposes of image management and status enhancement (Sweeney and Hodder (eds), 2002: 1). The body is viewed as flexible and plastic, 'a lifestyle accessory, a thing to be sculpted, shaped and stylized' (Hancock and Jagger (eds), 1998: 3). In addition, the body is perceived as the site upon which political, social, and cultural interventions play themselves out in relation to medicine, disability, work, ethics, old age, sexuality, reproduction, food, clothing, adornment, and disease (Hancock and Jagger (eds), 1998: 1). As a result, *body discourses*, reflective of specialized interests, have proliferated so that one can speak about medicalized bodies, consumer bodies, old bodies, homosexual bodies, disabled bodies, working bodies, desiring bodies, ethical bodies, deviant bodies, dead bodies, nude bodies, Classical bodies, and gendered bodies (Sweeney and Hodder (eds), 2002: 1–11). Women's bodies in their complexity are investigated according to issues pertinent to their bodies, including pregnancy, childbirth, menstruation, menopause, reproductive technologies, advertising and the shaping of female bodies, the beauty industry, eating disorders, body image, cosmetic surgery, and body-building (Brook, 1999: vi, ix–xiv).

In concert with this interest, a number of theoretical constructs are offered that conceptualize the historical development and location of the body in society and culture. First, there is the notion that the body is intimately linked to a set of social practices that are culturally determined. In this view, the body's potential is realized through a range of socially regulated practices in which the body is trained, disciplined, and socialized. Daily activities such as walking, experiencing shame, stigmatization, eating, and dressing, attend and train the body — they furnish a medium of culture. In such a view, the body is a powerful symbolic form of culture, a surface on which the central rules, hierarchies, and even metaphysical commitments of culture are inscribed — it is also, as anthropologist Pierre Bourdieu argues, itself a practical, direct locus of social control (1984). Through table manners, toilet habits, and other seemingly trivial routines, rules, and practices, culture becomes reified through the body (Baker, 1998: 241).

A second construct conceptualizes the body as a system of signs — that it conveys symbolic and social meaning through ritual, ceremony and religious practice. Best known for this approach is the work of Mary Douglas, who shows that dietary laws offer a means of conceptualizing social relations, purity and pollution (1978; O'Neill, 1985: 51). Douglas focuses on the significance of body metaphors in the *contexts* of danger, uncertainty and ambiguity (impurity), and safety (purity), within traditional social systems. According to her, these metaphors are characteristically associated with the orifices of the human body (Douglas, 1978; Neyrey, 1991). The religiously constructed body is thus both pure and impure and, in that ambiguous state, dangerous. In this questionable condition, the religiously constructed 'body' is situated in liminal areas where it can be used to mediate and negotiate behaviors and social expectations. The interplay of purity and impurity in the context of the body permits societies to construct religious boundaries that control social interaction, speech, behavior, and sexuality (Douglas, 1978; Neyrey, 1996: 87–96). Furthermore, it is clear that body parts and bodies are 'loaded with cultural symbolism; public and private, positive and negative, political and economic, sexual, moral and often controversial; and so are the attributes, functions and states of the body and the senses — they are not simply physical phenomena but also social' (Synnott, 1992: 1; cf. Malina, 1986: 22–23, 31). Ancient societies regarded the physical body and its various parts — such as face, eyes, buttocks, feet, heart, belly, navel, genitals, head, right arm or hand, teeth, hair — as the loci for which honor is claimed and displayed (Neyrey, 1998; Pilch, 1981; Synnott, 1992; Staubli and Schroer (eds), 1999: 85–90).

A third approach to the body understands the human body as a system of signs that stand for and express relations of power — as a system of signs, the body expresses hierarchies of power and authority that limit and control access to power (Turner, 1991: 25–27). Malina suggests that 'body' refers to the physical person as a living human being in which the physical body functions as the portable roadmap of the social body and by which it serves as the primary vehicle of communication. 'People use their individual physical bodies as portable roadmaps of the social body: the individual physical body replicates the social body' (Malina, 1986: 22, 31, 198).

Significant for this chapter is the work of Arnold van Gennep. He focuses on how the body 'is used to symbolize the social transitions of the individual in society, i.e., transitions of the individual in the social body are inscribed on the physical' (van Gennep, 1960: 52; Berquist, 2000: 33–34). The life of individuals in societies is made up of a series of transitions or passages — such as birth, marriage, pregnancy, fatherhood and motherhood, passages from age to age, from occupation to occupation, from one religion to another, and death (Neyrey, 1991: 333–87). Usually, at the onset or during these passages or transitions, ceremony signals a change or transformation — thresholds are crossed, transformation takes place, new identities are assumed. These social processes are also physical and are often marked by eating and drinking, changes in hairstyle, modification of adornment and clothing, ritual cleansing, body-painting, and body mutilations (tooth removal, circumcision, clitoridectomy, subincision (Burton, 1999: 43). As Synnott points out, 'the person is made new, *either negatively or positively*, changed by a new role, and this requires a new body which in turn symbolizes, physically, society's new demands on the individual, and the individual's new rights and duties in society' (1992: 248, emphasis mine).

The idea of bodies in a state of flux is approached somewhat differently by Pierre Bourdieu. He develops the idea that bodies are both conveyers of symbolic reality and unfinished entities that develop or evolve in conjunction with a range of social forces. Subjected to social forces and human investment, bodies in the rough are continually being shaped and reshaped. Moreover, they are fundamental to the construction and maintenance of inequalities in social status (men and women, elite, peasants, social bandits, patrons, clients, artisans, etc.). He conceptualizes the body as having a form of physical capital — including such things as the interplay between the unfinished body and the social forces within society (a reciprocal exchange of influence); the management of the body to acquire status and distinction;

the body laden with symbolic forms; and the body as possessor of the power required for acquiring a range of resources (goods, services, honor) (Bourdieu, 1984; Shilling, 1992: 127). The body, as a form of physical capital, is of considerable value to societies where social, economic, political, and religious exchange is dependent upon clearly delineated social networks.

According to Bourdieu, it is also clear that bodies occupy a *habitus*, i.e., a socially constituted system of tradition, custom, evaluation and response that shapes the symbolic forms imposed on the body (Bourdieu, 1984: 190; Keenan (ed.), 2001: 32). While *habitus* contributes significantly to the development of the unfinished body, it is also located within the body and has influence on every detail of embodiment. How humans treat their bodies 'reveals the deepest dispositions of the *habitus*' (Bourdieu, 1984: 190). A body dressed, for example, is one mode of *habitus* (table manners, eating habits, food, education, language, blowing one's nose, walking) invested with symbolic capital and considerable cultural power (cultural capital goods) available to humans in their interaction with others (Bourdieu, 1984; Keenan (ed.), 2001: 32). Bodies are the central setting for creating and negotiating social reality. Bodies as organic entities take up space but also constitute space upon which to inscribe gendered social roles and relationships. In the words of Baker, 'bodies not only move through, inhabit, exceed, imagine, and otherwise take up space, but they are themselves space — and place — overlapping and intertwining with countless others' (Baker, 1998: 221).[2]

A fascinating example of how bodies and clothing function to delineate social boundaries is found in Meisch's intriguing analysis of the Christianization of the Incas by the Spanish conquistadors (1532–33) in Peru, Bolivia and Ecuador (2000). When the Spaniards first encountered the Incas, they were struck by their sumptuously dressed bodies and the quality of the textiles they produced. The Incas' attitudes to stylized clothing and textiles and what they each symbolized were carried directly into their myth of origins, which tells the story of how their ancestors first emerged fully dressed with fine and handsome clothes — symbolic of their civilized status. Indeed, they believed that all ethnic groups first appeared in their own regions attired in their own distinctive clothing. They therefore regarded the story of all humanity's descending from one naked couple as being absolutely absurd. Their ancestors were gods fully attired, and each nation was dressed in its own distinctive clothing. For the Incas, the clothed body was an essential signifier not only of their civilized status but also of their humanness. Clothing embodied the essence of nations and persons — indeed, not to have the body draped in clothing implied a lack of culture and civilization.

An enemy's garments could be used to harm him in effigy. When animals were sacrificed to the gods, they were often attired with fine garments and gold ear ornaments. Funerary rituals involved washing the clothes of the deceased and, sometime later, either rewashing them or burning them for the deceased to use in the afterlife. Nobility were buried dressed in their finest garments and jewelry, and placed beside them were new garments carefully folded, along with other valuables. Not only did clothes signify identity, belonging, and boundary concerns, but they also indicated resistance to the imperialistic rule of the Spanish. The Incas signaled their resistance to Spanish rule by covering their bodies in traditional dress (Meisch, 2000: 68–80). The body dressed was a powerful medium of expression that communicated humanness, personal and ethnic identity, status, and belonging, boundaries between gods and humans, and resistance to foreign oppression. For the Incas, the surface of the body, *vis-à-vis* its adornment, was a site for the display of differences between groups in their society and between themselves and the conquistadors (Wyke, 1994: 134).

As this examination of body and culture demonstrates, the body's gestures, stances, initiatives, positions, and desire are not simply the result of the external stimulations that would provoke them but are the result of cultural and social understanding of the body and its functions (Lingis, 1994: ix). Individuals, therefore, presuppose a number of bodily identities — assumed identity, attributed identity, optative identity, sexual identity, gendered identity — all constructed through the experience of the body in social context (Lingis 1994: xi). These identities are the result of a 'collective exercise requiring enormous amounts of negotiation, experimentation, living together, talking, and narrating stories . . . with the express purpose of consolidating complex arrangements of relationships between women, men, and God' (Cameron and Miller (eds), 2004: 7).

In the ancient world, as in the modern, the human body 'is a cultural costume: it is decorated from birth to death by diverse cultural

traditions and is therefore at all times a medium of cultural communication' (Burton, 1999: 2). It is natural to suppose, therefore, that the
GLAE utilizes the body surfaces of Eve and Adam to designate rank and
relationship between females and males, to authenticate their identities, to define power personally and socially, and to keep their desires
in check (Porter (ed.), 1999: 1). Body and adornment discourses are
critical to regulating the body's dangerous potential to disrupt social
relations and organization (Brydon and Niessen (eds), 1998: 1). The
narrator of the *GLAE* is aware that the bodies of Adam and Eve are
most dangerous in moments of ambiguity and permeability, because
in such states breaches in wholeness threaten undesired social changes
between males and females and between humans and God (Berquist,
2000: 18–52). Thus, in the exercise of narrating the failure of the first
humans, bodies, nakedness, and clothing are integral features of the
story to help the narrator work out the complex relationships he envisions as existing between women, men, and God.

CONTEXTUALIZING THE STORY

In the Genesis account, after Eve and Adam violate the commandment
of God, one of a number of consequences is immediately apparent.
They recognize at once their nakedness and in their shame desire to
cover it up. They do so with a variety of materials, but are subsequently
vested with 'designer' skins fabricated by God. The *GLAE* 15–30 records
the incident somewhat differently from Genesis. As Adam is about
to die, he instructs Eve to recount to their children the story of their
transgression. She calls her children together and narrates how she, as
guardian of her portion of Paradise, was seduced by Satan into taking
and eating the forbidden fruit. Unbeknown to her, however, Satan had
poured upon the fruit the poison of his wickedness and, upon eating it,
her eyes were opened to the realization that she had been stripped of
the righteousness with which she had been clothed (*GLAE* 20.1). She
wept and asked why he had deprived her of the glory with which she
had been clothed (*GLAE* 20.3). Receiving no answer, she in her nakedness sought to find leaves that would hide her shame (*GLAE* 20.4).
She could not find a single leaf because, after she had eaten of the
fruit, every tree shed its leaves, with one exception — the fig tree. The
tree from which she had eaten had not shed its leaves and so, taking

leaves from it, she fashioned for herself a girdle (*GLAE* 20.4-5). Having covered her shame, she persuaded Adam to eat of the poisoned fruit by promising to reveal to him a great mystery — the knowledge of divinity. As soon as he ate, his eyes were straight away opened to the shame of his nakedness and he reproached Eve, 'O wicked woman! What have you done to us? You have deprived me of the glory of God?' (*GLAE* 21.6).

The *GLAE* does not indicate explicitly that Adam covered his shame with a girdle made out of leaves or that God fashioned 'designer' skins for him (Gen. 3.21). As Eve had been, so also Adam was at first clothed in divine glory — a kind of celestial mantle that covered his somatic surface — but with the mantle gone, the shame of his exposure would have driven Adam eventually to cover up his nakedness. Yet, not only do Adam and Eve hide their naked bodies by covering them up, they also hide their bodies from the face of God, fearing him because of their nakedness and the shame it precipitated. God called to Adam in a terrible voice, 'Adam, where are you? And why did you hide from my face?' (*GLAE* 8.1). Adam responded to the question; 'It is not because we think we can't be found by you, Lord, that we hide, but I was afraid, because I am naked, and I was ashamed before your might, Master' (*GLAE* 23.2). God replied, 'Who showed you that you are naked, unless you have forsaken my commandment, which I delivered you to keep' (*GLAE* 23.3). Adam expresses his disapprobation — turning to Eve he says, 'Why have you done this?' — and so begins the blame game. Eve in turn states, 'the serpent deceived me' (*GLAE* 23.5).

An Analysis of the *GLAE*

While several recent books offer fascinating assessments of the significance of the apparel of Adam and Eve in the Hebrew Bible and in certain post-biblical Jewish writings, none of them has dealt in a significant way with the issues of body, clothing and identity (Morris and Sawyer (eds), 1992: 74–90; Anderson *et al.* 2000: 55–81). Morris and Sawyer's *A Walk in the Garden: Biblical, Iconographical and Literary Images of Eden* concentrates on the *nakedness* and *garment* motifs of Genesis 2.25, 3.7, 3.21. They perform a valuable service by analyzing a fascinating and diverse set of biblical texts in which Adam and sometimes Eve are pictured as royal, kingly, angelic, or divine figures clad in glorious garments of light — "garments of glory that pious Jews hoped to receive at the eschaton" (Lambden in Morris and Sawyer (eds), 1992: 78–79). Moreover, Morris and Sawyer's collection of sources speculates about the nature of Adam and Eve's attire and concludes that Adam and Eve were initially dressed in splendiferous garments reflecting the glory of God. What those splendiferous garments might have been is subject to considerable debate in these sources. Consequently, some of them portray Adam attired in garments of priests handed down to him; others portray Adam and Eve clothed in garments of white; still others suggest that the first couple's clothes were made from the shining skin of the leviathan; some portray Adam and Eve initially clad in nail-skin — clothes variously described as smooth, tight-fitting, pearly, translucent and luminous, jewel-like; others suggest that their coats of skin were their fleshly skin or physical bodies; still others indicate that their post-Paradise clothes were made of either the skin or the fur of a goat, hare, lamb/sheep or weasel (Morris and Sawyer (eds), 1992: 89). It is clear from Morris and Sawyer's analysis that the issue of the garments that draped the bodies of Adam and Eve caused an ongoing debate. It gives testament to the importance of the altered body as a powerful medium that is capable of expressing the attitudes and values of both writers and readers.

It is instructive for us briefly to consider Gary A. Anderson's analysis of *Vita Adae et Evae* (2000 *et al.*: 58–81, 82–110).[3] He seeks to establish the relationship between *Vita Adae et Evae* and Genesis (2000 *et al.*: 58–59) and concludes that despite the loose connection between the *Vita* and Genesis, the *Vita* is nevertheless familiar with the exegetical material of Genesis 3 and that an examination of the way in which Adam and Eve are appareled will solve a number of puzzling differences between the two (2000 *et al.*: 59).

Genesis 3.22 records that God designs garments of skin for Adam and Eve and then clothes them. According to Anderson, three perplexing features of this text occupy the attention of commentators: first, why does God fashion garments of skin with which to cover the couple? Second, where did the material for the clothes come from? And, third, why was God compelled to clothe the couple himself? Did they require divine assistance in slipping on these garments (2000 *et al.*: 59)? Although a number of solutions are offered to explain the three perplexing features, Anderson presents one which, in his estimation, appears to resolve them. His solution is that rather than reading the phrase כָּתְנוֹת עוֹר as garments 'made of skin,' it should be read as 'skin like garments' that are being put on. Hence, the act refers not so much to covering human skin with outer garments made of skin, but rather to the transformation of Adam's angelic body to a mortal one. As Anderson states, 'Adam is to be changed from his former angelic and presumably impassable state to that of a mortal being: one prone to the needs of the body, illness and, susceptible to death. Adam has become mortal' (2000: 77). His conclusion addresses the issue of the surface of the human body and how it functions as a stage upon which power is applied and negotiated — Adam's transformation from an angelic being to a mortal one is symboled on his body (Sault (ed.), 1994: xi). Anderson does not, however, take into account human uses of dress and the body in addressing significant social and religious matters — determining issues of power and control, who has it and who does not, exercising epistemic control by putting limits on human desire for illicit knowledge, and in matters of defining the parameters of human sexuality.[4]

THE BODIES OF EVE AND ADAM

Eve and Adam were blissfully ignorant of their undressed state until the moment the veil was removed from their eyes — then shame set in at their undressed state. Eve remedied her nakedness by fashioning a girdle for herself from the same plant of which she had eaten, and Adam remedied his nakedness by acknowledging it and the shame it caused him before his master (*GLAE* 20.5, 23.2). The sequence of being in an undressed state, to self-dressing, to being dressed by God is a reflection of the transition from one state to another — the move from a paradisal to a non-paradisal world. In the act of covering up nakedness is implicated the radical discontinuity between the two worlds — from paradisal bliss to earthly torment. The body surfaces of Adam and Eve could be viewed as geography — a bodyscape — utilized by the *GLAE* to bring about separations between one place and another, one body and another, to describe and inscribe difference, and to create order through establishing limits (Baker, 1998: 222). In the *GLAE*, dress and bodily surfaces are used as instruments of social power (i.e., regulation, reward, coercion, legitimacy, information) to influence attributions of power (God has it), shifts in that power (humans lose it), and the assumption and negotiation of that power — that is, who ultimately determines borders, identities, and social hierarchies (Johnson and Lennon (eds), 1998: 3).[5] Appearance and social power are directly related.[6]

Moreover, bodies and clothing were also major sites for speculation on significant topics, ranging from identity, to the connection between humans and divinity, to knowledge, and to sexuality. Bodies, nakedness, and clothing were rhetorically charged discourses by those desiring to control and maintain the social structures of groups and individuals. In other words, the human body was integral to the formation of regulations and practices in order to avert illegitimate status aspirations and desires that might have challenged established social patterns. The bodies of Eve and Adam are the 'telling flesh' of society and an unfinished resource requiring constant human investment — eventually bodies, as they develop in response to a range of social pressures, come to embody the rules, sanctions, gendered hierarchies, and values of the societies within which they are located (O'Neill, 1985: 23; Shilling, 1992: 119).

These observations allow the conclusion that the *GLAE*'s body rhetoric was strategically designed to construct and legitimize a network of social relations, both between men and women and between humans and God. This body rhetoric also served as a critique of the dominant social systems, especially when these systems were under threat, served as religious commentaries to promote a particular theological line, and served as a warning to those tempted to break away from the socially sanctioned hierarchies. The network of social relationships fashioned by this body rhetoric was essentially hierarchical, and was clearly marked (naked to dressed) on the bodies of Adam and Eve to testify to the primal moment of the inception, institution, and legitimization of this social hierarchy. The boundaries established and reinforced between God, Eve, and Adam were a reflection of the desire to institute, reinforce, and regulate the boundaries between humans on a wide range of social practices (bodies sexualized by desire; power; knowledge). After all, it was important to maintain basic social patterns and the honor systems associated with these social practices (Berquist, 1998: 109). The rhetoric of body and dress in the *GLAE* was an expression of the desire to control and manage a number of important social issues: human aspirations for knowledge, sexuality, and desire.

Thus, in the estimation of the narrator of the *GLAE*, God has established boundaries around these issues that were not to be transgressed.

When human aspirations for knowledge, for example, breached those boundaries, the narrator set into motion a number of actions emblematic of transition and transformation. In the somatic actions of dressing undressed bodies, he not only symbolized Eve's and Adam's forcible shift from one place to another — from Paradise to earth — but also signaled the forcible shift from one kind of knowledge to another — one licit, the other illicit. Unruly flesh could potentially transgress established social norms and disrupt the balance of harmony and stability of God's created order. Thus the *GLAE* addresses the issue of unchecked human aspiration for knowledge — the desire of Eve and Adam for knowledge on par with God's — a knowledge above what it was legitimate for them to have. According to the narrator of the *GLAE*, the aspirations of Adam and Eve, which ultimately led to their shame, represented a potential loss to God, in regard both to honor and to power — Eve and Adam would have equality with God (*GLAE* 18.1-4). Indeed, the *GLAE* recounts, from Satan's perspective, the reticence of God to share knowledge with Eve and Adam: 'But God perceived this that you would be like Him, so he envied you and said, "Ye shall not eat of it"' (*GLAE* 18.4).

To the narrator, it is clear that such lofty ambitions would have not have pleased God and left the patron of the universe in danger of additional challenges. The threat of parity of knowledge with God, therefore, required that limitations be put on Eve's and Adam's ability to gain knowledge, wisdom, and power. These limits were made to operate on the materiality of Eve's and Adam's bodies which, in turn, had an effect on the social body.[7] Eve's and Adam's individual and corporate identities through dress signs and symbols clearly demonstrated where knowledge belonged in the order of things — they both had a knowledge that was commensurate with their position and role as humans (Keenan (ed.), 2001: 5).

Moreover, in his establishment of the social rank between females, males and God, the narrator of the *GLAE* signals a transformation of identity, status, and location made manifest by changes in dress (Arthur (ed.), 2000: 3; Ahmed and Stacey (eds), 2001). The bodies, undressed and dressed, functioned as an effective means of helping to forge new identities for Adam and Eve based on assigned or achieved positions within gendered social structures (Roach-Higgins and Eicher, 1992). The transition from nakedness to adorning the body with clothing strategically reminded Adam and Eve of who they were, who they were not, and where they belonged in the social order (Burton, 1999: 31). Those who heard and read the stories would also have been made aware of their place and position in the social orders to which they belonged.

Here once more, the act of being dressed was a signifier of human-ness, but it was also an act of being enveloped in *social skin* — designed to shape and communicate personal and social identity along with connecting and mediating the extremes between humans, society, and divinity (Arthur (ed.), 2000: 68, 77). This social skin, as reflected in bodily apparel, symbolizes the border between the body and the society that controls and molds it. The garment of skin that covered the skin of the physical body of Eve and Adam functioned as a second skin to signal the transformation of the identities of Eve and Adam — from garments of righteousness (Eve) and glory (Adam) indicative of high status to garments of skin indicative of low status and the shame it subsequently engendered.[8] Once again it reinforced where Eve and Adam belonged — they had been put in their respective places in the social order along with the rest of humanity that would follow them.

As pointed out earlier in the chapter, nakedness and sexuality have been connected and the perceptions generated of this union have been imputed to Eve. Thus, the recognition of nakedness and the shame it provoked in Eve have been taken to point metaphorically to the emergence of a precociously sexualized female body in the first female (from innocence to self-conscious awareness of her sexual body).[9]

An Eastern version of the story of the Fall makes this connection by portraying the first man and woman as sexless and only after the Fall do they become sexed beings 'where the halves of the forbidden apple were grafted unto them in the shape of breasts and testicles' (Rudofsky, 1971: 15). The *GLAE* drapes the body of Eve to cover strategically her offending body parts in order to signal the narrator's desire to constrain what, in his estimation, was out-of-control sexuality now under the burden of guilt and sin.

Even though sexual bodies were necessary for creation and for reproduction, the bodies of men and women were in the constant condition of desiring; that feeling which was directed to the attainment or possession of some object from which pleasure or satisfaction was expected. It was thus that 'desiring bodies were the cause for concern, debate, and reflection — desiring bodies were a nodal point of anxiety and apprehension' in ancient society — here seen to include generally all bodily appetites (Porter (ed.), 1999: 6; Berquist, 1998). Desiring bodies have the potential of challenging the integrity of the body physically and socially and, therefore, these somatic desires require careful guarding (Brayford, 1999: 163–65; Nussbaum, 1994: 78–101).

The allure of sexual desire was, to be sure, also celebrated but, more often than not, it was portrayed as a tempestuous storm that swept over humans, 'a snare rather than unmixed joy,' a tyranny, madness, wound, disease or fire that threatened the boundaries of the self, household and community (Zeitlin, 1999: 61–63; Nussbaum, 1994). Desire was represented as a 'condition of being radically at risk' a state made public by the body and its decoration (Porter (ed.), 1999: 7).

In ancient Israelite society, similar sentiments were expressed about the powerful, compelling potency of female bodily desire — it was a desiring body and body of desire full of erotic allure which, if not contained, would ensnare and delude the unwary. Hence, ancient Israelite societies gave expression to the danger of an out-of-control eroticism in a variety of ways. For example, Proverbs 5.3-5 and 7.10-23 read:

> For the lips of a loose woman drip honey, and her speech is smoother than oil; but in the end she is bitter as wormwood, sharp as a two-edged sword. Her feet go down to death; her steps follow the path to Sheol. She does not keep straight to the path of life; her ways wander, and she does not know it.
>
> Then a woman comes toward him, decked out like a prostitute, wily of heart. She is loud and wayward; her feet do not stay at home; now in the street, now in the squares, and at every corner she lies in wait. She seizes him and kisses him, and with impudent face she says to him: 'I had to offer sacrifices, and today I have paid my vows; so now I have come out to meet you, to seek you eagerly, and I have found you! I have decked my couch with coverings, colored spreads of Egyptian linen; I have perfumed my bed with myrrh, aloes, and cinnamon. Come, let us take our fill of love until morning; let us delight ourselves with love. For my husband is not at home; he has gone on a long journey. He took a bag of money with him; he will not come home until full moon.' With much seductive speech she persuades him; with her smooth talk she compels him. Right away he follows her, and goes like an ox to the slaughter, or bounds like a stag toward the trap until an arrow pierces its entrails. He is like a bird rushing into a snare, not knowing that it will cost him his life.

Another example comes from the Qumran community. It was preoccupied with the danger of male bodies caught up in the throes of
uncontained desire triggered by the sight of the female body bedecked
in finery (Barton, 2002: 217). 4Q184 portrays a female body attired and
bejeweled so as to ensnare: 'Her attire [. . .] her robes are gloom of
twilight, while her jewellery is infected with rot. Her bed is a couch of
corruption [. . .] pits of hell . . . her eyes are befouled with perversity,
her hands grip corruption tight, her thighs are pillars of darkness, a
horde of sins is under her hem . . .' (Abegg (ed.), 1996: 241). It is clear
from these passages and others that male desire expressed bodily was
presented as a condition of being thoroughly at risk — a condition that
required containment and from which male society required protec-
tion (Carson, 1999: 77–100). From the male perspective, it was not so
much his desire that required containment as it was the female body
that required regulation. In his misguided perception, it was the female
who was at the root of his problem.

Similarly, in Greek culture, female bodies were perceived as excessive, threatening, roasting a man with fire that brings him to premature
old age (Zeitlin, 1999: 60; Barton, 1999: 217). Male and female bodies
of desire in the Greek and Roman world were perceived as

> little fiery universes, through whose heart, brain, and veins there pulsed the same
> heat and vital spirit as glowed in the stars. To engage in intercourse was to bring
> one's blood to the boil, as the fiery vital spirit swept through the veins, turning
> the blood into the whitened foam of semen. It was a process in which the body
> was a whole, the brain cavity, the marrow of the backbone, the kidneys, and the
> lower bowel region — was brought into play — as in a mighty choir (Brown, 1988:
> 17; cf. Wyke, 1994: 146–48).

Galen mused about the oddity of the gods 'deciding to maintain the
human species by means of a pleasure so sharp and so potentially
anti-social, for "a very great pleasure is coupled with the exercise of
the generative parts, and a raging desire precedes their use'" (Brown,
1988: 17; Galen, *de usu partium* 14.9). The mixed potency of pleasure
and intense desire rendered the body at risk precisely at its most vulnerable moment — a body consumed by convulsive spasms and thus
out of control was potentially damaging to public decorum and social
concord. Augustine's contribution to Western culture was a sexualized

interpretation of sin where both sexuality and human nature were corrupted with the result that sexual desire and death were the punishments for original sin (Pagels, 1988; Steinberg, 1975).

Does the *GLAE*, however, present Eve's body as a corrupting influence on society? The *GLAE* reveals more than one depiction of Eve. The narrative supports the perception that Eve's recognition of her nakedness is not meant to signal her nascent moment of sexual awakening but the moment at which she challenged the maker for the control of a body that had been taken from her — she was, after all, of clay artfully compounded by the creator and therefore did not have the status to mount such a challenge. Yet, challenge she did in the attempt to reclaim her body — a body that while artfully compounded by the creator was nevertheless hers to re-create. Hence, the narrator of the *GLAE* framed the story in such a way that a double voice emerges — one voice suggests that Eve's challenge was indicative of her shameless disregard for her heavenly benefactor and her inferior rank before him, for she had disgraced herself and forfeited the honor bestowed upon her at creation (Rabichev, 2000: 3). And the other voice defies this view by characterizing Eve as seeking control of her body — a complex, alternate view competing with the dominant view of Eve's sinful sexuality. The question of the ideological motive that drove these perceptions and who stood to gain from it is important. For whom was female sexual desire a threat and why?

Regulating fleshly appetites of all kinds generally has been of concern to societies — this need to regulate the sexual desires of both the social body and physical body, in particular, has received considerable attention (Schroeder, 1997). Both female and male sexual desires were regarded differently and these differences were enshrined in the codes that established the boundaries of legitimate and illegitimate desire. As was pointed out above, the process of setting boundaries of female sexuality came from males who had 'vested' interests in keeping boundaries intact — domestic, social, family, kinship, and tribal. Hence, a preponderance of materials from the perspective of males features examples of out-of-control female desire that was in need of regulation (Pagels, 1988). The *GLAE* presents two visions, one in which Eve is held responsible for how she displays her body and its reception publicly and the other where she remains in control of her body — it remains within her power to display it in the way that she regards as appropriate. This raises the question of how females in reality actually expressed sexuality, both publicly and privately, and how males viewed the expression of that sexuality.

The ancient texts are a collection of androcentric idealizations of female sexual desire, both legitimate and illegitimate (Pagels, 1988). For better or worse, female sexual desire was regarded as more dangerous than male desire and thus it became the focus of legislation and description — it potentially threatened the honor of the male, the household, and society. While it seems clear that the descriptions of female eroticism do not reflect the everyday experiences of females, these visions of female desire nevertheless functioned rhetorically and symbolically as the means for social commentary and theological propaganda. It would seem that males projected their fears upon the females of society not only to protect their niches of power, domestic and otherwise, but also to regulate the female body and its sexual potential. Men had a vested interest in controlling female erotic desire because of political and ideological arrangements that were based upon the distribution of specific forms of social relations in society, whether of family, kinship, or religion (Turner, 1996: 127–28).

While male desire was not personified as a snare, it was nevertheless a risky fire that constantly threatened the boundaries of the self, the household and community and, therefore, also required regulation. Male bodies were not immune to desire and were displayed as being easily seduced by smooth words, beguiling glances, and provocative bodies decked out — leading their own bodies to rush off oxen-like to slaughter or bird-like into a snare (Berquist, 1998). As the male body exceeded its own limits — considered a body in perilous condition — so also it often transgressed the limits of household, community, and covenant. Desire was a good thing as long as it did not disrupt rank and reputation, undermine households, and destabilize social order. Adam's unrestrained desire challenged the creator for the control of a body not his own and interrupted the normal course of the unity of the heavenly hierarchies. Desire was a fearsome thing; because its foundations were cosmic, it threatened the very essence of God's power (Carson, 1999: 84).

CONCLUSIONS

When Eve and Adam came to a shameful awareness of their nakedness and began to cover up, it symbolically signalled that their fleshly desires had crossed the threshold of bodily, celestial, and social boundaries. It also indicated that corporal appetites were powerful and perilous, with the potential to put at risk both the physical and social body. Satisfying the appetites of the body could not be achieved through continually feeding the insatiable somatic cravings of humans and society but through the systematic regulation and control of the physical and social body. Furthermore, while the body 'had its rightful place in a great chain of being that linked humans to God,' when Adam and Eve participated in the liabilities of the desiring flesh, it had consequences for the issues of power, celestial and social order, the stable continuity of the human race, and communal concord (Brown, 1988: 27). Accordingly, they emerged dressed, forever consigned to the exercise of restraining or directing influences over their bodies situated in *habitus*. Altering the contours of Adam's and Eve's bodies served symbolically to enforce compliance to social expectation and to restore the 'balance of *their* [the] bodies that *had* [have] deviated from the norm *of what was noble in humans* (Berquist, 2000: 162; emphasis mine).

Chapter 4

THE EXONERATION OF EVE IN THE
KEY OF HONOR AND SHAME

For though the devil tempted Eve to sin, yet Eve seduced Adam. And as the sin of
Eve would not have brought death to our soul and body unless the sin had afterwards
passed on to Adam, to which he was tempted by Eve, not by the devil, therefore, she is
more bitter than death.

(Kramer and Sprenger, 1951: 47)

INTRODUCTION

This chapter directs attention to the two versions of what went wrong in Paradise between God, Satan, Eve and Adam as described in the *GLAE*. There is the much briefer version recounted by Adam (*GLAE* 7–8) and the much longer version recounted by Eve (*GLAE* 14.3–30.1). Each presents two perspectives on how Eve and Adam fell out of favor with God and their subsequent expulsion from Paradise. Both versions of the narratives have been highly influential in determining how Eve and Adam were viewed in terms of the issues of sin and sexuality. For example, Eve in the art of the Reformation (sixteenth century CE) was regularly portrayed as a temptress with noticeable sexual appeal, as the trickster who deceives Adam into ingesting the forbidden fruit, and the quintessential sinner responsible for sin's entry into the world (Miles, 1989; Hieatt, 1983: 290–304).

A good sample piece from this period is the painting of Hans Baldung Grien (1480–1545), a prolific German artist and innovative exponent of the *memento mori* iconography (Czarnecka-Anastassiades, 2007: 3). In his *Eve, the Serpent and Death* (1510–12), Baldung's imagination and popular sentiment combined to impart his ideas about social order through the representation of female and male sexuality (Hieatt, 1980). He portrays Eve with a sly, sidelong glance, a suggestive smile, a hidden, forbidden fruit in her right hand, a left hand grasping the serpent's tail, and death's hand gripping her arm. She is depicted as being in full complicity with death and utterly committed to the nefarious deed of disobeying her creator. She is rendered potent, powerful and with her beguiling speech convinces the hapless male to eat of the forbidden fruit (Hiett, 1983; Miles, 1989: 127). Moreover, Grien's depiction of Eve in a revealing, naked pose reflected the negative attitudes attached in his day to female nakedness. As discussed in the previous chapter, female nakedness was associated with sensuality, temptation, and shame, while male nakedness was associated with power, religious commitment, athletic prowess, and self-discipline (Miles, 1989). These associations exerted an influence upon Grien's depiction of Eve's body — in his estimation, her body was implicated in the deed that she committed and thus her body was the canvas upon which to display her betrayal.

Yet, in the *GLAE*, Eve's recollections of her part in the primeval transgression exhibit a remarkable ambivalence of attitudes to her culpability (Levison, 2000b: 40–41). Indeed, as Levison has argued in an earlier study subsequently modified, the details that Eve includes in her account 'tend, if not to exonerate her entirely, at least to win the affection and empathy of her audience' (1989; 2000b: 440).[1] She reiterates that the serpent entered Adam's portion first before it entered hers. It was a male serpent who deceived her. The devil in disguise was irresistible, as were his appeals to her. She recalls that 'Satan came in the form of an angel and sang hymns to God as the angels. And I saw him similar to an angel' (*GLAE* 17.1-2). In the presence of camouflaged intentions, feigning intense sorrow at her animal-like existence and ignorance, Eve nevertheless resists the attempt to mislead her out of fear that God would be angry with her: 'Then the serpent said to me, "As God lives! I am grieved on your account that you are like animals, for I would not have you ignorant. But arise, hither, hearken to me and eat and perceive the value of that tree'. But I said to him, "I fear lest God be angry with me as he told us"' (*GLAE* 18.1-2). It is clear that she is in a conflict of emotions, in which reticence and fear play into her resistance (Levison, 2000a).

Levison suggests that this display of reticence and fear signals her good intentions in the face of beguiling opposition (2000b: 40–41). While Eve is duped, she does not perceive herself to have fallen into the role of the wanton deceiver. She recounts that she had been coerced by the enemy to take an oath to give the fruit to Adam while she still believed that the fruit was full of glory. After the serpent had convinced Eve to open the way into Paradise and they had walked a little way, he turned to her and said, '"I have changed my mind and I will not give you to eat." These things he said wishing to trap me in the end. And he said to me: "If you swear to me that you will give also to your husband." And I said, "I do not know what sort of oath I should swear to you? Yet what I know, I say to you: By the throne of the Master, and by the Cherubim and the Tree of Life, I will give also to my husband to eat"' (*GLAE* 19.1-2).

Even after discovering the deleterious effects of the fruit, she swears to give the fruit to Adam. Of note is the oath that Satan suggests she swear. Apart from the social consequences of swearing an oath, Cartledge points out that vows in narratives serve both as plot devices and as characterizations of the person making the vow (1992; Berlinerblau, 1996). The oath serves as a plot device that permits the narrator to add depth to his characterization of Eve. The narrative highlights Eve's response — not only is she uncertain about the nature of the oath that she is to swear, but even in the face of uncertainty she will swear it. Yet it is not Satan's oath that she swears but instead one of her own — 'I do not know what sort of oath I should swear to you? Yet what I know, I say to you . . .' (*GLAE* 19.1-2). Swearing the oath, however, causes her great consternation; 'I wept also about the oath' (*GLAE* 20.3). Eve is depicted not as one simply engaging in a mindless verbal act devoid of deep regret and remorse, but rather as one deeply sorrowful for her verbal conduct. Even though the oath was a powerful performative that bound Eve to Satan, the binding was mitigated by her contrition — an emotion that would have been considered socially honorable and praiseworthy. Finally, Adam excludes Eve from the primeval transgression when he confesses that 'I alone have sinned' (*GLAE* 27.2; Levison, 2000b: 41). Based on his close analysis of the *GLAE*, Levison concludes that the 'autobiographical narrator, Eve, employs a variety of literary techniques to exonerate herself in her version of the primal transgression, curses, and expulsion from paradise' (Levison, 2000a: 255).

Adam, for the most part, is absolved of his role in the Fall of human-kind, but in seeking his absolution he both denigrates and exonerates Eve. Adam bemoans his dying — that it is on account of Eve's deed that he experiences death through her (*GLAE* 7.1). Adam imputes to Eve responsibility not only for his own death but also for the death of the entire human race: 'O Eve, what have you done to us? You have brought wrath upon us which is death which will rule over our entire race' (*GLAE* 14.2).[2] By implication, Adam also iterates that the virtue of his innocence protected him from disobedience to his creator, while the wickedness of Eve's gullibility opened her to the advances of the Devil — 'He gave us power to eat of every tree which is paradise, but, concerning that one only, He charged us not to eat of it, *yet she did*, and through this one we are to die' (*GLAE* 7.1, emphasis mine).

Not mentioned in Eve's version of this incident is Adam's conclusion that Satan entered his portion while he was praying. Despite Eve's being guarded by angels, she nevertheless succumbed to the advances of the Devil — 'and the hour drew near for the angels who were guarding your mother to go up and worship the Lord' (*GLAE* 7.2). Eve also takes the full blame for Adam's sickness — that it is she who brought it on: 'My Lord Adam, rise up and give me half of your trouble and I will endure it; for it is on my account that this has happened to you, on my account you are beset with toils and troubles' (*GLAE* 9.1-2). Adam's egregious behavior was imputed to Eve; 'And the enemy gave it to her and she ate from the tree. You know that I was not near her nor the holy angels' (*GLAE* 7.2). Indeed, it is she who 'gave also to me to eat' (*GLAE* 7.3a). Adam is portrayed as the innocent victim and sins solely because of Eve's treachery. Adam, however, eventually softens his position and takes full responsibility for his sin by confessing, 'I alone have sinned' (*GLAE* 27.2).

Yet the litany of accusations against Eve does not cease. A wild beast assailing Adam and Eve's son Seth formally accuses Eve with the rise of the rule of the wild beasts and the transformation of their natures from tame to wild. 'Then the beast cried out and said: "It is not our concern, Eve, your greed and your wailing, but your own; for it is from you that the rule of the beasts has arisen . . . On this account, our nature has also been transformed"' (*GLAE* 10.4–11.2). Eve is pictured as being dependent upon Seth to interpret a vision of a spectacular kind, weeping and constantly perplexed, unable to decipher its meaning.

Levison's observation that the testament of Eve appears to exonerate her and that it evokes a sympathetic response in the audience is attractive, but it does little by way of explaining Eve's remarkable monologue. Nor does it explain why the author chose to run parallel, contradictory storylines — one that focused on Adam and his admissions of shame and wrongdoing and the other on Eve and her confessions of shameful but justifiable culpability. Eve is presented as culpable and innocent — seemingly mutually exclusive points of view.

What are we to make of the two versions of Eve's story? The text forms of the *GLAE* developed in the context of everyday life and were thus utilized for various ideologically driven motives and contemporary notions of conduct befitting females, in terms of body, gender, and sexuality. So, for example, increasingly negative views of women as seductresses, tricksters, and sources of evil led to the telling of these stories to support a view of Eve as the prototype of all females, and this, in turn, continued to feed the popular imagination that women were indeed seductresses, tricksters, and sources of evil (Levison, 2000a). The commonplace quality of the stories in the *GLAE* thus permitted paradoxical stories of Eve to evolve in a single but multivalent version.

The commonplace quality of the stories of Eve, in certain social circumstances, deliberately played into the motifs of perversion and abuse (Greiner, 1999: 22) in which it was important to denigrate Eve. If Eve, however, was not the prototype of human failure but of human success, how then does her story play itself out? My argument is that the paradoxical elements in the story are an inherent part of a single discourse from two perspectives — one generated by views peculiar to the world of males with the propensity to denigrate Eve and the other peculiar to the world of females with the inclination to exonerate Eve. Pressures would have been exerted from the perspectives of males and females to avoid shameful acts and, depending on group and social circumstances, women's views of men's behavior and men's views of women's behavior would have differed radically. By blackening the reputation of Eve, Adam saved face; by setting herself free from reproach, Eve also saved face. Those who narrated the stories of Adam and Eve were interested in shaping attitudes and values with regard to what was considered appropriate and inappropriate behavior for males and females, from the perspectives of their social milieu.[3]

Levison has pointed out that, as unique exigencies emerged, early interpreters of the Adam and Eve cycle of stories were forced to adapt them to meet the specific concerns of particular social groups. Distinct emphases over different periods shaped and reshaped the constituents of what was considered appropriate behavior for males and females (Pitt-Rivers, 1977: 16). As Pitt-Rivers points out, variations in foundational stories are not uncommon even within the culture of a single region. He notes that 'while this has sometimes been taken to reflect differences between classes or factions in their struggles to impose their own evaluations upon their society, it must be pointed out that this is not merely due to the emergence of new social forces that require the rules to be altered, as it were, if they are to gain power, but to the fact that different elements of society behave in different ways and think in different ways, albeit within the framework of a common language' (Pitt-Rivers, 1977: 16). The two versions of the story provide an interactional context in which shameful acts are attributed to both Adam and Eve, each with their own consequences. We do not know with certainty the exigencies that the narrator of the *GLAE* faced, but we do know that differing perceptions of what counted for honorable and shameful conduct functioned as a type of discourse to inculcate socially appropriate behavior in both men and women. We need, therefore, to explore the cultural values of honor and shame and the unforeseen problems that are precipitated when standards of what is honorable and dishonorable differ between males and females.

The Grammar of Honor and Shame

While what counted as honorable and shameful in the ancient Mediterranean world was not defined in the same way everywhere (Swartz, 1988: 21), anthropologists have nevertheless shown that Greeks, Romans and Judeans regarded honor and shame as pivotal values in their social milieu. Honor has been defined as the 'value of a person in his own eyes, but also in the eyes of his society' (Pitt-Rivers, 1977: 1; Malina and Neyrey, 1991: 25). Honor has to do with self-regard and social esteem. Indeed, because honor only had value if it was acknowledged publicly by one's community, a person could not claim to have honor without its requisite recognition from the community. It was about how a person viewed themselves and how they were viewed by others — self-perception had to be congruent with public perception. In the words of Pitt-Rivers, 'the claimant of honor must get himself accepted at his own evaluation, must be granted reputation, or else the claim becomes mere vanity, an object of ridicule or contempt . . ..' (Pitt-Rivers, 1966: 22). Honor, then, is the claim to worth and the social acknowledgement of that worth (Malina, 1993: 32). Honor and shame had largely to do with status, reputation, and esteem, but also with integrity, rectitude, and probity and their gain or loss in the competitive push-and-shove of daily life. Given that honor was in limited supply, not all had it or could aspire to it and those who had it could not be guaranteed that in every social encounter it could be maintained. Maintaining honor required vigilance, wit, integrity, loyalty, magnanimity — moral qualities common to both sexes, but qualities that could be contested. All persons were constantly compelled to assess their own conduct relative to that of others around them.

Honor could be obtained in one of two ways: it was either ascribed or acquired. Ascribed honor was derived from birth and the standing that members of the family had as a result. In other words, honor could be symboled by blood and name — 'purity of blood, owed essentially to the behaviour of women, and renown principally to the behaviour of men, ensure together their collective honor which is degraded into shame if either blood or name is tainted' (Di Bella, 1992: 152). A name symboled 'being born into an honourable family [that] makes one honourable, since the family is the repository of the honour of past illustrious ancestors and their accumulated acquired honour' (Malina, 1993: 33, 38; Di Bella, 1992: 13, 151–65). Acquired honor could be gained by great acts of courage, athletic prowess, artistic accomplishment, and favors done for a beneficent person who had bestowed a gift upon you. As quickly as honor was acquired it could also be lost in the interminable game of challenge and response. What counted as honorable for a male might not count for what was honorable in a female — indeed honor could and did imply quite different codes of conduct required/demanded of each of them (Pitt-Rivers, 1977: 20).

MALE AND FEMALE HONOR AND SHAME

The honor of the male depended on the series of socially defined roles that he was either entitled or obligated to fulfill — courage, authority,

defence of his family honor, concern for prestige, the seeking of social
eminence, his position as husband and father, preserving the chastity of
his women, the ability to defend women from blemish, the generosity
displayed not only to insiders but also to outsiders, the poor and foreign
visitor, mercy shown to enemies, the accretion of prestige for his group
through his actions (Di Bella, 1992: 151). A good name was one of
the most valuable assets that a male could have. Thus, the avoidance
at all cost of the 'shameless ones' whose dishonorable reputation had
been well established 'through their habitual indulgence in conduct
which is shameful: petty thieving, begging and promiscuity in the case
of women' (Pitt-Rivers, 1977: 19). Keenly sensitive to shame, the male
was concerned about reputation both as a sentiment and the public
recognition of that sentiment (Pitt-Rivers, 1977: 20). This sentiment
made a male acutely aware of the pressure exerted by the court of
public opinion upon him, but also the esteem earned in consequence
(Pitt-Rivers, 1977: 20). At times, shame and honor were perceived to
be synonymous, since a good person was thought to have both. While
to feel shame was common to both sexes, given that both were sensitive
to maintaining reputation and that neither would expose themselves
to the risk of humiliation, when it was imposed externally and socially
recognized as such, it became humiliation (Pitt-Rivers, 1977: 21). For
the male, it was the avoidance of shamelessness — that which had the
potential to render him a dishonorable man. For the female, it was
also the avoidance of shamelessness — that which had the potential to
render her a dishonorable woman (Pitt-Rivers, 1977: 20).

While certain conduct defined honor and shame for both female
and male — the female had to conserve her purity and the male to
defend his honor and that of his family — not in all instances were
honor and shame synonymous. Shame that expressed itself in shyness,
timidity, and blushing was appropriate for the female but not for the
male, and honor 'when no longer equivalent to shame becomes an
exclusively male attribute as the concern for precedence and the
willingness to offend another man if provoked' (Pitt-Rivers, 1977: 21;
Di Bella, 1992: 151–65). A male who displayed timidity was likely to be
ridiculed and the female who displayed violence or attempted to usurp
the male prerogative of authority was likely to be regarded as acting
shamelessly. If she behaved indecorously, she forfeited her honor. The
honor of a kinship group and the criteria by which honor was granted

began with the females maintaining her sexual purity — in this way the continuity of the group was assured by reproducing it, and its immaculate genealogy was safeguarded by their fidelity (Di Bella, 1992: 152, 156). While Eve's infidelity may not have been sexual, her reputation, however, lay in ruins because of her deceitful behavior. Even if Eve had not committed adultery *per se*, she had nevertheless liaised in a questionable way with the Devil.

The division of labor between the sexes corresponded to the division of roles in the family structure. The virtue of maintaining sexual purity or maintaining loyalty to her husband and children was delegated to the female. In the eyes of Adam, Eve must not betray the trust of her husband, children, and children's children by consorting with the enemy (*GLAE* 15.1). An honorable woman, born with the proper attitude of shame, strove to avoid potentially embarrassing encounters that would expose her inadvertently to accusations of shameless conduct — here, in the case of her husband, children, children's children, and even wild beasts. If she committed adultery or betrayed her husband and children in some other way, she would have been perceived to be challenging the very foundations of the house in which she was domiciled. Adam was also fully aware that the virtue of maintaining and defending the sexual honor/fidelity of his wife and children was delegated to him. He knew that the honor of the household was established in male sexuality and its associated virtue of courage — namely to defend the honor of his wife and children by not permitting behavioral impropriety in his house. Specifically, his honor was bound up in the sexual purity of his wife and daughters, not in his own sexual purity (Pitt-Rivers 1977: 23). If they were in breach of the promise to remain loyal to him, not only did such a betrayal infringe on his rights but it also demonstrated publicly that he had failed in his duties (Pitt-Rivers, 1977: 24; Peristiany and Pitt-Rivers (eds), 1992; Di Bella, 1992: 13).

Adam was, above all, obligated to defend the honor of his wife on which his own honor depended. Should Eve commit adultery or betray him, her infidelity became his betrayal of household values — it brought dishonor to all of the other persons involved reciprocally in his honor. Preserving the dignity of an individual, whether child or spouse, 'was essential because the dignity of the individual reflected the dignity and esteem of the group/household' (Rabichev, 1996: 54). Were Adam unable to protect Eve from blemish, he would have been open to opprobrium by a judging public. He was, after all, enjoined with the social obligation of defending the honor of Eve — his failure tainted those around him and rendered him an object of scorn in public. In the public court of reputation, Adam had lost his good standing and was now a source of shame and disgrace to those in his household (Bechtel, 1991: 47–76).

Eve's betrayal publicly defiled the reputation of Adam — he had been unable to preserve the dignity and integrity of Eve. When Eve gave in to the enemy, she brought into public view Adam's inability to preserve her integrity. Thus, the public court of opinion rendered its verdict — her conduct, while not beyond reproach in her eyes, nevertheless did receive public opprobation — Adam, the one defiled, would have been regarded as dishonorable — 'it is the defiled one who will become the object of contempt, not the defiler' (Pitt-Rivers, 1977: 24).

Julian Pitt-Rivers, in his analysis of Andalusian attitudes to a cuckolded husband, notes that oddly enough, a wife could not have succeeded in this ambition of adultery or betrayal if unsupported by the authority of her husband (1977: 23). This gave rise to the deceived husbands being the object of ridicule and opprobrium and not the betrayer's/adulterer's social disgrace. The symbolism of the cuckold, *cabron*, meant literally 'the billy-goat.' In Spain, the billy-goat had horns — the horns were a phallic symbol and also the insignia of the Devil (Pitt-Rivers, 1977: 23). Adam had fallen under the dominion of Satan and had to bear the stigma of his befoolment by Eve when she was under his authority. Yet, as we shall see, in the *GLAE*, both Adam and Eve bore the stigmata of shame — shame was not an exclusive property of the female and honor was not an exclusive prerogative of the male — they both had honor to lose or gain, though for different reasons.

In an intriguing study of the expression of honor and shame among the poor in Cairo, Unni Wikan argued that shame rather than honor was of primary concern to both men and women (1984: 636). Her study showed that honor was not necessarily a binary opposite of shame (Wikan, 1984: 636). Honor and shame were ascribed through social interaction by significant others who were in the position to pass judgement on the behaviors of both men and women. This means that 'everyone is judged by some significant other to be blemished by shame and, since these verdicts are publicly spoken, there are not two categories of people — those endowed with honor (men) and those deprived of it (women). There is just one category, 'shameful people' (Wikan, 1984: 636).

Both men and women were concerned with honor, but shame rather than honor was a salient feature of their everyday lives (Wikan, 1984: 636). Hence, in everyday discourse, both men and women tended not speak of their own or each other's honor but rather they tended to speak of their shame (Wikan, 1984: 638). Thus, even if honor for the male rested ultimately on the female's sexual conduct, that did not mean that a woman had no honor to gain — this even after she had forfeited her honor because of illegitimate behavior. Indeed, a woman could gain value in her own eyes and in the eyes of the others around her even after her injudicious conduct had become public. Moreover, even if a woman's sexual conduct or loyalty were in question, that did not mean that men would have thought of her as having no value at all. Female fidelity and loyalty were not the essence of honor, nor was honor the absence of shameful acts. Indeed, the shame engendered by infidelity and disloyalty in women could be mitigated by such conduct as kindness, hospitality, generosity, and helpfulness (1984: 641). So while a shameful act might affect a woman's value in the eyes of men, some value derived from her positive behavior would nevertheless remain (1984: 644). This perceptual difference concerning what was honorable and what was not, especially when honor had been tainted by moral indiscretion, had to do with men and women only partially inhabiting each other's worlds of experience.

Wikan noted that 'there is the multitude of small women's worlds in which men also figure, but marginally and in partial capacities as husbands, brothers, sons, etc., and there is a single large world of the men that also embraces women, but in their partial, male-relevant capacities, as mothers, wives, daughters, sisters, etc.' (1984: 645). She goes on, 'both worlds contain standards for both men and women, but one is embraced by men, and the other is embraced by women. In the male world, females are interesting mainly in terms of their sexual trust-worthiness, because this is where they so strongly affect the lives of men. In the female world, hospitality, kindness, generosity, and a number of other qualities are highly relevant and have priority' (1984: 645). The value of women is determined such that what counts as honorable in the world of females may be different from what counts as honorable in the world of males (1984: 645). The impact of the shame of infidelity, for example, could be ameliorated in the court of women by noting their otherwise good behavior — their honor, while tainted, nevertheless could still be in force. The impact of the shame of female infidelity in the world of males could not be so easily ameliorated because the honor of a male was dependent upon a female maintaining her reputation in the public places within which men moved. Since in his eyes her feminine status precluded her from striving for honor, he judged her behavior by the codes of shame that kept the female in her place. As Marcus J. Swartz points out, 'from the perspective of community life, shame's most significant attribute is its role in promoting socially desirable or, at least, acceptable modes of behaviour and general qualities of well being' (Swartz, 1988: 21).

Men and women, however, viewed the matter of sexual impropriety and loyalty in different ways — especially in the way in which each responded to it publicly. Women were concerned about what others might think of them but the concern was not so much for themselves as it was for their husbands. They knew that a man's honor was dependent on the repute of a woman in the public world of a few friends, a number of acquaintances, and a host of strangers within which he moved (Wikan, 1984: 642). A woman's honor was not dependent upon recognition of her honor in the midst of an anonymous host of strangers. She was not a public figure in the way men viewed public space — 'the persons to whom she looks for personal worth and public esteem are not "out there" in an anonymous sea of "public opinion"' (Wikan, 1984: 642). Her public space was defined by a few acquaintances that she knew well and that knew her well. She had been socialized to be modest in a way that was oriented away from the public (Wikan, 1984: 642). In this way, women could socialize with all kinds of women, secure in the knowledge that they knew her and she knew them.

Men, on the other hand, were acutely aware that their every move was being scrutinized by numerous people who did not know them and formed opinions about them based on passing hearsay and incomplete evidence about who they were — they would have been mostly an unknown quantity in the public sphere (Wikan, 1984: 642). Their honor would always be on the line, open to the scrutiny of success or failure because their actions would be measured by the exacting standards of people who did not know them well. Thus, they would have had to be constantly on guard to protect their public image and that of their wives. This would have forced each man to 'steer a deft and elegant course with very few signals from that public who are his judges' (Wikan, 1984: 642, 646). A man would forfeit honor should he be found to fall short of the standards that prevailed in the public world of men. Because each woman was under the authority of a male, her failure became her male's responsibility. That male had failed in his responsibility and had to take the full blame for it and the public censure that would ensue. To the mutual concerns of the men in their world, hospitality, kindness, and generosity as expressed by women remained marginal and to the mutual concerns of women in their world, female sexuality remained marginal. Hence, adultery and other forms of betrayal were much less scandalous in the court of women than they were in the world of men (Wikan, 1984: 645). In such a world, a woman could seek justification for her actions — even to the point of being set free from the obligation for responsibility for misconduct that had shamed her family.

We will now apply the Mediterranean codes of honor and shame to select sections of the *GLAE*.[4] We hope to show that the values of honor and shame can help us to understand the apparently contradictory desire to both exonerate and denigrate Eve — each finding rightful expression in a multivalent narrative.

APPLICATION OF THE GRAMMAR OF HONOR AND SHAME TO THE *GLAE*

Lists of sanctioned and prohibited behaviors have long been a variable in the control of men and women. It is clear from the accounts of human failure in Paradise that the monumental issues of what constituted fitting behavior in both men and women were at stake — in particular, when their conduct was perceived to challenge the honor of Adam, Eve, and God. By placing the issue of conduct in the social milieu of what counted as honorable to Adam, Eve, and God — all of whom desired to avoid disgrace — its influence on behavior increased. After all, who would wish to defy what God, Adam, or Eve desired? Arguments about matters surrounding behavior were rhetorically constructed attempts to negotiate and define the conduct of the first humans — Adam's comment after his easy capitulation, 'O wicked woman! What have you done to us? You have deprived me of my Glory' (*GLAE* 21.6) was an

expletive that at the same time both blamed and shamed and through
shame also attempted to control the behavior of Eve. Adam, as arbiter
and guardian of his own honor, knew fully that his reputation was on the
line at the point when he was forced to admit that he had been duped
(Wikan, 1984: 646). And, duped he had been — 'O wicked woman!
What have you done to us' — and forced to concede that he was a
befooled man (*GLAE* 21.6). Hence, his obligation to point the finger
of blame at Eve — it was a desperate attempt to restore his honor. Yet,
all was not as simple as that — Eve strategically insinuated her point of
view into the storyline and rearranged the lines of argument.

The value that Eve had in her own eyes and in the eyes of the others
around her was measured by the standards in her society rather than
by those in Adam's society. Eve's female circle would have measured
her behavior in terms of honor as integrity and esteem from a different
perspective. Adam would have viewed Eve's conduct from the perspective of the standards in force in the world of men and Eve from the view
of the standards in force in the world of women. Both worlds contained
standards for Adam and Eve, but one was embraced by Adam and the
other by Eve (Wikan, 1984: 645).

The *GLAE* makes it clear that a division existed between the world of
males and the world of females. While Eve was explaining to her children the events that led up to her betrayal, she noted that both she and
Adam were guarding Paradise as each had been apportioned to them
by God — the west and the south for Eve and the east and the north for
Adam: 'Now I guarded in my lot, the west and the south. But the devil
went to Adam's lot, where the male creatures were. [For God divided
the creatures; all the males he gave to your father and all the females he
gave to me.]' (*GLAE* 15.2-3). Of note is that the Devil first visited Adam
in his lot, where the male creatures were, and then eventually entered
Eve's lot, where he initiated a sequence of events that ultimately forced
her to submit to his own devilish advances. Based on this division of
males and females into their respective areas, it is possible to argue that
what happened would have been seen from two different perspectives.
In the eyes of the women in Eve's lot, her betrayal would have been of
marginal concern and much less heinous than it seemed to the males in
Adam's lot. She was a noble woman, praiseworthy in many ways because
of the stiff resistance she had put up against such a beguiling force. In
the court of females, seeking Eve's exoneration would not have been

surprising for they would have desired to exonerate her from the banal reproach of capitulating to her passions without resistance. It was her praiseworthy character that trumped the betrayal — in their eyes, her honorable status had not been compromised.

In most evaluations of Eve's confessions, the assumption is made that the monologue is an admission of her principal faults that is designed to mitigate her failure before God and Adam. It is my contention, however, that Eve is not confessing failure, but rather explaining how she intends to rectify what she has done. The whole confession is a vindication of sorts. She mentions the motives that still actuate her: fear of disgrace, a sense of responsibility as mother to set an example for her children, the concern for the good repute of her husband and children — all laudable motives that soften the impact of her behavior. In the court of female opinion, Eve's otherwise good behavior mitigated the shame of her betrayal — acknowledging her admirable conduct was their way of saying how honorable Eve was. After Eve has called her children and her children's children together, she takes responsibility for her behavior by relating to them how she had been imposed upon by the enemy (*GLAE* 15.1). She recounts that the impostor, feigning genuine sorrow and solicitude, prevailed upon her by singing hymns like the angels, taking on the nonchalant pose of bending over the wall as one with no cares in the world, guising himself in the personal appearance of an angel so as to conceal his true identity, pretending genuine interest in her by asking 'are you Eve?' and enquiring what she was doing in Paradise (*GLAE* 17.1-3). He further falsely flattered her to obtain favor and serve his own purposes — 'you do well but you do not eat of every plant' (*GLAE* 17.4), was seemingly grieving to see Eve prostituted to such low and contemptible pursuits that were no greater than those of animals — 'I am grieved on your account that you are like animals' (*GLAE* 18.1), smugly asserting that 'I would not want you ignorant' (18.1), and smartly commanding her to 'arise, come to me, apply your ears privily to hear me, consume the fruit, and discern the value of that tree' (*GLAE* 18.1). The onslaught on her senses was overwhelming and irresistible. She had been hit from every angle and yet, even under the persistent verbal harangue of the Devil, she had remained a responsible actor with regard to her honor. She had not just mindlessly capitulated to the enemy's entrapment. Indeed, the Devil had endeavored to harangue Eve into betrayal of Adam and in the end succeeded but not without considerable resistance from her.

Eve's fear of disgrace stiffened her resistance to the advances of Satan — she did not simply capitulate, unresisting, to her passions. The fear of public humiliation, however, was not driven so much by concern for herself as by the desire to preserve the integrity of Adam and God in the eyes of the observing public. She was fully aware of Adam's constant need to protect her from reproach. She knew that he would forfeit his honor should he be found to fall short of the standards that prevailed in the public world of men. Because Eve was under the authority of Adam, her failure became his responsibility.

Yet, ultimately she did surrender to Satan. Why did Eve help the enemy to enter Paradise — what is it that he knew that she did not? Upon entrance into Paradise, Satan changed his mind and defaulted on his promise that he would give her to eat (*GLAE* 19.1). Based on the codes of honor and shame, the Devil knew exactly how to trap Eve — he knew that it was not Eve who would ultimately bear the brunt of her shameless behavior, but Adam. Aware that she would continue to resist him, what were the means at his disposal to soften Eve's resistance? In an act of calumny, the Devil pressured her into swearing an oath that she would give also to her husband to eat — if he ate, they were mutually consigned to each other's fate (*GLAE* 19.1). She acquiesced to his demands even though she was uncertain about the kind of oath she was to swear — 'I do not know what sort of oath I should swear to you' (*GLAE* 19.2). But swear she did, and almost immediately regretted her promise. She was clearly cognizant of the disgrace that she would bring upon Adam and herself and lamented the oath that she had sworn 'I wept also about the oath, which I had sworn' (*GLAE* 20.1). Oaths, however, were binding and non-retractable — indeed, even if Eve had desired to back out of the oath she was unable to do so for the enemy had 'descended from the tree and vanished' (*GLAE* 20.1). She called Adam and gave him to eat but took full responsibility for her actions — this despite having the Devil speak through her mouth: 'I spoke to him words of transgression which have brought us down from our great glory' (*GLAE* 21.2).

Another reason that explains why she did not yield unresisting to her passions was her fear that God would be angry with her (*GLAE* 18.2). She had no desire to disgrace her patron deity, who had gifted both her and Adam with life, children, knowledge, and Paradise. With such a benefactor and as the recipient of such beneficence, she was under the obligation to honor, worship, and obey him. Indeed, the only proper response that she could render to God was some form of praise, honor and gratitude (Neyrey, 2005: 486), not some form of defiance of his will. So the Devil raised the stakes, pulling a most attractive card from his deck and offering it to her, namely, knowledge. Do not fear, he said soothingly, as soon as you eat of it, you 'too shall be as gods, in that you shall know what is good and what is evil' (*GLAE* 18.3). Eve is offered equality with Adam and God on one of the fundamental mysteries of life — knowledge of good and evil. Yet, still she resists for the reasons presented above and so the Devil proceeds to tantalize her with the most attractive of all the cards in his deck. He informs Eve that God is involved in a bit of double-dealing himself by withholding knowledge that would make Adam and Eve his equals. The Devil demurely comments that 'God knew that you would be like him, and so he envied (ἐφθόνησεν) you and forbade you to eat of the tree' (*GLAE* 18.4). Worse, the Devil asserted to Eve, it was out of envy that God had handed the couple over to ignorance — for envy was not an ennobling emotion for God and appeared as an insult to the two humans.

In the ancient world, envy was an intense feeling like zeal or jealousy and, like jealousy, concerned possessing someone or something. Envy, however, had no positive quality. Envy was always evil and never virtuous (Elliott, 2007; Neyrey 1998b). Envy was the grief or distress of a person at the sight of valued goods possessed and enjoyed by a perceived rival, accompanied by the wish that the rival be dispossessed of the things causing happiness (Elliott, 2007; Neyrey 1998b).[5] Jealousy feared damage to self, envy intended damage to others (Elliott, 2007; Neyrey 1998b). In the context of the Garden of Eden, the Devil insinuated that envy arose when God saw Adam and Eve potentially possessing something of value and felt distress over the possession of the valued item and the happiness it would bring to its owners. Even if God, the benefactor, had given life, children, Paradise and partial knowledge to Adam and Eve — ostensibly positive acts — the envier begrudged the gift of full knowledge out of fear that this gift would result in his own loss (Elliott, 2007; Neyrey, 1998b). The feeling of ill-will occasioned by the contemplation of superior advantages possessed by Adam and Eve put God in breach of conduct unbecoming of a deity. Compared with the act of attributing shameful behavior to God, Eve's breach of conduct paled absolutely. She only desired something that should have been given to her in the first place and not denied her out of envy. Though still fearful to take the fruit (*GLAE* 18.6), she proceeded in this instance because of the unbecoming emotion of envy that had apparently driven the deity to keep knowledge from Eve and Adam.

Thus, these narratives attempted to prescribe shaming and honoring modes of behavior for males and females by presenting Adam as one whose honor failed him because of Eve's shameless behavior and by representing Eve as one whose honor, while tattered from the point of view of Adam, was nevertheless still intact. Presenting an exculpated Eve was a rhetorical flourish calculated to show that she was committed to setting right what had gone wrong — her stance was proactive, while Adam's was reactive because of his fear of disgrace. Eve was creating and controlling a situation by taking the initiative and anticipating events or problems, rather than just reacting to them after they had occurred. She had a sense of responsibility as a mother to set an example and she had a sense of obligation for the good repute of her husband and children. The exoneration of Eve in the context of honor and shame would have played a significant role in establishing social relationships between males and females, in promoting socially desirable and acceptable modes of behavior in them, and in imparting general qualities of well-being in and between humans.

CONCLUSIONS

It is not surprising that the author of the *GLAE* had Eve and Adam recount their respective stories of failures from the perspective of their own besmirched reputations. Adam, in defence of his failed bid to protect the honor of Eve, admits to his failure and even at points exonerates Eve by noting her other virtues. Eve confesses to the loss of her honor and the resulting shame it imputed to Adam, while at the same time outlining what she intends to do to set the record straight.

Nevertheless, as a householder under the obligation to defend his position as husband and father, to deal with strength in public transactions, to be daring and bold, and to run his household with authority, Adam had failed. Yet, that was one of only a number of failures. Little wonder that Seth notices his father's despondence and asks, 'Father Adam, what is thy complaint?' (*GLAE* 5.4). Adam responds, 'My children, I am crushed by the burden of trouble' (*GLAE* 5.5). Seth wrongly assumed that his father was yearning for the fruit of Paradise that he had once eaten and vowed that he would bring it to him even if it meant setting dung upon his head, weeping, and praying until the Lord hearkened to him (*GLAE* 6.1). Adam informed Seth that his sickness and trouble were the result of an event of much greater significance. The source of his greatest moment of shame emerged — he had been unable to control Eve's loyalty to him. She had acted shamelessly — under his nose she had switched her loyalties from him to the enemy 'who gave it to her and she ate from the tree' (*GLAE* 17). In his eyes, her shameless comportment threatened not only the very foundations of his household but also the order in society.

Eve's betrayal would have represented a serious infringement of Adam's rights and would have made publicly visible Adam's failure in his duty (Pitt-Rivers, 1977: 24). In the case of Adam, his manliness had failed him — because of Eve's behavior 'he had fallen under the domination of Satan and had to wear his symbol as the stigma of this betrayal' (Pitt-Rivers, 1977: 24; Di Bella, 1992). As we have pointed out, the responsibility for the failure was his and not that of the betrayer — in this case, Eve, who under pressure from the panderer had submitted to him. Neither was Eve ultimately responsible for what had befallen her — 'it was the panderer, not the libertine that was the prototype of male dishonour' (Pitt-Rivers, 1977: 24). While opinions of Eve's betrayal would have varied with time and group, her exoneration represented an attempt to set the record straight. Had this been seen by early interpreters, Eve would not have ended up as the quintessential seductress, trickster, and source of evil for humankind.

PART THREE

J.R.C. Cousland

INTRODUCTION

Part Three investigates the genres and generic influences upon the Greek and Latin 'Lives' of Adam and Eve. Genre is concerned with identifying different kinds of discourse, and the purpose of these chapters is to establish the genres of the Greek and Latin 'Lives' of Adam and Eve.[1]

Such an undertaking is essential for several reasons. First, a proper appreciation of the genre of a work is a *sine qua non* to interpreting it properly. Alastair Fowler, one of the leading modern theorists on the phenomenon of genre, rightly observes that 'Every work of literature belongs to at least one genre' (1982: 20).[2] Thus, even if one reads and interprets a work without considering its genre, one is still making tacit judgements about what kind of discourse it is. These judgements need to be made explicit and justified in any analysis of discourse.

In the case of the Greek and Latin 'Lives', however, both works would especially benefit from generic analysis. In the case of the *Greek Life of Adam and Eve* (*GLAE*), there has been a surfeit of hypotheses over the last century, but no appreciable agreement among commentators. Nor has there been a concerted examination of the question. In his recent and valuable study of the *GLAE*, Michael D. Eldridge laments the fact that, 'it is surprising that so far little serious attempt has been made to place the Greek life in relation to the genre or genres to which it lies closest with a view to gaining access to its intended meaning' (2001: 160–61). While Eldridge makes a valuable contribution towards this subject himself (2001: 160–72), it is fair to say that a more sustained treatment would be useful, and this is the topic of Chapter 5.

Chapter 6 treats the genre of the *Latin Life of Adam and Eve* (*LLAE*).

In 1992 Michael Stone wrote of the Latin *Vita* that he had found very few discussions that 'dealt in any detail with the purpose, shape or function of this version, nor with it in comparison with the Greek Apocalypse of Moses' (1992: 23). While this situation has begun to change, it certainly remains true that these features of the version have yet to be treated extensively. For instance, the historical survey of the *GLAE*'s genre that is offered in Chapter 5 (Table 5.1) is not really possible with the *LLAE* and, in fact, the situation of the Latin life is virtually the reverse of the *GLAE*. Very little has been done on the character of the work, and there are few surmises about its genre. Given the similarities between the Greek and Latin 'Lives', one might presume that the genre of the *LLAE* would be the same as that of the *GLAE*, but this presumption certainly warrants investigation. Chapter 6, therefore, sets out to explore the literary genre of the *LLAE*.

Genre

Establishing the genre of a work is not as straightforward a process as it might sound. Defining genre has long been a problematic enterprise, and the burgeoning of genre criticism over the last century has made the term 'genre' increasingly protean and hard to define.[3] Our English word 'genre' ultimately comes via the French from the Latin term *genus*, meaning 'sort' or 'kind,' and these 'kinds' are based on coherent and recurring patterns of literary characteristics. Typically, these are recurring patterns of form, content and function (Aune, 2003: 196). Here, however, theoretical agreement among scholars appears to come to an abrupt end. De Bruyn observes:

> Despite its long and impressive pedigree, the theory of genres is anything but a settled branch of criticism. The multiplicity of names that 'genre' has assumed in English — kind, species, type, mode, format — attests to the Babel-like confusion surrounding this discourse.[4] Indeed, because the concept of genre raises fundamental questions about the nature and status of literary texts, there are perhaps as many different definitions of 'genre' as there are theories of literature. (1993: 79; cf. Frye, 1957: 246)

If that problem were not sufficient, the very existence of genre has been called into question. Thomas Rosenmeyer, for instance, asks whether ancient literary genres are simply a mirage. He maintains that ancient authors were not especially concerned with adhering to abstractions like genre, and were more intent upon emulating individual authors (2006).[5] Alternatively, some scholars who do recognize the existence of genre simply discount its relevance. Maurice Blanchot affirms that:

> The book is the only thing that matters, the book as it is, far from genres, outside of the categorical subdivisions — prose, poetry, novel, document — in which it refuses to lodge and to which it denies the power of establishing its place and determining its form. A book no longer belongs to a genre; every book stems from literature alone, as if literature held in advance, in their generality, the secrets and the formulas that alone make it possible to give to what is written the reality of a book. It would thus be as though, the genres having faded away, literature were asserting itself alone in the mysterious clarity that it propagates . . . (Blanchot, 1959: 136, cited in Todorov, 1990: 13).

Blanchot, therefore, proposes that genre is irrelevant — all that matters are the lone pieces of discourse swimming in a vast sea of text. His assertion, however, is tantamount to saying that in biology the only relation between any of the world's individual living organisms is the mere fact of their being alive. Yet, even if the taxonomies provided by biological science (species, genus, etc.) are not absolute, they nevertheless demonstrate that there are clear family resemblances between different creatures. Overlooking such similarities may privilege the integrity of the individual text or creature, but it seems to be courting ignorance unnecessarily.

For this reason, many scholars continue to recognize an heuristic value in the use of genres. For them, genre serves as a propaedeutic for interpretation because discourse of any sort needs to be classified by genre for it to be properly understood and assimilated. This 'pre-assimilation' process is sometimes referred to as *Vorverständnis* — a preliminary approach to the word or text that guides subsequent interpretation (Hirsch, 1967: 71–102). Clearly, if a reader has no idea whether they are reading an epic poem, a phonebook, or a laundry-list, they will have a very limited understanding of what they are reading.[6]

This is where genre comes into play: it furnishes a convention that helps individuals to define and roughly categorize an artistic production. Conte describes it neatly when he observes, 'in order to be perceived, the world must take on a form, become a model of meaning; and the literary genre's communicative strategies help the reader to construct a situation or a whole imaginary world' (1994: 112).

One aspect of this convention is the recognition of various modes within genre, which are traits that help to characterize and influence genre itself. If, for instance, one were to speak of a 'narrative,' one could qualify this genre in a variety of ways: a cautionary narrative, a legendary narrative, an historical narrative and the like. David Aune distinguishes mode from genre in his observation that

> genres are usually identified in noun form (e.g., 'apocalypse,' 'letter,' 'church order,' etc.), [while] modal terms tend to be adjectival (e.g., 'apocalyptic,' 'hymnlike,' 'encomiastic,' 'mythic,' 'satiric'). They are applied more widely and never imply a complete overall external form or structure, because they are based on a selection of the features of the genre with which they are most completely connected. (2003: 307; cf. Fowler, 1982: 106–29)

It follows, then, that modes have a considerable influence on the ultimate character of a genre, although they are not themselves genres. Their influence ultimately promotes the emergence of new genres by modifying the constituents of an old one.

Genre's literary roots go back to the time of Plato and Aristotle, where two approaches to discourse were distinguished: the descriptive and the mimetic. The first category was characteristic of narrative poetry (epic), and the second of dramatic poetry (tragedy, comedy). The recognition that epic was actually a combination of the descriptive and mimetic categories occasioned a third, 'mixed' category, where narrative was interspersed with dialogue (Plato, *Republic* 392d–394c). Though Plato does acknowledge the distinctiveness of dithyrambic poetry (394c), it was not until after Aristotle (cf. *Poetics* 1448b–1449a) that lyric poetry came to be broadly recognized as a fourth category.

These categories were not merely distinguished by the differences in poetic metre, but also by the relation of the artist to the audience. In epic, the rhapsode recites for his audience face to face, while the dramatist is not seen by the audience but conceals himself behind the mimetic plot and characters. With lyric poetry, however, there is (conventionally) no audience — lyric poets recite for themselves (Frye *et al.*, 1985: 208).

These four categories exerted a powerful influence, and were gradually expanded upon by Alexandrian theorists, who added further categories such as elegy, threnos (lament), hymn, pastoral and the idyll. These categories then became codified by Quintilian (*Institutio Oratoria*) and Horace (*Ars Poetica*), and were immensely influential in late antiquity and the Middle Ages. Horace became regarded as the infallible arbiter of literary decorum, and genre was defined according to his dictates.

With the coming of the Renaissance, Aristotle's *Poetics* were rediscovered and Horace's influence became, if anything, even stronger (Fowler, 1982: 8). His *dicta* inspired neoclassical principles of generic usage, where each genre was regarded as having appropriate subject matter, language, characters and metre. Horace remarks, 'If in producing my work I cannot observe [and don't know] the required genres and styles, why am I hailed as "Poet"? Why prefer wanton ignorance to learning? Comic material resists presentation in tragic verse. Likewise the 'Feast of Thyestes' resents poetry that is conversation and worthy almost of the comic sock' (*Ars Poetica* 86–91 cited in Beebee, 1994: 2; his brackets). Thus, the extent and precision to which an individual work adhered to these generic principles determined its literary quality. The more a work strayed from these guidelines, the less successful it was and, correspondingly, the less it was esteemed (Garber, 1993; de Bruyn, 1993).

This brief overview reveals a fundamental transition that came to affect all subsequent genre criticism, notably the difference between *description* and *prescription*. Plato and the other Greek literary theorists were primarily bent upon exploring the types of literary representation, particularly where and how they differed from each other. In other words, their essential focus was upon defining the world around them. The fact that they advanced new genres, as did their Alexandrian successors, indicates that their focus was on description and completeness. They wanted to discover everything that existed, and to classify it.

Horace's typologizing of these findings added a new dimension. Suddenly a prescriptive element was introduced. Genres came to be regarded almost as if they were Platonic archetypes, disclosing a hypothetical, ideal form for each of the genres. Genres were fixed, immutable and part of the natural order of things: a law of nature. Hence, the pinnacle of literary achievement was to approximate this ideal as closely as possible. Aesthetics, not classification, became the *raison d'être* of generic theorizing.

This legacy has proved to be enduring. The Romantic period did see a notable shift away from these restrictive conventions, especially when the emergence of a 'new' literary genre — the novel — called into question the 'immutable' nature of generic laws. Nevertheless, the prescriptive understanding of genre has continued to exert a seductive influence over literary scholars up to the present day. Giving voice to a contemporary understanding of genre, Anda Schippers observes that 'definitions of genres tend to be *normative*. They describe the ideal . . . and often function as a criterion with which one may (or must?) measure the quality of individual [works]' (1999: 71).

This legacy has significantly affected scholarship, particularly in Germany, and the understanding of genre as a classificatory and pre-scriptive exercise has profoundly affected both Classical and Biblical Studies. It has led to the assumption among scholars that genres are ideal in form, with a perfect exemplar dictating the constitutive traits that a genre must have. A genre necessarily possesses a set and constant number of characteristic features. Absence in a literary work of one or some of these traits causes consternation, and the notion that the ideal form has somehow been subverted, or the literary work misread, since there must be a way to fit the round pegs into the square holes.

An example of this sort of classification can be seen, for instance, in Ethelbert Stauffer's taxonomy of the farewell address (discussed more fully, below), which includes 26 specific traits (1955: 344–47). Possible farewell addresses can then be evaluated against this ideal and favored or faulted accordingly.

Not only is this type of classification ineffective and unrealistic, it also promotes an implicit hierarchicalizing of genres, based on aesthetic considerations. As Roest and Vanstiphout observe:

> The classification and interpretation of the different genres (tragedy, comedy, epic, satire etc.), was to have provided subsequent generations with the necessary and sufficient tools for literary analysis. The central assumptions are that each subject requires an appropriate form and style; that there is a perfect model for each type of art; and that therefore there is a hierarchy of genres — with tragedy at the top. Generic boundaries are seen as preconditions for literary production, and for understanding by the reader. (1999: 132)

Along with the presupposition that prescription overrides description is the cognate assumption by scholars that genres are somehow unchanging and immutable. They are represented as static, idealized, 'hypostases.' Of course, those genres that have long been perceived as fundamental — epic, tragedy, lyric — have been relative constants in Western literature, but others, such as the novel, are generally accounted recent innovations. As Fowler pithily observes, 'the character of genres is that they change' (1982: 18). That is to say, genres are not immutable; their use and emergence are historically conditioned and in an ongoing state of flux. Marincola, for instance, argues 'that innovation constantly modified traditional forms, so that it is dangerous to assume uniformity of treatment by authors writing in the same genres' (1999: 282). New traits are added to the mix, and others are left behind. These traits can even extend to modes and genres themselves: 'One must keep in mind that just as elements are assimilated within a tale, whole *genres* are also assimilated and intermingled' (Propp, 1968: 100). Part of the process of the development of genres results from the departure of a literary work from one distinct genre to a hybrid form that may eventually result in another (new) genre. Just as in the colour spectrum one colour shades imperceptibly into another, so also genres merge into each other, and can be mapped out (Scholes, 1977: 46–48). Like distinct colours, genres retain their precision to the degree in which types of writing depart from them (Todorov, 1990: 14).[7]

This ongoing change of genres is consistent with ongoing changes in literature, style and literary sensibility. At least since the time of Vico it has been recognized that different types of literary discourse tend to dominate different periods of history. Where the epics of Homer and Virgil were the touchstones of Classical civilization, a latecomer, the novel (hence its name) dominates our age — Odysseus has been supplanted by *Ulysses.*

With genre and literature both in flux, the process of generic analysis is necessarily in flux as well. Hence, it follows that the indicators of genre may vary widely over time. Genre is invoked to draw attention to commonalities between various individual works of art. These commonalities are established by *comparanda.* But which *comparanda?* Is form more important than content? Is length more important than function? What about the work's relation to the audience? Would moderns classify a work in the same way as their ancient forebears? If not, how do we know that we are ascribing to a work a genre that would even have been recognized by ancient authors?

The policy followed here, therefore, will be to attempt to be mindful of the various elements that have been used to point out 'family resemblances' in the 'Lives'. This, of course, also includes differences. Fowler observes that, 'Every genre, too, has multiple distinguishing traits, which however are not shared by each exemplar' (1982: 18).

What, then, are the types of elements that can be analyzed to find these family resemblances? To give a characteristic instance, one can reference Richard Burridge, who in his study of the genre of ancient biography devotes a chapter to various types of generic features (1992: 109–27):

A. Opening Features
    1. The title
    2. Opening formulae/prologue/preface

B. Subject
    1. Analysis of the verbs' subjects
    2. Allocation of space to various subjects

C. External Features
    1. Mode of delivery (i.e. relation of artist to audience)
    2. Metre
    3. Size and length
    4. Structure or sequence
    5. Scale
    6. Literary units
    7. Use of sources
    8. Methods of characterization

D. Internal Features
    1. Setting
    2. Topics and motifs
    3. Style
    4. Tone/mood/attitude/values
    5. Quality of characterization
    6. Social setting and occasion
    7. Authorial intention and purpose

Analysis of the Greek and Latin 'Lives' in light of the criteria Burridge provides would require far more space than is available here, so in the following two chapters only some of the more salient features will be considered. Obviously, the process of selecting 'salient' features is a highly subjective enterprise, but in what follows, especially for the *GLAE*, my discussion will largely be a response to the evaluations that other scholars have made about the genre of the work.

A Note on Texts

As Johannes Tromp has recently stressed, literary approaches to the 'Lives' are necessarily subordinate and ancillary to stemmatical considerations (2004). Until recently, this has been one of the unresolved and perennial problems facing scholars of the Adam and Eve literature — namely the relation of the variations both in the Greek and Latin manuscripts and those of the other 'Lives'. The proliferation of versions and recensions of the lives of Adam and Eve has presented scholars with a mare's nest of interpretive problems, and it is obvious that any generic evaluation requires an established text and tradition history to function.

Fortunately, research on the *Lives of Adam and Eve* has made great strides in recent decades, and many of the textual problems that dogged earlier commentators are slowly being resolved. Much of this can be credited to Tromp's exemplary critical edition of *The Life of Adam and Eve in Greek* (2005) — his stemma outlining the development of the various textual traditions constitutes a milestone in the interpretation of the *GLAE*. The fortunate consequence of this edition is that issues that were formerly occluded by uncertainties about the text and provenance have now been brought into sharper focus, and scholars are now able to address more specifically literary issues arising from the text.

Tromp argues that all present manuscripts derive from three hyperarchetypes that were largely similar and that the great diversity of the extant manuscripts is due to later elaboration (2004: 208 n. 8). These findings have confirmed longstanding speculation that the earliest text forms were in Greek, and that the variants in other languages arose from these Greek versions, diverging at different points from one hyperarchetype (Tromp, 2005: 103–07).[8] For the purposes of the next two chapters, I will presuppose the correctness of Tromp's stemma and his reconstruction of the hyperarchetypes.[9]

It is obvious that the Latin versions and the modifications made to them will reflect developments within the text that are subsequent to the hyperarchetypes of the Greek text. The examinations that follow, therefore, will presuppose the validity of Tromp's analysis and conclusions. There is as yet no comparable edition of the *LLAE*, so I rely on the text of Lechner-Schmidt (1990) as found in the second edition of the *Synopsis* edited by Anderson and Stone (1999).[10]

Chapter 5

NONE OF THE ABOVE? —
THE GENRE OF THE GLAE

'Nomen est omen.'

INTRODUCTION

The purpose of this chapter is to establish the genre of the *GLAE*. The above introduction explained the fundamental importance of genre studies for a proper appreciation of any piece of literature. Given the complications associated with definitions of genre, and the varied conceptions of its applicability to the *GLAE*, it is perhaps not unexpected that scholars should have emerged with multiple interpretations. The following is a listing of just some of the generic classifications.

As this overview will make evident, there has been little in the way of a consensus this past century. Not only do commentators differ widely in the generic categories they choose, but they themselves are also reluctant to propose just one possible genre. Almost every commentator advances more than one option. If, however, the various options are distilled, they appear to resolve themselves into five generic categories, namely: rewritten Bible, midrash, apology, apocalypse, and bios (ancient biography). The following discussion will consider each of these in turn, after a brief discussion of the features within those *GLAE* itself that may help to define it.

GENERIC INDICATIONS FROM THE *GLAE*

Discussion of genre needs to begin with the indications provided by the work itself, and here, the incipit frequently furnishes valuable insights.

Table 5.1: Generic classifications of the *GLAE*

Author	Year	Classification
Wilhelm Meyer	1878	a revelation (187)
C. Fuchs	1900	haggadah arising from a midrashic approach to a Scripture (II.510)
L.S.A. Wells	1913	part of a cycle of legendary matter (123)
J.L. Sharpe	1969	midrash[1]
Marcel Nagel	1972	midrash (I.XXXV)
A.-M. Denis	1982	hagiographical midrash ('midrash hagiographique . . . parfois sous forme de testament;' 2)
G.W.E. Nickelsburg	1984	a testament genre though modified for the author's narrative purposes (111) (cf. Nickelsburg, 2005: 331–32)
M.D. Johnson	1985	a midrashic narration (249)
D.J. Harrington	1986	a rewritten biblical narrative (239)
'Schürer'[2]	1986	biblical midrash (III.757)
D.A. Bertrand	1987	a mixed genre or 'a pious legend (haggada)' ('légende pieuse (haggada);' 53–54)
J. Levison	1988	a narrative expansion of Scripture (163) and an apologia with a hortatory element[3]
A.M. Sweet	1992	'a work of mixed genre, encompassing aspects of both pre-rabbinic narrative midrash and Greco-Roman biography' (44)

The incipit of the *GLAE* begins as follows: 'The story (*diegesis*) and the

Author	Year	Classification
M. de Jonge and J. Tromp	1997	a 'farewell discourse' or 'testament' (45, 47)
M. Eldridge	2001	'a variant form of rewritten Bible' or 'midrashic novella' (172)
T. Knittel	2002	no specific genre adequately accounts for its features (94)
J. Dochhorn	2005	testament/death narrative; rewritten Bible/narrative exegesis (112–24)
O. Merk and M. Meiser	2005	testament (as well as haggadic midrash, legend and expanded Bible; 2005: 186 cf. Merk and Meiser 1998: 769–70)

history (*politeia*) of Adam and Eve the first-created, revealed by God to Moses (*apocaluphtheisa para theou Mōsēi*) his servant, when he received the tablets of the law from His hands, having been instructed by the Archangel Michael' (0.1). As is well known, this superscription gave rise to Tischendorf's title *Apocalypse of Moses*,[4] even though Moses is mentioned nowhere else in the *GLAE* (Tischendorf, 1866: x).[5] Though the revelatory aspect of the work is important, the words *diegesis* and *politeia* also furnish an indication of the character of the *GLAE*. The former is 'an orderly description of facts, events, actions, or words; *narrative, account*' (BDAG s.v.), and the latter, 'behavior in accordance with standards expected of a respectable citizen, *way of life, conduct*' (BDAG s.v.). *Diegesis* is often used in historical contexts (Lk. 1.1; Polybius 3.4.1; Diodorus Siculus 11.20.1; Josephus *Ant.* 20.157; *B.J.* 7.42), and it likely has something of that sense here — readers are being offered a narrative of the events that occurred after the protoplasts' eviction from the Garden. *Politeia*, however, further specifies the nature of the narrative — it is connected with the protoplasts' *ethos*, their manner of behaving. The *GLAE*, then, appears to be presenting an account both of their lives and their conduct.

As the word 'account' suggests, the *GLAE* is also a narrative. Although the narrative character of the *GLAE* has sometimes been overlooked, it is fundamental to a generic appreciation of the life (cf. Eldridge, 2001: 162; Knittel, 2002: 90). Whatever else it may be, the *GLAE* is fundamentally a prose narrative, and displays the features that typically characterize a narrative. It is a chronological account with an omniscient third-person narrator that also includes dialogue and, more unusually, an extensive monologue by Eve. All of the scholars' definitions above concur on this point, even when they disagree elsewhere in their proposals.

REWRITTEN BIBLE

One of the most popular of these proposals is a 'rewritten Bible' (Dochhorn, 2005; Eldridge, 2001; Harrington, 1986; Hayward, 1990: 597; Levison, 1988; Merk and Meiser, 1998).[6] The designation 'rewritten Bible' is a category proposed by Geza Vermes (1973: 67–126) and signifies 'a narrative that follows Scripture but includes a substantial amount of supplements and interpretative developments' (Schürer, 1986: 3.1: 326). Though Vermes' designation is modern, the phenomenon to which it refers is ancient and well attested, especially in the Second Temple period, and includes a broad range of 'parabiblical' literature, including such works as *Jubilees*, Philo, *De Abrahamo*, and *1 Enoch* 6–11.[7]

Using Vermes' definition as a point of departure, it is evident that the *GLAE* is indeed 'a narrative that follows Scripture.' The literary form conforms to that found in Genesis — a prose narrative with a third-person omniscient narrator, interspersed with dialogues among the characters. Moreover, the narrative construction of at least part of the work 'follows Scripture,' since some of it is directly reliant on the story of the protoplasts in Genesis. A quick overview of the episodes in the work makes this evident (Table 5.2).

How do these two works relate to each other? With respect to generic features in common, one might suppose that the functions of the two works can be presumed to overlap. To take but one function of the early chapters of Genesis, for instance, one detects a pronounced concern with aetiology.[9] They are designed to describe how humans through

Table 5.2: Overview of episodes in the *GLAE* and Genesis

GLAE	*Genesis*
Birth of Cain and Abel (1.2-3)	Gen. 4.1-2
Murder of Abel (2.1–3.3)	Gen. 4.3-16
Birth of Seth (4.1-2)	Gen. 4.25; cf. 5.3
Assembling of the children (5.1-3)	—
The Fall as the cause of illness (6.1–8.2)	—
The journey to Paradise (9.1–13.2)	—
Adam's lament (14.1-2)	—
Eve's account of the temptation (15.1–21.6)	Gen. 3.1-6
God's punishment (22.1–26.4)	Gen. 3.14-24
Adam's request (27.1–29.6)	—
Eve's conclusion (30)	—
Adam's death (31.1-4)	Gen. 5.5
Eve's repentance (32.1-2)	—
Adam's heavenly ascent (32.3–37.2)	—
Michael and Adam (37.3-6)	—
Dialogue between God and Adam (38.1–39.3)	—
Adam's burial (40.1–42.2)	—
Eve's death (42.3–42.8)	—
Eve's burial (43.1-4)[8]	—

their own disobedience lost their privileged position in Eden and were suddenly subject to death, labor, and the pains of childbirth. In other words, Genesis accounts for the human condition. The same holds true for the *GLAE* narrative, which essentially amplifies the message in Genesis. With it, however, goes a hortatory function that is merely latent in Genesis; Eve, after recounting to her children the story of her own and Adam's disobedience, concludes: 'Now then my children, I have shown you the way in which we were deceived; and do guard yourselves from transgressing against the good' (30.1). A terse but explicitly moral precept is drawn from the behavior of the protoplasts.

Both works also display pronounced similarities in the characters, setting, subject matter, plot and theme. The *GLAE* resembles a movie sequel in repeating the chief features of its 'forebear.' The characters Adam and Eve, Cain, Abel and Seth, the serpent, and God, all appear again. Some of the same settings, such as Eden, re-appear, and the subject matter of Eve's deception is recapitulated when she is deceived a second time. Her disobedience, therefore, serves as a major theme in both works.

This is not to overlook important differences. Satan and the angels assume far more important roles within the text and, from the perspective of setting, the heavenly realms are unique to *GLAE.* So, for that matter, is the emphasis on the *Endzeit* as a counterpart to the *Urzeit* of Genesis. A further discrepancy is to be found in the plots of the two works. A glance at Table 5.2 reveals that despite some reliance on Genesis, the bulk of the events in the *GLAE* are unique and, from Chapter 31 onward, the plot ceases to have any correspondence with that in Genesis.[10] So even though the *GLAE* is partly reliant on Genesis 1–3, its expansions and elaborations are so extensive that they do not constitute 'rewriting' so much as writing *de novo* (cf. Aune, 2003: 412).

Nevertheless, these points of departure are also consistent with Vermes' definition, since these departures constitute the substantial 'supplements and interpretative developments' that Vermes suggests one should expect. When this observation is factored together with the points of agreement, this brief sketch would suggest that 'rewritten Bible' is a generic category that would suit the *GLAE* particularly well.

The chief difficulty with this conclusion, however, is whether 'rewritten Bible' can be considered a valid generic category. First, there is substantial disagreement about the corpora of texts that have been interpreted as examples of a rewritten Bible (Alexander, 1988: 99; Aune, 2003: 411–12; Harrington, 1986: 239; Hayward, 1990: 597),[11] with the result that the parameters of those works said to embody rewritten Bible either overly reduce the specificity of the genre or expand it beyond the point of usefulness.

Philip Alexander has addressed this problem by proposing a more focused genre of rewritten Bible — one with 'distinctive characteristics' (Alexander, 1988: 100, 116–18). In the end, he examines four 'rewritten' works (*Jubilees, Genesis Apocryphon, Pseudo-Philo* and Josephus's *Antiquities of the Jews*), and emerges with nine principal characteristics. Examples of rewritten Bible should be: 1) free-standing 2) narratives, 3) covering a substantial part of the Bible 4) serially 5) that also draw on non-biblical tradition. 6) They are not intended to supersede the Bible, 7) and although they are interpretive, 8) they are not exegetical; 9) rather, their narrative presents a single interpretation of the original (Alexander, 1988: 116–18). Such commonalities are compelling evidence, and have convinced scholars such as Eldridge, who affirms that, 'Alexander has set out sufficiently clear and valid differentiae to enable one to speak of a genre called "rewritten Bible"' (Eldridge, 2001: 167).[12]

This judgement, however, may be a bit precipitate. Tromp, for one, has pointed out that 'rewritten Bible' lacks a specific form, which is a 'prime criterion for the definition of a genre according to the modern standards of literary criticism' (Tromp, 2002: 40). The 'rewritten Bible' has no distinctive form: the forms it assumes are as varied and protean as the biblical texts that serve as their exemplars. In fact, the one mirrors the other and replicates its form (modifying, like funhouse mirrors, the overall image[13]). Moreover, the number of 'rewritten Bible' forms is proportional to the number of Scriptural forms: the wider the formal ambit of the latter, the more forms are found in 'rewritten Bible.' The number of generic forms will parallel each other.

Alexander's endeavor, then, is a laudable attempt to limit this multivalence, by reducing the formal parameters. Nevertheless, he offers no rationale for his selection of the four works except that they are 'normally included in the genre' of "rewritten Bible"' (1988: 99–100).[14] And, on the basis of his comparisons, he concludes that 'they represent a definite literary genre' (1988: 116). Yet it is hardly a coincidence that all four works that he has selected model themselves, at least in part, on the narrative of Genesis. Is it surprising, therefore, that they should reflect the features of Genesis when they have all been modeled on it? If, however, he were to add other works of the rewritten Bible to the mix, many of the generic traits he adduces would disappear, and others would appear. As Harrington remarks, 'it is tempting to place all these books . . . under the broad literary genre of "rewritten bible," but unfortunately the diversity and complexity of the material will not allow it' (Harrington, 1986: 243).

The fundamental reason for this problem is that the generic features of 'rewritten Bible' as a whole do not generally share basic commonalities with each other except in their mutual reliance on the Bible or Scripture. Where genre is usually thought to consist of family resemblances, there are few such resemblances in the rewritten Bible. To pursue this metaphor, 'rewritten Bible,' instead of being a family connection, is more like an assemblage of people who have gathered together to celebrate one individual, where this individual is the only acquaintance they all have in common. Of course, a few of these people could be related to each other and demonstrate family resemblances, but that is not the basis for their assemblage. Their chief relation is not with each other, but the one person they all know.

Halpern-Amaru aptly observes that 'each author not only assumes but requires that the reader relate the rewriting back to Scriptures,' a process requiring the interpreter to unravel the 'implicit as well as explicit relationship to the sacred one' (1994: 4).[15] This is not to deny that 'rewritten Bible' can be free-standing; it can exist on its own, but in much-diminished form. Like a film sequel, it is only fully appreciated and understood by an audience that is familiar with its predecessor. Or, to use another metaphor, 'rewritten Bible' is ultimately epiphytic. Its life is largely dependent on the host.

In sum, the genre of the rewritten Bible is essentially a reflection of the genres or modes present in the Scriptures. Its generic features are largely derivative and the only feature they all share is a dependence on Scripture.

What then is to be said about classifying the *GLAE* as a rewritten Bible? Evidently, the answer depends on the status of 'rewritten Bible.' If one continues to suppose that the rewritten Bible is a legitimate genre, then the answer is clearly 'Yes.' The analysis conducted above, however perfunctory, indicates that, apart from some differences in emphasis and content, the *GLAE* corresponds closely with the criteria for 'rewritten Bible' as set out by Vermes. It is no wonder, therefore, that so many of the scholars listed above have used it to classify the *GLAE*. If, however, 'rewritten Bible' is not to be accepted as a viable genre — as is argued here — then the *GLAE* cannot be accounted an instance of 'rewritten Bible,' and other possibilities need to be pursued.

The recent volume on 'rewritten Bible' by Koskenniemi and Lindqvist emerges with a similar observation:

> The only reasonable solution seems to abandon the use of the term 'rewritten Bible' as a definition of a genre. If a group of narrative works meets enough criteria to be bundled together by scholars, let them be labelled with a more appropriate term. In our opinion, the biblical tradition was reworked in many different genres, although each of them rewrote the Bible. Thus as it is used today 'rewritten Bible[16] is not a literary genre. (2008: 15–16)

Midrash

Another of the popular approaches to *GLAE*'s genre has been to characterize it as 'biblical midrash' (e.g. Denis, 1982; Eldridge, 2001: 172; Johnson, 1985; Merk and Meiser, 1998; Schürer, 1986: 3.1: 757–61; Sweet, 1992) or as (h)aggadic midrash (Bertrand, 1987). This approach is at least as old as Fuchs (1900), and has received renewed popularity in Vermes' advocacy (Schürer, 1986: 3.1: 757–61). Like 'rewritten Bible,' however, it is a term that is far from transparent, in part because it has such a broad range of significations, and can be interpreted in an exceedingly broad fashion.[17] Le Deaut, for instance, notes that it 'is pervasive throughout the whole Jewish approach to the Bible, which could in its entirety be called midrash' (1971: 268–69). Alexander expands this notion further: at 'its broadest it [midrash] may be applied to the whole range of early Jewish Bible interpretation as found e.g. in the Septuagint, Jubilees, the Qumran Pesharim, Genesis Apocryphon, Philo, the NT, Josephus, the Targumims, as well as in the classic rabbinic commentaries' (1990: 453). Given such a vast purview, one might do better to ask: what does not constitute midrash?

Fortunately, midrash can be reduced to more manageable dimensions by dividing it into constituent components. Within the context of early Rabbinic literature, Midrash is often said to embody three different senses. One is the interpretation of the Hebrew Bible; a second is the exegetical interpretations resulting from this process, and the last, the assemblage of these interpretations into literary collections (midrashim) (Fraade, 2000: 549).[18] Of these three senses, the first is the one most germane to our discussion. It is likely that it constitutes the earliest form of midrash and would have provided the compositor with literary models to guide their productions.

This first sense can be further differentiated into Halakhic and Haggadic/Aggadic categories. Halakhic midrash was concerned with exegeting Scripture in order to gain a more detailed and precise understanding of Jewish law.[19] Haggadic/Aggadic midrash, by contrast, interpreted Scripture in order 'to enlarge on biblical history and evolve religious and moral ideas through a systematic combination of separate scriptural passages' (Schürer, 1973: 1.69).[20] What, then, is to be made of assertions that the *GLAE* is an instance of the Haggadic midrashic approach to Scripture (Bertrand, 1987: 53–54; Fuchs, 1900: 2.510; Merk and Meiser, 1998: 186)?[21]

Without doubt, Haggadah/Aggadah involves an exegetical dimension. While the *GLAE* does not contain the commentaries on individual verses that often appear in midrash (Porton, 2003: 202–03), the narrative nevertheless appears to be designed to answer questions that arise from a careful reading of the Genesis narrative. Dochhorn (2005: 115–22) and Eldridge (2001: 169–72) both regard the *GLAE* as a narrative designed to elucidate difficulties raised by Genesis 3.22–5.3. These include such questions as whether the protoplasts ever repented, and whether they would be resurrected. As Dochhorn rightly emphasizes, these problems are not resolved by exegesis, but by 'narrative exegesis' (2005: 117).[22]

Unfortunately, the notion of 'narrative exegesis' does not correspond particularly well with the concept of Haggadic/Aggadic midrash. We do not, in Vermes' phrase, have 'a systematic combination of separate scriptural passages' (Schürer, 1973: 1.69). Verses from Genesis 3.22–5.3 are not used as exegetical pegs on which to structure individual commentaries. Instead, we have a lengthy narrative that does not at all conform to the attenuated form of exegetical midrash. More significantly, as can be seen from Table 5.2, the majority of the work is not reliant on Scripture *at all*. It is an entirely new production. To describe the *GLAE* as midrash, therefore, is highly misleading.

Lastly, and most seriously, Haggadic/Aggadic midrash suffers from

the same fundamental deficiency as 'rewritten Bible.' Since it, too, can
be applied to Scripture globally regardless of its genre, it shows itself not
to be a literary form but a literary *process*. Like 'rewritten Bible' it is not
a literary genre, but an exegetical method or approach (cf. Aune, 2003:
304; Eldridge, 2001: 164; Sweet, 1992: 33#106).[23] The midrashic process
has had some influence on the *GLAE*, but the latter is not midrash.

Apology

If it is not midrash, can the *GLAE* be characterized as an 'exoneration'
or apology of Eve?[24] There are various features in the *GLAE* that could
be construed in this light, particularly Eve's extensive first-person narrative. This feature is unusual and highly emphatic within the work,
both by virtue of its length and its placement right at the heart of the
GLAE (Eldridge, 2001: 142). The use of Eve's own point of view is also
exceptional — first of all, that she should be chosen over Adam to
recount their history and, second, that she should have a chance to
express events from her own perspective. Point-of-view narratives typically, by their very nature, create sympathy for the narrator. Moreover,
the non-ironic juxtaposition of Eve's point of view with that of the
GLAE's third-person omniscient narrator appears to imbue her with
his authority; at a surface level, their narratives do not seem sufficiently
different from each other to call Eve's reliability into question. She
assumes the status of a reliable narrator (Eldridge, 2001: 183).

These and related features have brought a number of scholars
to argue that part or all of the *GLAE* is calculated to exonerate Eve
(Kvam *et al.* 1999; Levison, 1989, 2000b; Sweet, 1992; van Houten, 1994:
301–02). The most influential advocate for this position has been Jack
Levison, who has addressed this topic in several publications.[25] In a
pioneering article he argues that reading 'Eve's account independently
from the remainder of the *Apocalypse of Moses* allows us to hear the voice
of a unique author sympathetic to Eve' (Levison, 1989: 137). That is
to say, that the tenor of the monologue or testament (*GLAE* 15–30) is
different from the 'frame' of the work as a whole (*GLAE* 1–14, 31–43)
and betrays a more sympathetic voice.[26] While the 'frame' of the *GLAE*
may not be well disposed toward Eve, the 'monologue' — or at least
some recensions of it — are thought to exonerate her.

Levison's analysis found an enthusiastic audience, and his assessment has since been echoed by other commentators. Kvam, Schearing, and Ziegler, for instance, affirm that 'No other source from this period [200s BCE – 200 CE] presents Eve in such a sustained sympathetic light as that found in the *Apocalypse of Moses* 15–30' (Kvam *et al.*, 1999: 43).[27] Thomas Knittel in his extensive study of the *GLAE* is also convinced that Eve is exonerated by the stylistic alterations in the 'monologue' (Knittel, 2002: 179). A.M. Sweet's Notre Dame doctoral dissertation, 'A Religio-Historical Study of the *Greek Life of Adam and Eve*,' sees this sympathetic perspective extending to the whole of the *GLAE*, not simply to the 'monologue' — 'This emphasis,' she remarks, 'certainly makes it plausible that the author was a woman, concerned to correct the predominant negative view of Eve' (Sweet, 1992: 24).[28]

In the decade following his first article, careful consideration of the divergent textual traditions of the *GLAE* has led Levison to modify his views (Levison, 2000a). In the sequel to the above article, 'The Exoneration and Denigration of Eve in the *Greek Life of Adam and Eve*,' he recognizes that the various Greek text forms offer varying assessments of Eve and her behavior (2000b: 259–60), ranging from 'exoneration ([text forms] DSV) to denigration ([text forms] ATLC, NIK)' (2000b: 267). For those text forms that denigrate Eve, this denigration extends to the 'monologue' as well as to the narrative 'frame.' Only the text form represented chiefly by M absolves Eve from guilt and 'contains significant material which is sympathetic toward Eve' (2000b: 274). Nevertheless, Levison has come to see both the exoneration and denigration of Eve as tendencies that affect the entirety of the various text forms, not simply the monologues themselves (2000b: 275).

This point, however, has serious repercussions for his argument. Above all, it needs to be reiterated that Levison's second essay has withdrawn from the notion that the testaments (i.e. monologues) of all the Greek 'Lives' exonerate Eve. He now delimits her exoneration (including the monologues) to only *two* of the four text types — his Text Form I (DSV) and Text Form II (R and M) (2000a: 42–44; 2000b: 267; cf. Tromp, 2005: 14–15). Accordingly, his conclusion to the second article is distinctly puzzling when he suggests that Eve's exoneration is more widespread than he had supposed:

> Both the exoneration and denigration of Eve are more widespread in the *Greek Life of Adam and Eve* than I suggested a decade ago. The first and third text forms,

represented by ATLC and NIK, tend to denigrate Eve throughout the *Greek Life of Adam and Eve*, including Eve's Testament, where I had discerned elements of exoneration. The second text form, represented principally by M, tends to incorporate substantial elements that exonerate Eve, even in *GLAE* 1–14 and 31–43, where I had discovered elements of denigration. (Levison, 2000b: 275)

He had supposed that Eve's testament in the first and third text forms also exonerated her, where he now determines that they are actually denigratory. How then is the exoneration more widespread? It is possible that he means that he is now taking into account all the various text forms and that this perspective is more 'widespread,' but the fact remains that, by his own admission, half the text forms denigrate Eve.

This finding, however, seriously undercuts his argument that the first two text forms exculpate Eve. Although he amasses thirteen features in the *GLAE* that are thought to exonerate her, they are of uneven weight.[29] The two strongest features of his case are, in my view, Eve's monologue (point 1) and her visions (point 13).[30] Levison interprets both features as indications that Eve is focalized and privileged. This may be so. Yet, it is remarkable that these two features occur in *all* the text forms, including those that Levison would regard as denigratory to Eve. If these features were as favorable to Eve as he argues, why would the editors of the non-sympathetic text forms retain them, when it is clear that they have chosen to excise or attenuate other features in their text forms? The strong implication is that the editors of these denigratory text forms did not regard them as exonerating Eve. And if they, early in the generative process of the *GLAE*, did not regard them as exculpatory, it seems that modern commentators need to be wary of finding apologies that may not be there (however appealing the notion). In any event, these findings certainly cast doubt on the *GLAE*'s being an apology designed to exonerate Eve.

Apocalyptic

If not an apology, what about an apocalypse?[31] Apocalypse, it will be remembered, was one of the first classifications of the *GLAE* (Meyer, 1879: 187; Tischendorf, 1866: x). Since these scholars' time, its apocalyptic components have not been emphasized so much as other features; but recently, this view has been advocated more strongly

(Bertrand, 1987: 50; Dochhorn, 2005: 269).

With respect to 'apocalyptic' as a categorization, John Collins' definition of 'apocalyptic' is often taken as normative: 'a genre of revelatory literature with a narrative framework, in which a revelation is mediated by an otherworldly being to a human recipient, disclosing a transcendent reality which is both temporal, insofar as it envisages eschatological salvation, and spatial insofar as it involves another, supernatural world' (Collins, 1979: 9).[32]

Given this definition, there are certainly features of the *GLAE* that are suggestive of an apocalypse. It is a story. Divine revelations are mediated to human recipients not just once but several times, with Moses, Eve, and Seth all having been enabled to participate in heavenly realities (Incipit, 32.4–38.4(?)). The temporal reality of the vision is chiefly concerned with Adam's immediate translation to the divine sphere 900 years after his creation. One of the seraphim takes him to the Acherusian Lake where he is washed thrice and led before God and deposited in the third heaven (37.3-5).

There is an eschatological timeframe in view also: God bids Michael to 'leave him [Adam] there until that fearful day of my reckoning, which I will make in the world' (37.5). The narrative continues with contemporary events (albeit in the heavenly sphere) until God predicts to Adam that 'I will turn their joy to grief and your grief will I turn to joy, and I will return you to your rule, and seat you on the throne of your deceiver' (39.2). Satan and his cohorts will be condemned and chagrined at seeing Adam's glorification (39.3). Last of all, God promises the Resurrection to Adam and his seed (41.3).[33]

Evidently, then, there is a definite eschatological component to the visions, and an ongoing vacillation between the *Urzeit* and *Endzeit* (Bertrand, 1985: 112–15; Knittel, 2002: 256–57).

Various features of the supernatural world are disclosed in this process: among other features, the seven heavens (35.2), a chariot of light (33.2-3), the seraphim (33.3, 37.3), the Archangel Michael (38.1, 40.1, with Gabriel and Uriel 40.2), the ranked assemblages of angels (35.2, 38.2), heavenly censers, bowls, lyres and trumpets (33.4, 37.1, 38.2), the darkened sun and moon (35.4–36.3), the Acherusian Lake (37.3) and God, himself, enthroned (37.4).[34] In short, there is a broad variety of apocalyptic tropes.

Collins' 'apocalyptic grid,' outlining characteristic traits of apocalypses (1998: 7), demonstrates substantial overlaps with the tropes found in *GLAE*. He isolates twelve traits that help determine whether a work is an apocalypse.

1. Cosmogony
2. Primordial events
3. Recollection of past
4. *Ex eventu* prophecy
5. Persecution
6. Other eschatological upheavals
7. Judgment/destruction of wicked
8. Judgment/destruction of world
9. Judgment/destruction of otherworldly beings
10. Cosmic transformation
11. Resurrection
12. Other forms of afterlife

Of these twelve traits, the *GLAE* displays about half. It is evident, therefore, that there are a number of traits that would help to characterize the *GLAE* as an apocalypse. Though these categories are far from precise, one could reasonably argue that the *GLAE* displays elements of at least categories 2, 3, 4, 7, 9, and 11. Of the fifteen 'apocalyptic' works Collins deems to be apocalypses and which are anatomized by Collins in his grid, the number of apocalyptic features found in the *GLAE* surpasses five of the 'apocalypses' included there, matches three (or five) of them in 'apocalyptic' traits, and is exceeded by six. It is on a similar footing, therefore, with works such as *1 Enoch* 1–36, the astronomical book, *2 Enoch,* and possibly *Jubilees* and the *Apocalypse of Weeks.*[35] Its median position in this grid of related 'apocalypses' would strongly suggest that the *GLAE* is, at least in part, an apocalypse.[36]

Does this conclusion mean that the *GLAE* should be dubbed an apocalypse in its entirety? Probably not — numerous indicators suggest that the *GLAE* is not, or at least not all of it, a literary apocalypse. There are various reasons for this supposition. Most importantly, what might be described as the nub of the apocalypse (33.2–43.2) occupies less than a quarter of the overall *GLAE*, and even these chapters have lengthy, non-apocalyptic descriptions of Adam and Eve's human story as it evolves on earth.[37] For the rest, the *GLAE* discloses very little that could even be designated apocalyptic, much less apocalypse. The apocalypse genre only comes into its own in the final quarter where it contextualizes the events of Adam's life in a heavenly framework, and explains how these events are finally resolved.

What is notable about the resolving of these events is that they pertain to only one individual; the final segment is more concerned with individual eschatology than with corporate humanity. The focus of God's judgment is largely on one man, and the reversal it describes — Adam's transition from being a sinner to an exalted exemplar of the *imago dei* — is again confined to one man. Naturally, there is a sense in which the experience of Adam embodies and foreshadows that of all humans, and in which he reflects the coming judgment and potential forgiveness of all the dead, but the cosmic tableaux so characteristic of many apocalypses are absent except at Adam's demise.[38]

In sum, Bertrand's judgement that only part of the *GLAE* is an apocalypse seems to be warranted (1985: 109). The work as a whole does not conform to the standard perceptions of an apocalypse. This conclusion appears rather unusual — that only part of the work is an apocalypse — until one recognizes that this composite formation is by no means uncommon. It is characteristic of a number of the works deemed 'apocalyptic' by Collins: such works 'are composite in character and have affinities with more than one genre' (1998: 4).[39]

Bios and Testament

If the *GLAE* is only partly an apocalypse, what about the remainder of the work? How should it be classified? One possibility advanced by Sweet is that it conforms to the ancient genre of *bios*, that is, Greco-Roman biography: 'In view of the fact that the subject of the *Bios* [*GLAE*] is the life of Adam and Eve from creation to death, it is appropriate to consider the document in terms of the Graeco-Roman literary genre of biography or *bios*' (1992: 36).

The origins of the *bios* are a matter of dispute, and despite various conjectures, its ancient origins remain obscure (Momigliano, 1993) as do, for that matter, its particular boundaries.[40] In fact, it may be better to speak of 'tendencies' of the *bios* since, if Dihle is correct, 'ancient rhetorical and literary theory seems never to have granted biography the status of a genre that can be formally characterized as such' (1991:

374; cf. Cox, 1983: 6–7). He adds that, apart from the *Lives* of Plutarch, most 'other textual forms that are ever and again called biographies or included in the history of biography do not meet the criteria according to which they could be assigned to the category of biography' (376).

Not unexpectedly, therefore, the *bios* is also broadly accommodating: it constitutes 'an inclusive literary form into which a variety of shorter literary forms may be inserted' (Aune, 1988: 123). Burridge usefully suggests that the *bios* is best conceived as a spectrum or continuum with history at one end and encomium at the other (1992: 65; cf. also his figure 1, p. 66). In between these poles, *bios* sketches 'the significance of a famous person's career (i.e. his character and achievements), optionally framed by a narrative of origins and youth, on the one hand, and death and lasting significance on the other' (Aune, 1988: 27; cf. Cox, 1983: 4–12).

This sketch shows a number of commonalities with the *GLAE*. There is a definite chronological development in the *GLAE*, as the narrative *diegesis* unfolds. The work's concern with the *politeia* of the protoplasts is also noteworthy, since *bioi* often focus on the *ars vivendi* of those portrayed. Yet, *bioi* can also be consistent with the *ars morendi*, showing the accord between the manner in which the individual dies and the manner in which they have lived.[41]

Nevertheless, the sharp distinction between life and death becomes a pivotal point of differentiation for the *GLAE*. When the latter is considered in detail, it is evident that the work is very largely focused not on the life of Adam, but on his death. The terminal sickness of Adam that begins at 5.2 is anticipated as early as 1.1, which records the expulsion from Eden and portends Adam's approaching death. Adam's death and its complications continue to dominate the work until 42.2, whereupon the focus shifts to Eve's own death for the last couple of chapters (42.4–43.1).

Moreover, Adam's sickness and death provide a frame for Eve's monologue, which, as was noted above, occurs right in the middle of the work. There would seem to be little doubt that Eve's words are designed to furnish a commentary on the deaths of the protoplasts, and for this reason a number of scholars (de Jonge and Tromp, 1997: 45; Merk and Meiser, 2005: 69–70; Nickelsburg, 1984) have proposed that the *GLAE* should be interpreted as a testament or farewell discourse.

According to the useful definitions and distinctions advanced by Collins (1984) and Kolenkow (1986), testaments and farewell discourses, though similar, can be readily distinguished: if a farewell address constitutes an independent literary form, it is classified as a testament, whereas, if it forms part of a longer work, it is a farewell address or discourse.[42] Here, although Eve's actual monologue occupies only fifteen chapters, the *GLAE* obviously meshes thematically with the death of the protoplasts, and so it is more likely to be a testament.

The number of specific features said to characterize the genre vary widely. As noted in Part Three's introduction, Ethelbert Stauffer, for instance, furnishes a prescriptive template for the farewell discourse, amassing 26 distinct characteristics (Stauffer, 1955). Similar templates have been advanced by other scholars (cf. Aune, 2003: 182–83; Von Nordheim, 1980: 234–36). Yet the problems associated with prescriptive generic constructions were shown in Part Three's introduction to be too procrustean and delimiting. If a potential testament does not conform to all or many of Stauffer's criteria, does this mean that it cannot be classified as a legitimate 'testament'?

Instead it is, perhaps, optimal to focus on the core features (advanced by Aune) of what are generally regarded (or explicitly designated) as testaments. These can be reduced to three main elements: 1) a patriarch's biography, 2) a revelatory speech by the patriarch, and 3) a forecast of the future from the deathbed (Aune, 1987: 233).[43] Kolenkow has convincingly argued that ethical instruction is also a necessary constituent (1986: 262–64), so a fourth element should be added to this template, notably 4) paraenesis (cf. Eldridge, 2001: 152–53).

Generally speaking, these traits are present in the *GLAE*, but the manner in which they occur is certainly idiosyncratic. As to 1), the *GLAE* furnishes details of the *bios* of Adam, but it is the life of Eve, the matriarch, that is given most prominence. With respect to 2), there is no lack of valedictory material — the *GLAE* contains not one but two farewell speeches, one each by Adam and Eve (7.1–8.2, 15.1, 30.1) — but the more revelatory speech is delivered by Eve while Adam is on his deathbed.[44] With 3) we do indeed have a forecast associated with the patriarch on the deathbed, but by this point Adam is already dead, and it is God himself who furnishes the prediction (39.1-3, 41.1-3).

Finally, with regard to 4), there is ethical instruction delivered, but by Eve, not by Adam. Levison has suggested that 'Eve's testament is paraenetic. She tells the story of the transgression in order that her children may avoid such transgressions' (1988: 168). His observation is certainly true, but it is also the case that Eve's paraenesis is brief compared to the extended exhortation characteristic of many other farewell discourses (cf. Eldridge, 2001: 153).[45]

Are these idiosyncratic features enough to discount the *GLAE*'s being a sort of testament? Eldridge convincingly argues that although some of these features are 'peculiar,' they are sufficiently prominent within the *GLAE* to argue that it is a testament: 'The writing does not precisely fit any of the usual models but there are several close, albeit not exact, parallels; these indicate that the farewell address in the *Greek Life* is best taken as a confession by Eve leading to a moral summons of a more general character' (Eldridge, 2001: 159). It is, however, a testament of a distinctive kind; its unusual features indicate that it is a testament that has come under the influence of a particular mode. The mode in this instance is confessional, which makes Eve's monologue an example of a 'confessional' testament.[46]

Eldridge notes that 'the closest parallels are the confessions found in certain of the *Testaments of the Twelve Patriarchs* that are followed by a general warning, for example, *T. Reub.* 3.11–4.1, *T. Jud.* 12.1–13.2, 13.3–14.1, *T. Gad.* 1.2–3.1' (155).[47] There are indeed substantial affinities between Eve's confession and those of the patriarchs. The latter do not attempt to cover up or vindicate their misdoings. Like Eve, they are forthright about the wrongs they have committed, and they each finish with a moral exhortation to their children. In the *Testaments*, each confession is succeeded by a lengthy exhortation counselling their children not to commit the sins that their fathers had committed. That of the *GLAE* is the somewhat more attenuated, 'Now then, my children, I have shown you the way we were deceived; and do guard yourselves from transgressing against the good' (30.1).

The distinction in emphasis between the lengthy confession (15 chapters) and the laconic exhortation (8 words) reveals that, for the author/redactor, the importance of Eve's confession resides in the account of Eve's past. The readers and implied readers of the *GLAE* are given an explanation of how humans have ended up in their particular predicament. Her confession informs humans about the Fall, about the Devil, and the way in which God's will was subverted. Eve's acknowledgement of her lapse is the only reparation that she is ultimately capable of making to all her progeny. And, in knowing these details, humans are far better equipped to deal with the realities with which they are faced. This ethical encapsulation is not without importance, but far more important is the knowledge — won at such cost — that she passes on to her descendants. The focus of Eve's testament, therefore, is not on attempting to vindicate Eve and her actions, but on having her confess to all humanity the mis-steps that she has made. It is only when humans are armed with this knowledge that they can understand the world around them and endeavor to please God.

The foregoing discussion argued that in spite of some of the similarities with the *bios* genre, the *GLAE*'s pronounced emphasis on death and dying and the manner in which it frames Eve's monologue indicates that the *GLAE* is a testament. Its idiosyncrasies suggest that it is a confessional testament whose chief purpose is to explain to the protoplasts' children (and to readers in general) how humans became subject to sin and death, and how the world they inhabit came to be ordered as it is. Eve's testament gives a first-person account, and urges her hearers not to act as she had done.

MISCHGATTUNG

From the above findings, the *GLAE* appears to embody features of two distinct genres — apocalyptic on the one hand, and confessional testament on the other. It is, therefore, a composite genre. The phenomenon of the composite genre (*Mischgattung*) is well known. Conte gives an admirable account of it:

> Even if, operatively, genres can be thought of as pure, their real action (in texts) is subject to many possible deformations and concomitances: they can undergo procedures of combination and aggregation, inclusion and selection, reduction and amplification, transposition and reversal; they can undergo functional mutations and adaptations. Contents and expressions that are already strictly codified can also become dissociated, so that they can be reassociated with other expressions and contents (1994: 154–55 n. 2).

This process is what allows genres to change and new genres to emerge. The notion that genre must be unchanging and absolute, as was shown in the introduction to this part, is based upon fundamental misapprehensions. Genres change and develop over time, as does literature itself when it leaves behind features of one genre and appropriates others in their stead.

In Jewish literature, this process was commonplace in the Second Temple period and thereafter; mixed-genre literary works were common in both the biblical and Classical spheres. Michael Fishbane has established that the mixed genre was a characteristic feature of Jewish literature, especially with regard to legal exegesis. He observes:

> early Jewish literature was not quick to transform the genres it inherited from ancient Israel. This is particularly noteworthy given the fact that these genres had *already* been mixed with exegetical content in ancient Israel. Early Judaism in some ways, then, perceived the exegetical *Mischgattungen* of the Hebrew Bible as *Gattungen* in their own right, and built on them for their own purposes. (1985: 274)

And as was noted above, Collins remarks that this process was very much at work within apocalyptic literature.

In the Classical sphere, as well, both in the Hellenistic and Roman periods there was an ongoing emergence of 'novel' genres through the recombination and modification of existing genres (Aune, 1981: 46; Burridge, 1992: 58–59).[48] This process, as Kroll remarks, was very much characteristic of Roman literature at the opening of the Common Era (Kroll, 1964: 202–24).

CONCLUSION

What then is to be said about the genre of the *GLAE*? If someone were to ask 'Which of the above scholarly positions have you followed?,' the answer would clearly be 'None of the above.' The *GLAE* does fit readily within the generic categories 'rewritten Bible' and 'Haggadic/Aggadic midrash.' Yet, as neither can properly be classified as a literary genre, other options need to be taken into account. Despite arguments that the monologue of the *GLAE* exonerates Eve, it does not conform to the genre of apology. Rather, the presence of characteristic features of apocalypses suggests that part of the *GLAE* is an apocalypse. These features, however, are not characteristic of the whole work, and it is the elements of Adam's demise in relation to the monologue that suggest that it is also a testament — one influenced by the confessional mode.

In sum, it is a hybrid of apocalyptic and confessional testament.

Yet, if the *GLAE* is, in truth, a *Mischgattung*, what is to be made of the fact that none of the above scholarly commentators have emerged with a similar description nor, with the sole exception of Sweet, have they explicitly classified the *GLAE* as being of mixed genre? Doesn't this undermine the findings presented here? Probably not. Although none of the above scholars makes the precise identification I do, almost all tacitly agree with my identifying the *GLAE* as a mixed genre. Nearly every one of them posits more than one generic option for the *GLAE*: none of them seems satisfied with just one surmise about its genre. This, of itself, speaks strongly for a mixed genre. Further, if more of the above scholars had rejected 'rewritten Bible' and 'midrash' as genres, as is done here, they would very possibly have emerged with findings similar to mine.

It is unclear just why the *GLAE* is a hybrid of apocalyptic and confessional testament. The easiest explanation is that, as the *GLAE* was assembled, the testament and apocalypse were incorporated from two distinct sources, and fused together in the redacted 'life' without major editorial modifications. The testament and apocalypse remained largely 'unmixed' and were able thereby to retain their characteristic traits — hence the rather uncommon hybrid of testament with apocalypse. Nevertheless, they fit together reasonably well, because of the *GLAE*'s focus on death and its aftermath.

The following chapter will focus on the Latin *Vita*, and investigate whether a similar hybrid is to be found there.

Chapter 6

THE LATIN VITA — *A 'GOSPEL' OF ADAM AND EVE?*

'The Lineaments of Gospel books . . .'

Matthew Roydon

As noted in the introduction to Part Three, Michael Stone remarked of the *Latin Life of Adam Eve* (*LLAE*) or *Vita* that he had found very few discussions that 'dealt in any detail with the purpose, shape or function of this version, nor with it in comparison with the Greek Apocalypse of Moses' (1992: 23). It has been analyzed far less, and in some instances it seems as if judgements about the *GLAE*'s genre are tacitly supposed to apply to the *Vita* as well.

The previous chapter sought to argue that the genre of the *GLAE* was essentially a mixed one. The core of it was a testament, but in combination with a limited apocalypse that imparted a mixed character to the work as a whole. What, then, do these findings suggest about the genre of the Latin *Vita*? Should it also be classified according to these same criteria?

Such a judgement would hardly be unexpected. According to Tromp's stemmata, the Latin versions are derived from the Greek hyparchetype γ and they, along with the Armenian and Georgian versions, have a common Greek ancestor in Tromp's #50; (Tromp, 2005: 100–01), although the Armenian and Georgian versions go on to diverge from the Latin.[1] On the strength of this common ancestry, one might presuppose that the *GLAE* and the *LLAE* are largely consonant with each other, and that despite a few vicissitudes, the tenor of each

121

is the same. James Charlesworth says as much when he affirms that the two works are 'virtually identical' (2003: 268).

Making this assumption would be a mistake. Levison has observed that,

> Each redactor combines the unique and synoptic material according to a particular *Tendenz*. The dominant purpose of ApMos [the *Apocalypse of Moses*] is to provide hope for its readers by presenting Adam as a forgiven sinner who endures the pain of existence, faces death with uncertainty, but receives mercy after death. In contrast, the dominant purpose of *Vita* is to exonerate Adam and to denigrate Eve, thus presenting the readers with a perfect penitent, a righteous figure who receives mercy during life and after death. These variant concerns of the respective redactors result in the adaptation of common material to produce divergent portraits of Adam. (Levison, 1988: 164)

The first indications of this divergent *Tendenz* emerge when the episodes in each 'Life' are set side by side.

As Table 6.1 demonstrates, there is a superficial continuity between the episodes of the two works. Careful scrutiny, however, discloses notable differences in content and sequence — differences that have been increasingly emphasized by recent scholarship (though see already Meyer, 1879: 194–95; Nagel, 1974: 1.XXXI–XXXII). De Jonge and Tromp affirm that the *Vita* is a 'writing very different in form and content' from the other 'Lives' (1997: 59). Anderson points out that the 'Latin version has a number of unique features . . .: it has a substantial penitence narrative at the beginning of the tale (pericopes 2-6), and it lacks Eve's extended account of the fall (pericopes 15-29)' (2000d). Further, two lengthy segments in the *Vita* (10.3–17.3, 25.1–29.10) — some eleven chapters in all — are not found at all in the *GLAE*.[3] More strikingly, the fourteen chapters of Eve's 'testament' are missing from the *Vita*, as well as several other episodes (30, 32.1-2, 38.1–39.3). In addition, the order of the episodes has also been significantly altered. The *GLAE* adheres to the order of Genesis in opening with the birth of Cain and Abel, Eve's portentous dream, and the murder of Abel by Cain. The *Vita*, however, puts off these events until chapter 22 and replaces them with the penitence of the protoplasts. Where the testament of Eve forms the *GLAE*'s centerpiece, dominating the entire work (to say nothing of eclipsing Adam's own ancillary testament[4]), the

Table 6.1: Comparison of episodes from the *GLAE* and the *LLAE*

GLAE	*LLAE*
Birth of Cain and Abel (1.2-3)	21.3–22.3
Murder of Abel (2.1–3.3)	22.4–23.2
Birth of Seth (4.1-2)	23.3–24.2
Adam's revelation concerning Seth	**25.1–29.10**
Assembling of the children (5.1-3)	30.1-4
The Fall as the cause of illness (6.1–8.2)	31.1–34.2
The journey to Paradise (9.1–13.2)	35.1–43.2
Adam's lament (14.1-2)	44.1-4
Eve's temptation (15.1–21.6)	—
God's punishment (22.1–26.4)	—
Adam's request (27.1–29.6)	—
The need of the protoplasts (29.7-9)	1.1–4.3
Repentance (29.10-13)	5.1–10.2
Adam, Eve and the Devil	**10.3–17.3**
Eve's conclusion (30)	—
Adam's death (31.1-4)	45.1-3
Eve's repentance (32.1-2)	—
Adam's heavenly ascent (32.3–37.2)	46.1–47.1
Michael and Adam (37.3-6)	48.1-3
Dialogue between God and Adam (38.1–39.3)	—

(continued)

GLAE	LLAE
Adam's burial (40.1–42.2)	48.4-6
Eve's death (42.3–42.8)	49.1–50.3
Eve's burial (43.1-4)[2]	51.1-3

testamentary elements of the *Vita* are far less substantial (Adam: 30.1-3, 32.1–34.2; Eve: 49.1–50.3[5]).

Are these changes significant enough to signal a change in genre? Certainly, the number of elements that the two lives share would suggest that any differences are not likely to be that considerable. And there are similarities, to be sure: the generic features that were detected in the *GLAE* can also be discerned here. Though the genre of apocalypse is there, some apocalyptic features are still in evidence. Of the various traits of apocalypses mentioned in the chapter above, the *Vita* demonstrates some of the same features as the *GLAE* does: one could reasonably argue that the *LLAE* displays some elements of categories 2, 3, 4, 7, 9, and 11 (Collins, 1998: 7).

On the other hand, these elements are very considerably attenuated. The *LLAE* 'apocalypse' occupies roughly one-fifth of the space that the *GLAE* 'apocalypse' does (8 verses in the *Vita* compared to 41 in the *GLAE*). Key elements such as the divine throne or the washing of Adam by the seraphim in the Acherusian Lake are absent, and the balance of the account is much compressed and subordinated to the larger narrative. These elements would seem to argue against finding an integral apocalypse within the *Vita*. Rather, it is safer to say that 'apocalyptic' functions as a mode and that apocalyptic has tinctured the text as a whole.

Yet, if the *Vita* no longer contains an apocalypse, what about the genre of testament? The previous chapter determined that although it was unusual, the genre of the *GLAE* was partly that of a testament. Can the same be said for the *Vita*? As was determined last chapter, the core features of what are generally regarded as testaments tend to display four main elements: 1) a patriarch's biography 2) a revelatory speech by the patriarch 3) a forecast of the future from the deathbed (Aune, 1987: 233) and 4) paraenesis (Kolenkow, 1986: 262–64).

Certainly, in the *Vita* there is patriarchal biography and something of revelatory speech by the patriarch. However, Adam does not himself give a forecast from his deathbed, while Eve only utters a brief prophecy — 'On account of your conspiracies, our Lord will bring upon your race the wrath of his judgment, first by water and second by fire. By these two will the Lord judge all the human race' (49.3). Finally, paraenesis is altogether absent. Taken together, the *Vita*'s minimal testaments and the absence of some of the more common testamentary features would indicate that it does not belong to the genre of testament. There is no doubt that the testamentary mode has influenced the genre, but it is not a testament *per se*.

If it is not a testament, what genre is it? The clearest indication comes from the end of the work itself where the work seems to be classified as a life or lives. Eve adjures her children to take tablets of stone and earth and 'write on them *my whole life, and that of your father* [*omnem vitam meam et patris vestri*], which you have heard from us and seen' (50.1, my italics). One would expect that these tablets would certainly include the substance of the *LLAE*. In contrast with the *Apocalypse of Moses*, then, the *Vita* is aptly named — it does indeed provide an account of the lives of the protoplasts.[6] Further confirmation is provided by the narrative itself, which relates the episodes of their lives in a manner that appears consistent with the form of the ancient *bios*. What form of *bios*, however? As was discussed in the previous chapter, the *bios* is a genre that is not amenable to ready classification, and possesses broad parameters.

What then of the *Vita*? Is it a *bios*? I would like to argue that it remains a *bios*, but has been influenced by another generic mode, namely that of gospel. In recent years, it has been increasingly established that gospels are a form of *bios*, and need to be interpreted as such. This view is something of a recent rediscovery. In most of the last century it was commonplace to assume that gospels were not *bioi*, but rather a hitherto unknown genre.[7] Following the lead of Martin Dibelius and Rudolf Bultmann (who were reliant on K.L. Schmidt's influential description of the gospels as *Kleinliteratur*), scholars came to regard the gospels as popular and lengthy expansions of the Christian *kerygma*.[8] These expansions resulted in a new genre, of which Mark was the first example. Mark then served as a template for Matthew and Luke.

This once firmly entrenched consensus, however, has broken down over the last few decades (Aune, 1987: 206). While some scholars have continued to support a *sui generis* gospel genre (e.g., Guelich, 1991), it is fair to say that a majority now regard the gospels as a distinctive subgenre of the *bios* (Burridge, 1992; Shuler, 1982; Stanton, 1992; Talbert, 1977).[9]

If this is the case, then gospels and *bioi* are actually related, though I would argue that, for the *Vita*, it is as modes that the gospels have produced an 'evangelical' *bios*.

The 'Gospel' of Adam and Eve

As this is (so far as I know) a novel surmise, and likely to be a contested one, I would like to take the balance of this chapter to argue that the Synoptic Gospels have furnished a modal influence on the *Vita* and have imparted to it a structural and thematic armature or framework, around which the *Vita* has been reorganized. Themes and *topoi* from the life of Jesus have helped to serve as an organizing principle for the narratives and furnished them with an overall coherence.

When one compares the details of the Synoptic Gospels and the *LLAE*, a number of parallels in content emerge. Some of these are sufficiently prominent that even a casual reader would notice similarities between the Adam and Eve traditions and events from Jesus' life. Adam immerses himself in the river Jordan, where Jesus is later baptized. Adam and Eve fast in the wilderness for 40 days, just as Jesus did. Jesus is tempted in the wilderness and so is Eve. Jesus and Adam both rebuke Satan, he departs, and they are furnished with food (or the wherewithal for food) by angels. Later, both Adam and Jesus experience the anticipatory pains of death. Adam gives up his spirit, as does Jesus. Both deaths are accompanied by portents, notably 'eclipses,' and each corpse is swathed in linen.[10] Given all the above points of overlap, it is difficult to discount the cumulative impression they present. Consider the parallels listed in Table 6.2.

Not all of these parallels are equally convincing, and in some cases the points of overlap appear tenuous at best. On the other hand, some events are so markedly similar — such as immersion in the Jordan — that they cannot help but conjure up familiar echoes, even if their details differ. A narrative that opens with the protagonist's lustration in the Jordan and ends with his burial in a linen shroud sounds far too familiar to be coincidental.

Table 6.2: Parallels between the Synoptic Gospels and the *Vita*

Narrative detail	Gospel	Vita
spirit	Mt. 1.20, 3.16	*Vita* 13.2
driven into wilderness	Mt. 4.1; Lk. 4.1; cf. Mk 1.4	*Vita* 1.1
hunger	Mt. 4.2; Lk. 4.2	*Vita* 2.1, 2.2
animals	Mk 1.13	*Vita* 8.3
fasting for 40 days	Mk 1.13; Mt. 4.2; Lk. 4.2	*Vita* 6.1a
temptation by Satan (food)	Mk 1.13; Mt. 4.3; Lk. 4.2,13	*Vita* 9.4-5
immersion in Jordan	Mk 1.9; Mt. 3.13; (Lk. 3.21 with 4.1)	*Vita* 6.2, 7.2
penitence	Mk 1.4; Mt.3.2; Lk. 3.3	*Vita* 4.3
rebuke of Satan	Mt. 4.10	*Vita* 11.2, 16.3
departure of Satan	Mt. 4.11; Lk. 4.13	*Vita* 17.2
angelic provision of food	Mt. 4.11	*Vita* 22.2
proleptic pains	Mt. 26.38	*Vita* 36.2, 40.1
giving up the spirit	Mt. 27.50	*Vita* 45.3
'eclipse'	Mk. 15.33; Mt. 27.45; Lk. 23.44	*Vita* 46.1
linen shroud(s)	Mk. 15.46; Mt. 27.59; Lk. 23.53	*Vita* 48.1a

The supposition of an influence by the Synoptic Gospels can help to account for some of the structural peculiarities found in the work. For one, it may explain why the *Vita* begins with the penitence of Adam and Eve.[11] As was noted above, the *GLAE* opens with the murder of Abel by Cain. This order is what one would expect because (barring Eve's dream) it is the order of Genesis: 'He drove out the man; and at the east of the garden of Eden he placed the cherubim, and a sword flaming and turning to guard the way to the tree of life. Now the man knew his wife Eve, and she conceived and bore Cain, saying, "I have produced a man with the help of the Lord." Next she bore his brother Abel' (Gen. 3.24–4.2). The narrative then proceeds with the Cain and Abel story.

The *Vita*, however, puts off this episode until book 22. So why does the editor not follow the scriptural order as the *GLAE* does? I would suggest that he has sought to align the experience of the first Adam with that of the last Adam. Starting the protoplasts off with fasting, temptation, and immersion in water means that the start of their earthly life corresponds at its onset with the features of Jesus' ministry. This also explains in part why Eve's testament is not in the *Vita*: the events that she describes are appropriated and expanded by the *Vita*'s narrator and resituated at the beginning of the *LLAE*. The focus has moved from Eve's past experiences of sin to the abolition of sin in the future coming of Jesus.

The supposition of an underlying Gospel mode can also be used to explain some other anomalies in the *Vita*. One particularly puzzling passage is the reference to Adam's fasting for 40 days (6.1). This detail does not fit the narrative especially well, since Adam and Eve had already been without food for 23 days (*Vita* 2.1, 3.1, 4.1); the dignifying of their hunger by proclaiming it as a fast certainly makes a virtue out of a necessity. Why should God impute any sort of favor to Adam and Eve for fasting when they could not eat even if they wanted to? Nor do we hear of Adam's eating after the completion of his fast (17.3). The only reference to food is when the angel Michael brings seeds to Adam and teaches him the art of cultivation (22.2). By this time, however, Cain has already been born. At 18.3 it is stated that Eve is three months pregnant. As 63 days appear to have elapsed since their expulsion, Cain was likely conceived in the Garden. But this means that Adam and Eve do not receive the wherewithal to live for at least six more months, and possibly longer: 22.2 relates that 'Adam took Eve and the *boy* [*puerum*] and led them to the East' before Michael appeared with the seeds. So the 40-day fast becomes all the more anomalous as Adam and Eve are not furnished with food for almost a year.[12] The inference, therefore, is that the author has added the 40 days of fasting to his account in order to parallel the behavior of other notables. But although figures other than Jesus do fast for 40 days, the protoplasts appear to resemble Jesus most closely.[13]

This hypothesis of a modal influence by the gospels raises a number of questions. If the *LLAE* is an 'evangelical' *bios*, one would need to address the following questions, at the least:

1. Why are the commonalities in plot and structure so minor?
2. Why are the commonalities in content limited?
3. If the *Vita* has a Christian subtext, why is it not made more explicit — something that occurs with great frequency in much of the other Adam and Eve literature (Stone, 2002; de Jonge and Tromp, 1997: 75)?
4. How is it that the *Vita* is reliant on all the Synoptic Gospels?
5. Why is Jesus paralleled to both of the protoplasts?
6. Is there a Christian *Nachleben*?

The balance of this chapter proposes to address these questions seriatim.

Why Are the Commonalities in Plot and Structure not more Obvious?

As was stated above, some of the 'episodes in common' appear tenuous. The 'animals in the wilderness' figure in both the *Vita* and the Synoptic Gospels, but, apart from the mere fact of there being animals present, there seems to be little other points of overlap between the accounts. The same holds true with the lengthy repentance narrative. The *Vita* explicitly states that the protoplasts immersed themselves only up to their necks. In other words, their immersion was only a penitential act — there is no reference here to baptism: 'Although a requirement for a ritual bath was that the water reach to one's neck and in proselyte baptism a Woman was in water to her neck for decency, Eve and Adam's standing in the water was an act of penitence' (Ferguson, 2009: 67; cf. Nagel, 1974: 2.196). Such is the view of Everett Ferguson in his comprehensive new study of baptism. It is thus only in a very superficial sense that parallels can be drawn. Yet, even if they are undeniably superficial, why should they be drawn at all?

The most satisfying solution to this problem is to suppose that the redactor is engaging in typology — a hermeneutic that 'sees in persons, events, or places the prototype, pattern, or figure of historical persons, events, or places that follow it in time' (Fishbane, 1985: 350).[14] Typology is especially associated with the emergence of Christianity, and Paul is reputed to be the originator of the word *typos* in this sense (*1 Cor.* 10.11; cf. *Rom.* 5.14; cf. Goppelt, 1982: 4–5). Here, the figures and events in Hebrew Scriptures are regarded as prefiguring figures and events concerning Jesus, which are considered as 'antitypes' ('copies,' 'representations;' cf. *1 Pet.* 3.21). For instance, Moses' saving Israel by putting a bronze serpent on a pole ('type') is an anticipation of Jesus being lifted up on the cross ('antitype'). The one historical event foreshadows the more important historical event where Jesus' death saves all of humanity. It can, therefore, be conjectured that the same process is at work in the *Vita*, and that the editor is trying to show how the protoplasts' actions and circumstances anticipate those of Christ. Here, exactitude is not necessary, so long as the protoplasts furnish a 'type' that seems to accord with an 'antitype' in Jesus' experience.

Of course, one of the inherent difficulties of using typological interpretation is uncertainty about whether a passage is typological or not (Goppelt, 1982: 19). Sometimes the correspondence is straight forward, but on other occasions this connection can be much more obscure. The episode of Moses and the serpent, for instance, bears scant resemblance to Jesus' crucifixion, but the two are a common example of type/antitype.

Fortunately, in the case of Adam and Jesus there is little difficulty in making this equation, since it is an instance of typology that Paul develops himself. The link between the 'first' Adam and 'second' Adam originates in *Romans* 5 and *1 Corinthians* 15, where the two figures are contrasted to illustrate the sinfulness of the first Adam and the redemptive character of the second Adam.[15] The connection is obvious to anyone acquainted with Paul's letters. Hence, everyone who could draw this correspondence that Paul himself had sanctioned and advocated.[16]

Nevertheless, these typological episodes appear somewhat muted — could they not just as easily be described as random coincidence? In in my view, initially the parallels probably *were* random coincidence. The parallel features, for instance, of immersion that are common to both works seemingly went unnoticed until one editor/ traditor recognized the parallels and decided to use features of the Synoptic Gospels as the antitype for types found in the *Vita*. That is to say, events within the *Vita* were retroactively made types for the 'antitypes' that were discerned in the Gospels.[17]

Why Are the Commonalities in Content Limited?

The same might be said to have happened with the structure of the work. The Synoptic Gospels furnished a rudimentary template or armature to frame the *Vita*. Since the latter and the Gospels are both examples of *bioi*, it is not unexpected that they have similar lineaments. Just as clearly, however, their structures are only approximate, with the bulk of the parallels occurring at the beginning and the end. Both works have independent plots, and many of the central features of Jesus' ministry are without parallel.

That said, the beginnings of the *Vita* and the Synoptic Gospels both describe an embarkation into a new phase of life. More importantly, the protagonists' sufferings and deaths occupy a very substantial part of the narrative: the ongoing focus of the two stories is about the inexorable movement towards death. So, in terms of these broad structural outlines, there is a certain structural coherence.

This type of coherence can be observed in other instances of 'parabiblical' literature, where both structure and *topoi* are informed by earlier textual models. Devorah Dimant, for instance, has shown how the *Testament of Job* provides a framework to the book of *Tobit*. She offers the following correspondences (1988: 418).

Dimant's conclusions are worth citing at length:

> These affinities with the book of Job are notable because they are present without any explicit reference to Job or the Book of Job. Moreover, the materials of the plot are not taken from Job or a similar biblical figure, but are independent of them. The use made by *Tobit* of biblical motifs differs, then, in purpose and form from that of narratives of the rewritten Bible or pseudepigraphic biography type. In the case of a 'free narrative' like Tobit, the author achieves a Job-like plot. The referential value lies in the coincidence of motifs and some of the terms, but it leads to a comparison between the new and old texts, and not to an integration

of the old in the new, as was the case in the pseudepigraphic or 'rewritten bible'
narratives. (1988: 419)

Her remarks are very suggestive for the *Vita* and the Synoptic Gospels,
and may point to a related phenomenon at work. Nevertheless, the
Vita cannot be considered a 'free work' in the sense of *Tobit*. As was just
noted, the *Vita*'s framing process was probably carried out retroactively,
where features of the *LLAE* were restructured to put them in line with
features of the Gospels. Still, when Dimant's chart (Table 6.3) is compared with the Gospel/*Vita* parallels listed in Table 6.2, some suggestive
resemblances emerge. It will be noticed, for instance, that the motifs
in common tend to cluster at the beginning and end of both works.
The effect is to frame the story without replicating the plot. Moreover,
as Dimant remarks, the features of the plot are independent: the *Vita*
and Gospels tell their own stories.

Table 6.3: Some commonalities in parabiblical literature

Motifs	Job	Tobit
The hero is pious and righteous	1.1, 8	1.6-12, 16–17
	2.3	2.2-5
He is prosperous	1.2-3	1.13
He is deprived of his possessions	1.14-19	1.15-20
He is crippled by illness	2.7-8	2.9-10
His wife works for others	31.10 (LXX)	2.11-14
He is provoked by his wife	2.9	2.14
He prays and wishes to die	3 *et passim*	2.1-6
His vindication and restitution of health/wealth	42.11-15	14.2-3
He dies in old age with progeny and wealth	42.16-17	14.11-12

If the Vita *Has a Christian Subtext, Why Is It Not Made More Explicit?*

If the foregoing arguments have some merit, why is the work not explicitly Christian? If the *Vita* has a Christian subtext, no effort has been made to bring it the fore, in contrast with a great deal of the later Adam and Eve literature (Stone, 2002; de Jonge and Tromp, 1997: 75). This question has not gone unnoticed by commentators. George Nickelsburg observes that, 'Especially noteworthy is the total absence of Christian soteriology with reference to the future salvation of Adam and of humanity in the resurrection of the dead. This absence stands out the more because such elements enter the later manuscript tradition.'[18]

Can it be said that there actually is evidence for Christians producing pseudepigraphal literature without an obvious Christian 'thumbprint'? Christian overlays are for the most part easily discerned: as Vermes tellingly remarks, 'the obviously Christian additions are patently different from the rest of the work' (Schürer, 1987: 3.2.758).

Detailed work by Johannes Tromp on the qz-text of the *GLAE*, however, has led him to differ with Vermes' assumption that Christian scribes were always predisposed to make mention of Christ: 'The qz-text shows . . . that other Christian editors of the *Life of Adam and Eve* could actually insert eschatological passages that contain no mention, or allusion, to Christ. This suggests that some editors of this writing thought that overly explicit references to the Saviour would be anachronistic and illogical in a story about the protoplasts' (Tromp, 2004: 206).[19]

Nor, by all accounts, was this phenomenon in any way unique among pseudepigraphal and other types of literature. James Davila has recently devoted an entire volume to aspects of this question, and concludes:

> A look at selected Christian sermons, scriptural commentaries, and poetic epics shows that Christians did write Old Testament pseudepigrapha, that at least some did not find it incoherent that a Christian could write a work that dealt with Old Testament themes and yet never mentioned a Christian doctrine or quoted the New Testament or other early Christian literatures, and that Christians did update explicitly Christian works to make them look more Christian or doctrinally acceptable. (Davila, 2005: 229)[20]

Clearly, then, Christians could produce works that were not explicitly Christian. Was, however, the *LLAE* one of these works? Why, given the myriad opportunities within the narrative for doing so, would the author not wish to introduce explicitly Christian features?

As possible solution is that the author wanted the work to be regarded as prophetic in its limning of Jesus. The *Vita* introduces in the figure of Eve the problem of sinful humanity, condemned to keep sinning and passing on corruption to future generations. How are humans to be delivered from this strait? The figure of Adam furnishes the prospect of hope — of a second Adam who would correspond to the first Adam in essential features — one who undergoes temptation, fasting, immersion and who ultimately dies, only to be resurrected and enthroned in heaven by God. One would not need to know much of the story of Jesus to recognize these parallels. The fact that the document was regarded as prophetic would also provide it with notable impact.

This impact would affect non-Christians and believers alike. One need only consider the reaction by Christians to the *Sibylline Oracles*. Augustine, Lactantius, and the emperor Constantine, for instance, all regarded the Christ-acrostic in the eighth *Sibylline Oracle* (8.218-50) as incontrovertible proof of the veracity of the pagan prophets. None of them had any suspicion that it might be a Christian forgery.[21]

If, however, the *Vita* was regarded as a Jewish production, then Christians could proclaim that the Jews' own texts furnished prophetic anticipations about Jesus as the second Adam. Here the correlations are even more explicit than with some of the prophetic proof texts that Christians used to establish their case. While symbolic prophetic discourse offered room for dissent and counter-interpretation, narrative events would be more difficult to discount.

How Is It That the Vita Is Reliant on All the Synoptic Gospels?

Would potential hearers or readers recognize all the narrative events alluded to? The commonalities adduced above are not derived from one Synoptic Gospel but from three (Matthew, Mark and Luke). Can we assume that potential hearers or traditors would have had ready access or familiarity with all the synoptic gospels? Is it likely a compositor would instinctively jump from one Gospel to another and then intercalate the various events of Jesus' life?

Evidence suggests that, in fact, this procedure would have been far from unusual in the second and third centuries CE. At least two factors help to substantiate this conclusion. The first is the manuscript evidence for the three Synoptic Gospels. Most of the earliest papyrus fragments of the gospels had been part of codices, some of which evidently contained several gospels at once, giving rise to the supposition that the gospels circulated as a body of texts, not simply as one scroll (Stanton, 2004).

Second, there is much to support the view that harmonizations of the Synoptic Gospels would also have been commonly available. A harmonizing of the Gospel accounts is at least as old as Justin Martyr (Petersen, 1997: 72–73), and Helmut Koester and others have drawn attention to the prominence of harmonization in Justin's writings, as well as to Justin's own possible reliance on harmonized sources.[22] Martin Hengel observes that Justin Martyr's references to the apostles' 'reminiscences' show clear signs of harmonization, and he further postulates that Justin 'possessed notes of some sort of private "Gospel Harmony" without John for his personal use in catechesis, to which he resorted freely and which may have inspired his pupil Tatian to write his new precise and more elaborate literary Gospel Harmony' (Hengel, 2000: 20).

Justin's 'Gospel Harmony' was evidently not the only one to precede Tatian. Eusebius relates that Ammonius of Alexandria produced a harmony (or possibly a synopsis), using Matthew as the framework (Eus. *Ep. ad Carpianum* 1), while Jerome writes that Theophilus of Antioch (late second century CE) 'put together into one work the words of the four gospels' (*Epistula ad Algasium* [121] 6 cited in Petersen, 1997: 74). Tatian's own harmony, the *Diatessaron*, 'proved itself one of the most popular editions of the Gospels ever produced' (Petersen, 1992: 2.189), and its influence endured for centuries — in some instances, for a millennium. It served as the basis for an array of later versions, including the Old Syriac version of the New Testament, and the Armenian and Georgian versions of the Gospels (Trebolle Barrera, 1998: 238; 358–59).[23]

So despite Irenaeus' famous assertion that there are four Gospels because there are four winds (*Haer.* 3.11.8), many nascent churches seem to have preferred one single, prevailing, wind. The reasons for such a choice are easy to isolate. Having to make use of multiple scrolls or codices was expensive, inconvenient, and awkward. Reducing three or four gospels to a single, authoritative, internally consistent exemplar would have been an obvious choice.[24]

Also worthy of consideration are the harmonizing tendencies manifested in the transmission of Gospel citations by late first- and second-century authors. Petersen's study of the early Gospel traditions observes that harmonization 'seems to be omnipresent and prominent... We conclude that for second century writers there was no clear demarcation among gospels in the same way we distinguish them from each other' (Petersen, 2002: 54).

Hence, the above discussion suggests that harmonizings of the Gospels were pervasive and influential from a very early period. One would suppose, therefore, that it would be far from unusual for Common Era editors to be aware of a harmonized form of the Gospels or to be readily disposed to look at the life of Jesus from a harmonized and synoptic point of view. The same, of course, could be said for their readers.

Why Is Jesus Paralleled to Both of the Protoplasts?

If the Synoptic Gospels can be harmonized, how is this to be done with Adam and Eve? If Jesus' *bios* was the ostensible model for the *LLAE*, how does the redactor make the lives of *both* Adam and Eve correspond?

It appears that the issue is handled in two different ways in the *Vita* — one where the protoplasts are treated as a unity, and one where the differences between them are strongly emphasized. In the former instance, a look at Table 6.2's parallels between the *Vita* and the Gospels illustrates how much Adam and Eve act as a unit. They both experience expulsion and hunger, and undergo ritual immersion. Though the main focus of the work is on Adam's death, Eve's own death soon follows. As Eve's closing words suggest, the work really is about 'my whole life, and that of your father' (50.1). Their lives are intimately connected.

This intimate connection, however, breaks down at various points where the variant behavior of Adam and Eve is exploited to bring out the fundamental disparities between the two figures. Here, each of the protoplasts is intended to represent different facets of God's divine economy. Adam prefigures Christ, so he is best described as representing the Gospel (ante)type, the outworking and anticipation of the Gospel events to come. He is a figure of the future Christ, and his presence speaks for the final reconciliation of humans with God. Eve, by contrast, embodies sinful humankind — the fallen, fallible character of humanity with its weak, sinful, side: one governed by the body and its desires. Accordingly, she exemplifies humans apart from Christ.

Adam has been refashioned in the *imago Christi*. Throughout the *Vita*, Adam and Christ, the second Adam, are explicitly compared. As was noted above, Adam's 40 days of fasting correspond to those of Jesus. Moreover, there are distinct features in the temptation narratives: After Adam's rebuke of the Devil while undergoing penance, the Devil replies: 'O Adam, all my enmity, jealousy, and resentment is towards *you* [*ad te*], since on account of you I was expelled and alienated from my glory . . . on account of you I was cast out upon the earth' (12.1). The Devil then adds, 'By a trick I cheated your wife and caused you [Adam] to be expelled through her' (16.3). Adam cries out, 'O Lord my God, in your hands is my life. Make this adversary of mine be far from me, who seeks to ruin my soul. Give me his glory which he himself lost' (17.1-2). The *Vita* then relates: 'Immediately the Devil no longer appeared to him.' This episode is certainly redolent of the temptation narrative in Matthew where Jesus says '"Away with you Satan! For it is written 'Worship the Lord your God and serve only him.'" Then the devil left him' (Mt. 4.10-11).

The import of this exchange is not simply that Adam's behavior is seen as parallel to that of Jesus, where both resist the Devil, but that Adam, like Jesus, completes his act of penitence successfully. And though the *Vita*'s compositor cannot quite skirt around Adam's transgression, he nevertheless leaves Adam with something of an unfallen sensibility. The animals that mourn with him at the Jordan are by no means hostile, in contrast to the serpent that later bites Seth and reviles Eve (*Vita* 37.1f.).[25] Moreover, only Adam's prayers are regarded as efficacious; Eve in the throes of her labor-pains begs Adam to pray to God on her behalf (*Vita* 20.2b). His prayers are heeded by the angel Michael, who informs Eve: 'Blessed are you, Eve, on account of Adam, for his prayers and supplications are great. I was sent to you that you might receive our help' (*Vita* 21.2).

Eve, by contrast, appears to epitomize the state of sinful humanity. The sinfulness associated with Eve in the *Vita* is relatively obvious, since it is repeated with some frequency. Even Jack Levison, who has argued for the exoneration of Eve in the *GLAE*, finds no exoneration here; the *LLAE*'s purpose is 'to exonerate Adam and denigrate Eve, thus presenting the readers with a perfect penitent, a righteous figure who receives mercy during life and after death' (1988: 164).

The *LLAE* repeatedly has Eve inculpate herself for the transgression. As early as 3.2 Eve says to Adam, 'it was because of me that the Lord grew angry with you.' At 5.3 she continues, 'I brought labor and tribulation upon you.' More surprisingly yet, after her second seduction by Satan, Eve says to Adam: 'you did not take part in either the first or second collusion [*praevaricationem*]. But I conspired and was seduced, because I did not keep the commandment of God' (18.1). Readers are left wondering just how it was that Adam did not participate in the first collusion. Similarly, in Adam's farewell address, she gainsays her husband's remarks and assumes the blame herself. 'When Eve saw him, she began to cry and she herself crying said, "My Lord God, transfer his pain over to me, since it was I who sinned"' (35.2).

Nor is she alone in blaming herself; the same theme recurs in the mouths of various other characters in the *Vita*. When Eve is confronted by the serpent at the gates of Paradise, it reviles her, asking 'Tell me, Eve, How could you open your mouth to eat the fruit which God commanded you not to eat?' (38.2). Adam himself takes up the refrain at 44.2: 'Adam said to Eve: What have you done? You have brought on us a great affliction, fault and sin unto all our generations. What you have done will be passed on to your children after my death.' These are Adam's final words to his wife. The *Vita*, therefore, does its best to sublimate the misdeeds of Adam; while it does not entirely expunge them, at almost every opportunity it devolves the guilt and blame on to the figure of Eve.

And, if her deception by the devil was not enough, she is portrayed as being especially fallible in other respects: her bodily appetites betray her. She gives in to her physical hunger and to the cold.[26] She falls down before the Devil, after emerging from the Tigris. Her fall evidently indicates her corporal weakness — note Adam's comment at 6.1a, 'You cannot endure the same number of days as I' — but could also conceivably hint at obeisance to Satan.

Further, when Eve and Seth go in search of the oil of life, Seth is bitten by the serpent. Eve exclaims, 'O cursed beast, why are you not afraid to cast yourself at the image of God, but dare to fight against it? Why have your teeth prevailed?' (37.3). The serpent scathingly replies, 'O Eve, was our malice not ever against you? Isn't our anger against you?' (38.1). The serpent does not mention Adam; the animals' (serpents'?)

enmity at their change in status is directed solely at Eve (cf. *GLAE* 11.2 'our nature has also been transformed').[27] This would suggest that their enmity is not directed at Adam. If so, this circumstance helps to explain a scene from their penitence. Why is it that Adam is able to enlist *omnia animantia* (8.3) to form a wall around him and lament for him? And why is Eve left entirely to herself in the Tigris when Adam fully recognizes that she 'cannot do as much as I' (6.1a)? The answer would seem to be that once she ate of the forbidden fruit, all the animals became hostile towards her. This sets her up for a second failure; where Adam is well protected from the Devil's deceptions, Eve has no such armor. Her first lapse makes the second inevitable. Sin carries its own momentum with it.

Less obvious, perhaps, are the various ways in which Eve is consistently associated with death. The most important of these emerges in her inability to sustain life, and in the fact that she is appointed to the interring of the dead. She is unable to heal or restore life, as is proved by her abortive quest with Seth to obtain the oil of mercy to relieve Adam's pains. Adam is left to suffer until his death, whereupon Eve assumes the role of his undertaker. Her name, therefore, becomes cruelly ironic — she may produce living children, but death, not life, is their ultimate outcome (cf. Gen. 3.20).[28]

In sum, Eve is made to represent fallen humanity. It is only through Adam's redemptive activity that she is saved, just as humans are only saved by Christ's salvific actions. It is this fundamental disjunction between Eve and Adam that helps to explain the curious quasi-sinless status of Adam. It can be explained by reference to Jesus. He was sinless, as Adam was and will be again. At the same time, he was subject to death like Eve. So the two protoplasts bring together both aspects of the human experience. While it would be going far too far to say that there is some form of syzygy at work, it might be described as an anticipation of the concept, which became increasingly elaborate in gnostic thought.[29]

Is there a Christian Nachleben?

The final question concerns the *Nachleben* of the typology in the *LLAE*: Are they at all consistent with similar patterns in other early Christian literature? While it is not possible to discuss the issue here in any depth, there do seem to be similar patterns, especially in Syrian literature.[30]

Some of the poems of Ephrem the Syrian, for instance, draw strong connections between the experiences that Adam and Christ share:

> In the month of Nisan our Lord repaid
> The debts of that first Adam:
> He gave his sweat in Nisan in exchange for Adam's sweat,
> The Cross, in exchange for Adam's Tree.
> The sixth day of the week corresponded to the sixth day of creation,
> And it was at 'the turn of the day' [Gen. 3.8]
> That He returned the thief to Eden.

(*Church* 51.8)[31]

Ephrem's explicit reference to the 'first Adam' presupposes a 'second Adam' and the careful parallelism also demonstrates that the same form of typology is in view here. As Brock remarks, 'Ephrem perceives a detailed pattern of complementarity between the processes of fall and restoration: all the individual details of the Fall are reversed, so that we are presented with a series of contrasted types, with Adam/Christ and Eve/Mary as protagonists' (Brock, 1992: 32).

This phenomenon is even more pronounced in the *Cave of Treasures*.[32] The extent of the dependence of the *Cave* on the *Vita* is debated, though Ri observes a number of parallels that are specific to the two works (Ri, 2000: 198, cf. 198–201). Most important for our purposes is that the *Cave* actually uses the story of Jesus to construct an entire narrative of Adam's experience, which is then interpreted as the 'type' corresponding to the 'antitype' of Jesus' life. The author develops a lengthy series of parallels, where the key moments of Jesus' crucifixion are juxtaposed with events from the fall of the protoplast (or protoplasts). For instance, 'At the third hour of Friday a crown of glory was placed on the head of Adam, and at the third hour of Friday the crown of thorns was placed on the head of Christ' (Budge, 1927: 222).

In fact, the author demonstrates that the events of every three-hour period in Jesus' life on Good Friday correspond closely to the events of the Fall in Eden, which also takes place on a Friday. 'At the same hour in which the Son of Man delivered up his soul to His Father on the Cross, did our father Adam deliver up his soul to Him that fashioned him'

(Budge, 1927: 73). What is more, the locale for Adam's tomb is none other than Golgotha, so that when Jesus' blood trickles downward, Adam is redeemed. It is apparent, therefore, that the details of Adam's life have been consciously modeled on the features of Jesus' life to develop additional correspondences between them.

Both of the above texts, therefore, demonstrate the development of a biographical impulse on the story of Adam that uses Jesus' own story to furnish the needed details. In the *Cave of Treasures*, these details are almost entirely extrapolations of features of Jesus' own life; in the poem of Ephrem, this process is more subdued. Nevertheless, both show the strong influence of Jesus' *bioi* on the construction of Adam's life(s), and indicate that this process was by no means uncommon in early Christianity.

This chapter would argue that the process in the *Vita* was more circumscribed. The details of Adam and Eve's lives were already there, so they have merely been shaped by the Gospels, not written *de novo* as was the account of Adam in the *Cave of Treasures*.

CONCLUSION

Taken together, all the features treated above suggest that the *Vita* has been strongly influenced by the gospel mode or, as Roydon's poem puts it, it displays the 'Lineaments of Gospel books.' Of course, the *Vita* is not a Gospel itself, but has merely assumed some gospel overtones in the same way that it has been influenced by the apocalyptic genre. Unlike the *GLAE*, however, the *LLAE* is not a hybrid: it is a *bios* that has been shaped by evangelical and apocalyptic modes. And while the *GLAE* and the *LLAE* share a strong apocalyptic element, the *Vita*'s testamentary features are negligible.

Accordingly, the genres of the two 'Lives' are not the same. One is a hybrid compounded of apocalypse and confessional testament, the other a *bios* strongly influenced by apocalyptic and evangelical modes.

These two chapters on the genres of the *GLAE* and the *LLAE* prompt several conclusions:

1. The genres of the *GLAE* and the *LLAE* do not readily conform to procrustean attempts to categorize them as one genre. Their

respective genres have been significantly influenced by other genres and/or other modes.

2. Genres change. While the *GLAE* and the *LLAE* have notable similarities, they have shifted sufficiently that they no longer belong to the same genre.

3. The 'Lives' are in a continuum with earlier generic forms, and themselves serve as the basis for further generic transformations.

CONCLUSION

'and so they went out . . .'

Lucille Clifton

Lucille Clifton's pregnant phrase not only describes the experience of the protoplasts, but also the trajectories assumed by the multiple stories associated with them. Just a single one of these story forms, the *Greek Life of Adam and Eve*, has given rise to five of the essays in this volume. These essays, inspired by the *GLAE*, could also be said to have 'gone out' in their attempts to draw attention to features of the *GLAE* that have been discussed less fully in modern scholarship.

Daphna Arbel, for instance, builds on Levison and Tromp's observation that the text forms of the *GLAE* developed in the context of everyday life. Drawing on Bakhtin's concept of *heteroglossia* as well as on observations related to the collective, flexible, and variable nature of everyday-life stories, she demonstrates in her first chapter (Chapter 1) the multivocality of the *GLAE* and shows that a single version can contain an entire spectrum of perceptions, narratives, and counter-narratives about Eve. In several traditions, Eve is cast as a transgressor of God's way, as Adam's deceitful wife, and as being attracted to the sins of the flesh. Yet, the same single text contains contradictory traditions in which Ev is represented as an ethical figure, as Adam's dutiful wife, and as a figure who beholds transcendent visions.

Arbel's second chapter (Chapter 2) explores yet another way in which the *GLAE* speaks about Eve with more than one voice. The narrative appeals to traditions about Eve's culpability for inflicting death

on Adam and all humanity. Yet, it also contains counter-traditions about
Eve who is entrusted with Adam's obsequies. In these, Eve is associated
with a set of cultural funerary norms according to which women were
perceived to act publicly with authority, to voice their feelings, and
to employ their skills of consolation, as well as with traditions about
women's spiritual virtues and abilities to partake in transcendent heavenly realities. So, again, Arbel suggests, the *GLAE* reveals an array of
traditions and counter-traditions about a blameworthy and a venerable
Eve. These may have circulated in the cultural context of everyday life
in which the *GLAE* seems to have emerged and may have been, in turn,
incorporated into its framework.

On the topic of honor itself, Dietmar Neufeld adopts an intriguing
approach to the *GLAE* by recognizing in his first chapter (Chapter 3)
that it is not a small drama that simply unfolds in the broad confines of
Eden and the heavenly realms. Rather, the whole narrative is quintes-
sentially a tableau with a vast number of witnesses — not only the angels
and the children of the protoplasts, but humankind *in extenso*, whose
members are the actual recipients of the social modeling and values
couched within the narrative.

One aspect of this, of course, is the complex role of clothing and
dress within the human experience. The Adam and Eve narrative
offers a remarkable locus for bringing out all the variegations in divine
and human figuration and dress. These variegations extend from the
glorious appearance of the archangels and seraphim, to the glory of
the prelapsarian couple, to their physical loss of glory, their subsequent
nakedness, and their final garbing in mundane human clothing. All
these permutations of appearance and dress establish a complex social
framework and hierarchy. Thereby, the social embodiment of Adam
and Eve assumes emblematic importance for the implied readers and
hearers, and serves as a means of codifying experience. In particular,
the transition from glorious nudity to shameful nakedness marks the
movement of Adam and Eve into a social and cultural *habitus* where
humans are forever marked by what they do or do not wear.

Neufeld's second chapter (Chapter 4) addresses the related issues of
shame and honor and their social repercussions. In this case, humans
are also 'clothed' by those around them — not with literal clothing but
with a social fabric of approbation or contempt. The effect, however,
is similar in many ways. Society provides the matrix in which these

culturally shaped values operate. Neufeld contends that these values operate differently for males and females, and that males tend to be more vulnerable to societal opprobrium than women are, and that this insight is fundamental for assessing the behavior of the protoplasts in the *GLAE*. After Eve's 'seduction' by Satan, she and Adam each respond in a socially appropriate manner, but the consequences are more severe and far-reaching for Adam. He is unable to recover his lost honor, and his resultant suffering and death are emblematic of this loss. Eve is both more resilient and repentant, and the depth of her monologue gives expression to both of these features.

J.R.C. Cousland's first chapter (Chapter 5) continues with a discussion of the *GLAE* from the standpoint of genre. He determines that generic study of the *GLAE* is both necessary and important, not least because of the widely discordant views among scholars attempting to identify its genre. For Cousland, 'rewritten Bible' and midrash prove to be unsuitable generic categories because they are not authentic genres, but rather literary processes. Nor does the *GLAE* appear to be an apology or a *bios*. Instead, it displays distinct characteristics of two genres that together form a mixed genre (a *Mischgattung*), notably that of testament and apocalypse. Such a finding is not unexpected because in literature mixed genres are relatively commonplace and help to explain how genres change.

A specific example of this shift in genres can be seen in Cousland's second chapter (Chapter 6), which offers the volume's only study not devoted to the *GLAE*. Here he moves from a discussion of the Greek to the Latin 'Life'. Because of the notable differences between the two 'Lives', he establishes that their genres are different as well. The *Latin Life of Adam and Eve* (*LLAE*) presents an example of ancient biography, the *bios*, but this *bios* has been refracted and altered by another literary mode, namely that of the 'gospel.' The balance of the chapter explores this notion and concludes that it is highly likely that the synoptic gospels provided the template that helped to guide the transformation of the *LLAE* from one genre into another.

These last two chapters indicate, therefore, that at least two of the 'Lives' differ significantly in their generic composition. There is no single genre that can be taken to be constitutive of the books of Adam and Eve, and, in fact, mixed genres may well predominate over single genres. These findings cohere well with the observations of recent scholars about the multivalent nature and forms of the narratives. The books of Adam and Eve are not so much an example of 'unity in diversity' as 'similarities in diversity.'

Hence Clifton's phrase, 'and so they went out,' represents an invitation to take account of the multivalence of these narratives. When they are assessed together, our conclusions demonstrate just how radically the biblical traditions enshrined within the books of Adam and Eve have been transformed and redeployed to suit the circumstances and needs of their authors and editors. Their multivalence — particularly that of the *GLAE* — has continued to influence our own interpretations. While Arbel, Neufeld, and Cousland have worked together closely in bringing this volume to fruition, they have not attempted to influence or change each other's views on interpretative matters. Rather, inasmuch as these books of Adam and Eve took on a life of their own as persons and groups utilized them in different ways, so also Arbel, Neufeld, and Cousland wished to take possession of them from their own perspectives and methodological proclivities.

And so once more, the stories of Adam and Eve have gone out and stirred the imagination. Hearers and readers of these narratives have and will continue to impose their culturally and socially conditioned impulses onto them — impulses that are of necessity driven by the peculiarities, sensibilities, concerns of each person, group, and age, investing the stories with new meaning. And another retelling of the stories waits just around the corner — a transformation in which the narratives of Adam and Eve will once more be taken and spun out to reflect the meanings being sought — religious and cultural — on such issues as gender, sin, and redemption. Each retelling, far from being value-free, is charged with the unconsciously and consciously driven anxieties and ideologies that govern the imagination of every reader or hearer. Hence, the authors have attempted to show that, in their retelling, the stories are not only transformed but that they also become transformative themselves.

NOTES

Part One: Daphna Arbel

1 A nuanced examination of Eve and her role in the first sin has been offered by John Levison. As he has persuasively demonstrated, the *GLAE* contains diverse depictions of Eve and her role in the primary sin: the short textual unit in *GLAE* 7–8, commonly referred to as Adam's account of the transgression, presents Eve as the primary agent of the transgression. In contrast, several text forms of the *GLAE* 15–30, known as Eve's account of the sin, convey diverse views regarding Eve and her sin including 'exoneration' (DSV) and denigration (ATLC, NIK). See, in particular, Levison, 2000a: 251–75; 2000b: 21–46. The following two chapters, as noted, will not examine the theme of the sin but rather will focus on other traditions.

2 Obviously, feminist criticism includes a variety of characteristics and represents diverse methodologies. For discussion of various reading alternatives, including methods of 'reading against the grain,' see discussions and references: Fuchs, 2008: 45–65; Reinhartz, 1997: 30–38; Rooke (ed.), 2007; Schüssler Fiorenza (ed.), 1993; Schüssler Fiorenza, 1985.

   Charlotte Elisheva Fonrobert has succinctly articulated strategies of 'reading against the grain,' which will be adopted here. '"Reading against the grain" can take various forms, just as its goals can be variously formulated. One may, for example, search for lapses in ideological coherence of a text or set of texts, or one may interrogate texts with respect to traces of possible choices not made. One can locate what appears to be the "repressed" of a text; one can emphasize what the text hides, embedded in overt rhetorical structure; or one can highlight what are only moments of disturbance in the overall dominant ideology of the text. What characterizes most of such readings is the highlighting of the cultural, textual or rhetorical construction of gender' (Fonrobert, 2009: 9).

3 See Levison, 2003: 15. For a full discussion, see 1–16.

4 See Tromp, 2004: 205, 218. For a full discussion, see 205–23.

5 Tromp, 2004: 218.

6 Mikhail Bakhtin, 1981. See also Clark and Holquist, 1984.

7 Bakhtin coined the term to allude to the multiplicity of actual languages, but it can be introduced into poetic and narrative genres. On *heteroglossia*, see Pam Morris's explanation: '*Heteroglossia*' (the Russian "*raznorechie*" literally means "different-speech-ness"), refers to the conflict between "centripetal" and "centrifugal," "official" and "unofficial" discourses within the same national language. "*Heteroglossia*" is also present, however, at the (q.v.) micro-linguistic scale; every utterance contains within it the trace of other utterances, both in the past and in the future. The discursive site in which the conflict between different voices is at its most concentrated is the modern novel (q.v.).

   'One way of representing *heteroglossia* in the novel is by a hybrid construction, which contains within it the trace of two or more discourses, either those of the narrator and character(s), or of different characters (q.v. "quasi-direct discourse").' See Morris (ed.), 1994: 248–49.

8 Nancy Glazener, among others, has made this clear. As she has noted, Bakhtin's own work is not markedly feminist 'and was conspicuously silent about feminism and the social effects of gender differences.' See Glazener, 2002: 155. For a full discussion, see 155–76.

9   Feminist critics, in diverse contexts, have drawn on Bakhtin's writings in order to replace
    assumptions about homogenous patriarchal discourses with alternative views about
    traditional and subversive elements that are normally integrated in cultural discourses.
    For discussions of biblical traditions and counter-traditions related to representations
    of feminine figures, see, for example, Pardes, 1992; Fentress-Williams, 2007: 59–68. On
    normative and subversive gender traditions in Rabbinic texts, see, for example, Hasan-
    Rokem, 2000, 2003. On *heteroglossia* in early Christian context, see Castelli, 1994: 73–98.
    On the dialogic character of the Bible and its parts, see Reed, 1993.

10 Here I adopt the fundamental perspective on gender famously articulated by Judith Butler,
    who has established the foundation for theorizing and articulating concepts of gender
    formation (Butler, 1990).

Chapter 1: Traditions of Sin and Virtue

1   On the primacy of the sin of disobedience in Genesis 3, see Von Rad, 1972: 75; Meyers,
    1988: 72–79, 87. Compare Frymer-Kensky, 1992: 120–21, 127, 140–43; Wenham, 1991:
    90; Westerman, 1984: 53, 275–78; Trible, 1978: 72–143; Barr, 1993: ix; and Bird, 1998:
    129–51 especially, 135–36.

2   In this chapter, I confine myself to the *GLAE*'s version and translation included in the
    Synopsis of the Books of Adam and Eve by Anderson and Stone, because of its accessibility.
    Other Greek versions of the *GLAE* can be found in Levison (2000b) and in Tromp (2005).
    References to other MSS will be mentioned in relevant discussions. When I refer to the
    GLAE, I mean only Anderson and Stone's version.

3   On the literary nature of the *GLAE* and its merged traditions, see Tromp, 1997: 25–41.

4   On the two accounts, see de Jonge and Tromp, 1997: 20, 52–54; Levison, 1988: 164–74;
    1989: 135–50; 2000a: 251–75; 2000b: 21–46.

5   See Levison, 2000a: 159–60, which carefully analyzes several text forms that convey varying
    views of Eve and her sin, including exoneration (DSV) and denigration (ATLC, NIK).

6   On Eve's pain, see Anderson, 2000d: 3–42, especially 23–32.

7   See Levison's discussion of this idea and its reflection in several *GLAE* scenes: 2004: 519–34,
    especially 525–30.

8   For discussion of Satan in the *GLAE*, see Stone, 1993: 143–56; Anderson, 2000a: 83–85;
    2000b: 141; Piñero, 1993: 191–214.

9   Italics here and in the following note are mine.

10 On the designation of the serpent as the enemy, compare *GLAE* 2.4; 7.2; 5.1; 25.4; 28.3.
    See parallel versions of the Adam and Eve books: *LLAE* 11.3, 39.1; *Arm.* 17.1, 20.2, 28.3;
    Geo. 17.1, 7.2, 28.3, 39.1, 39.2. Compare also *Test. XII Patr.* (*T. Dan* 6.3), *T. Job* 7.11, 47.10;
    3 Bar. (Gr.) 13.2; Mt. 13.24ff; Lk. 10.19. Examining Genesis 2–3 against the backdrop of
    the Ancient Near East and Israel, Gerhard Von Rad, among many scholars, has emphasized
    that the serpent, or snake, who has been too readily associated with the embodiment of
    evil, is, in fact, 'not the symbol of a "demonic" power and certainly not of Satan.' See
    Von Rad, 1972: 87; compare Westerman, 1984: 236; Hanson, 1972: 43. Sarna, 1989: 24;
    Soggin, 1975: 88–111, especially 94–100. For a survey of the role of the serpent/Satan in
    the history of interpretations, see Ansgar Kelly, 2006: 32–41; Winston, 1979: 121–23.

11 According to Genesis 3.6b, after Eve ate of the fruit 'she gave also to her husband with her.'
    On the sin of disobedience in Genesis 3, which does not involve elements of temptation,
    see von Rad, 1972: 75; Meyers, 1988: 72–79, 87. Compare Frymer-Kensky, 1992: 120–21,
    127, 140–43; Westerman, 1984: 53, 275–78; Trible, 1978: 72–143; Barr, 1993: ix; Bird,
    1981: 129–51, especially 135–36.

12 This is indicated in *GLAE* 20.1 as follows: 'And in that very hour my eyes were opened, and
    forthwith I knew that I was naked of the righteousness with which I had been clothed (upon),
    and I wept and said to him . . . .' As Levison notes: 'It is not the discovery of nakedness for
    the first time — which is surely the implication of Gen. 3.7 — but the discovery that the
    virtue that had clothed Eve is now lost that saddens her.' See Levison, 2004: 526.

13 It is true, as Levison has observed, that Eve is made to justify herself by explaining that she was bound by the oath she had selflessly given to the Devil when she still believed that the tree was valuable for both herself and for Adam: Levison (2000a). This explanation, nonetheless, only accentuates her culpability by contrasting her commitment to the Devil with her lack of commitment to God. When faced with the two options — moral obligation to God or to the Devil — Eve binds herself to her illicit pledge to the latter and consequently also deceives Adam.

14 The literature is quite large. See, for example, discussion and bibliography in Bal, 1987: 104–30; Bird, 1997: 174–93; Carmichael, 1992: 47–63; Frymer-Kensky, 1992: 108–17; Niditch, 1985: 36–38, 40–43; Pardes, 1992: 39–59; Trible, 1978: 72–143.

15 On the sexual aspect of the sin, see Levison, 1988: 169. On Jewish and Christian interpretations of Adam and Eve's sexual life in the Garden of Eden, see Anderson, 1989: 121–48. On later views regarding sexual aspects of the sin in Augustine's writings, see Anderson, 2001: 63–73; Clark, 1996.

16 The interpretation of Ben Sira's statement as a reference to Eve is widely accepted. See Trenchard, 1982: 8. For a different view, see Levinson's suggestion that the whole content of this passage is about the behavior of wives and not Eve: Levison, 1985: 617–23.

17 'Theophilus to Autolycus,' 1885: 105.

18 Tertullian, 'On the Apparel of Women,' 1890: 14. For a discussion of theological views shared between the *GLAE* and Irenaeus, Tertullian, and Theophilus of Antioch, see de Jonge, 2003b, especially 363.

19 Ambrose, 'Paradise,' 1961.

20 Neusner (ed.), 1985.

21 Tertullian, 'On the Apparel of Women'; Chrysostom, 1961, 1998, 'Homily on Genesis'.

22 See references and discussion in Clark (ed.), 1983: 29–31.

23 Ambrose, 'Paradise,' 1961: 301–2.

24 'On the Death of His Father,' 1894: 257.

25 On Philo's use of gender categories, see Taylor, 2003; Baer, 1970; Lloyd, 1984; Sly, 1990; Mattlia, 1996; van den Hoek, 2000.

26 Boyarin, 1993: 91.

27 Compare *Sabbath* 145b–146a, *Avodah Zara* 22b.

28 'Homily 1.' See also Heine's introduction, 20.

29 Ambrose, 15.73 in 'On Paradise,' 1961.

30 Augustine, 'Literal Commentary on Genesis,' XI: 42. See references and discussion in Clark (ed.), 1983: 40.

31 Eldridge, 2001: 85, 153–54. See also his view regarding Eve's speech being directed to the human community at large which, on a practical level, includes members or some branch of Early Judaism, whether Christian or Jewish, and perhaps Gentile sympathizers: 2001: 184–85.

32 For personified Woman Wisdom, see Camp, 1985; 1991: 1–39; Di Lella, 1991: 39–52; Fox, 1997: 613–33; McKinlay, 1996; Murphy, 1995: 222–33; Newsom, 1989: 142–60.

33 Eldridge, 2001: 122.

34 Eldridge, 2001: 199.

35 Zlotnick, 1966: 84, 164. On notions of gender in *Semahot* and related sources, see Wandrey, 2007: 269–88.

36 Archaeological evidence reflects similar customs. For example, ossuaries from the second half of the first century BCE, found in Jerusalem and Jericho, attest to the fact that women, especially those who were mothers, were buried in their husbands' burial plot; see Peleg, 2002: 65–73, especially 67.

37 On the account of Adam's death, see Tromp, 1997: 25–41.

38 The account of Adam's death develops further and provides additional details concerning heavenly sights and visions that are seen by both Eve and her son Seth. Our present discussion, however, is concerned solely with the above-cited passage, in which Eve is featured as the main protagonist, as well as the first and principal beholder of God's chariot.

39 Eldridge, 2001: 43–44. Sweet, 1993: 156.

41 Eskola, 2001: 112.

42 The term 'chariot' (מרכבה *merkavah*) is not explicitly mentioned in Ezekiel's first-person account in chapter 1 but is derived from *1 Chron.* 28.18, which refers to 'the chariot of the cherubim' that carried the ark of the covenant in the holy of holies. The term 'chariot' was applied to Ezekiel's vision later, by priest and author Yeshua Ben Sira from the second century BCE, who recounts how Ezekiel 'saw a vision and described the different orders of the chariot' (Ben Sira, 49.8). In a similar vein, the Septuagint replaces the Hebrew term 'vision' with the Greek term 'chariot' (ἅρμα) and it renders Ezekiel 43.3 as 'the vision of the chariot which I saw was like the vision which I saw at the river Chobar,' whereas in the Masoretic text Ezekiel states, 'The vision I saw was like the vision I had seen . . ..' Accordingly, in post-biblical tradition the vision of God's heavenly throne came to be known as the vision of the chariot — the *merkavah*. We can see this tendency, for example, in *Pseudo-Ezekiel* from Qumran (4Q385) that employs the term 'chariot' to describe the throne vision of Ezekiel. In most of the later references, Ezekiel's vision as described in the first chapter of the book of Ezekiel was combined with themes from Ezekiel's visions described in chapters 3, 10, and 43, as well as with themes from Isaiah 6 and Daniel 7.

43 On the image of the chariot-throne in a variety of sources, see discussions and references in Arbel, 2003: 8, 18, 23–29, 115–16; Baumgarten, 1988: 199–213; Davila, 2000: 249–64; 2000a: 87–90; Dimant and Strugnell, 1990: 331–48; Gruenwald, 1980; Halperin, 1988; Himmelfarb, 1992: 10–11, 16–7, 31, 64–5, 100; Elior, 2004: 63–81; Eskola, 2001: 1–123; Morray-Jones, 1992: 1–31; Nitzan, 1994: 163–83; Newsom, 1987: 11–30; Rowland, 1982: 95–8; Schäfer 1992; Scholem, 1941: 40–79, 1960; Schiffman, 1982: 15–47; Wolfson, 1994: 13–124.

44 References to chariots/thrones often appear in the context of privileged righteous figures ascending to heaven; therefore, the study of the chariot-throne tradition is often focused on the ascent theme. This present study, however, will not treat the theme of heavenly ascent. See, for example, Halperin, 1988: 47–67; 1988; Himmelfarb, 1992; Segal, 1980; Smith, 1981: 403–29; Tabor, 1986; Wolfson, 1993: 13–44.

45 Here I do not treat the ongoing discussion over whether literary descriptions of visions of the chariot-throne reflect authentic and genuine visionary experiences. For views in favor of seeing literary texts as reflecting visionary experience, see Merkur, 1989: 119–48; Rowland, 1982: 215–34; Stone, 1990: 31–33. For arguments against these views, see Himmelfarb, 1992: 95–114. On integral links between interpretative activities and revelatory experiences, see Wolfson, 1994: 74–124.

46 On the angels, eagles, and God's chariot, see Piñero, 1993: 191–214; especially 195, 197.

47 In a similar manner, for example, a passage in *3 Enoch* of the Hekhalot and Merkavah literature also envisions eagles as the creatures of the chariot. See *Synopse* §3, which describes Rabbi Ishmael's ascent to heaven in the hope of beholding God's chariot-throne: 'Then the eagles of the chariot, the flaming *ophanim* and the cherubim of devouring fire asked Metatron: "Youth, why have you allowed one born of woman to come in and behold the chariot?"' (Alexander, 1983: 1.257). It also is noteworthy that one Armenian version of the life of Adam and Eve replaces the eagles with 'four fiery beasts,' presumably to conform the passage to Ezekiel 1, as Halperin has suggested. See Halperin, 1998: 101.

48 Levison, 2003: 15. For a full discussion, see 1–16; Tromp, 1997: 25–41; 2004: 205–23.

49 Tromp, 2004: 222–3.

50 Tromp, 2004: 221.

51 On the nature of everyday-life stories see Hasan-Rokem, 2000: 1–15; 2003: 1–27. For a compelling discussion about female storytellers and folktales, see Virginia Burrus's suggestions about women's folktales that were preserved in the late second-century *Acts of Paul and Thecla.* Burrus, 1987: 53–57, 67–80.

52 Bakhtin, 1981.

Chapter 2: Eve, Funerary Practices, and Adam's Death

1 For a comprehensive discussion see Johannes Tromp, 1997; compare, D.A. Bertrand, 1983. For a discussion of funerary practices in the *GLAE*, see M. de Jonge, and J. Tromp, 1997: 70–75.

2 Tromp, 1997: 36.

3 Jonge and Tromp, 1997: 71.

4 In this chapter, I use the *GLAE*'s version and English translation included in Gary A. Anderson and M.E. Stone (eds), 1999. Compare Greek versions of *GLAE* included in four text-forms in J.R. Levison 2000b; M.E. Stone (ed.), 1993; and J. Tromp, 2005. References to other MSS will be mentioned in relevant discussions. When I refer to the *GLAE*, I mean only Anderson and Stone's version.

5 For a variety of biblical and post-biblical views regarding the afterlife, see a very comprehensive discussion by Segal, 2004: 120–638. For discussion of afterlife beliefs in the first centuries CE, see especially 351–95.

6 Levison, 2000a: 268–69.

7 Levison, 2000a: 268; compare Levison, 2000b: 95.

8 For observations regarding inconsistencies between the portrayals of Eve's sin in Genesis and in later interpretive traditions, see Bal, 1987; Bird, 1997; Carmichael, 1992; Frymer-Kensky, 1992: 108–17; Meyers, 1988; Niditch, 1984: 36–38, 40–43; Trible, 1978: 72–143.

9 Ben Sira seems to display one of the first examples: 'From a woman sin had its beginning and because of her we all die' (25.24). See Trenchard, 1982: 8. Levinson suggests that the whole content of this passage is about the behavior of wives and not Eve, in Levison, 1985.

10 Levison, 2004: 529. For a full discussion of both the *GLAE* and Romans 1.18-25, see 519–34.

11 Levison, 2003: 15. For a full discussion, see 1–16.

12 Tromp, 2004: 220; cf. 205–23.

13 Tromp, 1997: 219.

14 Brown, 1981: 24.

15 Recent work on the ancient world has demonstrated its complex nature and the fluidity of boundaries between pagans, Jews, and Christians. See, for example, Segal, 1986; Kraft, 1975; Boyarin, 1999.

16 Van der Toorn, 1994: 119. Compare, Starr Sered, 1994: 89–118; 120–33; Young, 1993: xxi. For detailed information regarding women's funerary practices, see Corley, 2002.

17 Padel, 1993: 5.

18 See Goff, 2004: 34–35. On women, birth–death, and pollution, see also Stears, 1998: 89–100, esp. 89–93.

19 See Erwin Rohde's classical study, 1925: 31–32.

20 See Alexiou, 1974; Burkert, 1985: 192; Garland, 1985: 23–24; Kurtz and Boardman, 1971: 143–44. Men also performed similar practices, but typically in battlefield situations where women would not ordinarily be present. See Holst-Warhaft, 1992: 103–14; Sourvinou-Inwood, 2004: 160–88. Compare interpretations of images of everyday life in Classical art as markers of social structures and prescribed norms related to women and funerary practices: Sourvinou-Inwood, 1995: 328–37; Stears, 1995: 109–31.

21 Women relatives usually performed these tasks, but at times they were undertaken by domestic servants or an undertaker; cf. Rush, 1941: 106, 117–25. For Greek views about afterlife and examples of how anxiety about death was reduced by deploying figures like Charon, see Sourvinou-Inwood, 1995: 303–61.

22 The most complete discussion of later customs of Jewish mourning can be found in the tractate 'Mourning,' or *Semahot*. See the translation and commentary by Zlotnick, 1966, *The Tractate 'Mourning'*. For women and mourning practices, see De Ward, 1972a: 1–27; 1972b: 145–66; Feldman, 1977; Safrai, 1987: 1.728–92, esp. 773–87; Corley, 2003: 61–72; Kraemer, 2000: 14–71. According to *Semahot* 12.10, for example, men are allowed to prepare only men for burial, but women prepare corpses of either sex. In Acts 9.36-7,

women prepare the body of Tabitha in Joppa by washing it. Compare Mt. 26.12; Mk 14.8, 16.1; Lk. 23.56, 24.1; Jn 19.39-40.

23 Corley, 1993: 102–06.

24 See views regarding the grief expressed during the Greek *prothesis*, which was thought to confirm that the person was really dead and not merely sleeping: Garland, 1985: 30; Kurtz and Boardman, 1971: 144.

25 Garland, 1985: 33. For discussions of women in vase representations and illustrations, see Ahlberg, 1971: 72–87, 97, 102–08, 114–21, 129, 179, 225–27, 230–31; Havelock, 1981: 102–65, plates 26, 34, 35, 40, 41, 88, 89, 90, 91, 92, 93, 94, 95, 96, 97, 98; Vermule, 1979: 11–23, figs 6, 7, 8A, 9, 10, 13, 16; Kurtz and Boardman: figs 43 and 44.

26 The wailings uttered during these rituals were thought to raise the spirit of the dead from the grave. See Alexiou, 1974: 108–09; Holst-Warhaft, 1992: 131–33.

27 Toynbee, 1971: 44–47; especially plates 9 and 11; Rush, 1941: 109, 163. Compare: Corbeill, 2004: 67–106. According to Anthony Corbeill, various acts of self-degradation that are shared by grieving women in numerous cultures — such as tearing the hair, scratching the cheeks, beating the breasts — acquire new meaning in a Roman context. Rather than representing the women as targets for the pollution of death, these actions in fact celebrate the uniquely feminine power of giving and nurturing life. See, for example, Corbeill's examination of textual and visual evidence, which suggests that beating the breasts represents a metaphorical 'breast feeding' of the corpse to ensure immortality in the afterlife.

28 See Archer, 1999: 259, 280–90; Goitein, 1988: 1–33, esp. 23–27. For Ancient Near Eastern images of weeping women, see Kramer, 1983: 69–80; Van der Toorn, 1994: 119–21.

29 Brenner and van Dijk-hemmes, 1993: 88–90; Day, 1989: 58–74.

30 *Pseudo-Philo* 40:6. See also Josephus, *Antiquities of the Jews* 5.264-66. See Alexiou, 1971: 819–63.

31 See the discussion and references in Schaberg, 2002: 215.

32 Feldman, 1977: 129–32.

33 Bloch-Smith, 1992: 96.

34 Fine, 2005: 143–44.

35 Baskin, 2002: 69. Compare Bar-Ilan, 1998: 60–74.

36 Ilan, 1997: 231.

37 Burkert, 1979: 107.

38 On the dirge-singers to Tammuz, see Goitein, 1988: 21–23.

39 For discussions of the Adonia, see Alexiou, 1974: 55–57; Griffiths, 1981: 247–73; Kraemer, 1991: 30–35; Simms, 1998: 121–41. Laments for Tammuz also persisted in Harran until the Middle Ages. See Burkert, 1979: 106, 109.

40 Heyob, 1975; Kraemer, 1992: 74. On Rome, see Heyob, 1975: 42, 54, 56; Kraemer, 1992: 72–73.

41 Parker, 1983; Shapiro, 1991: 629–56.

42 Holst-Warhaft, 1992: 2–3.

43 Stears, 1998: 96–97.

44 Although the best evidence comes from Athens, funerary legislation was also enacted in other places. For a discussion of all the pertinent legislation, see Garland, 1989: 1–15. See also Alexiou, 1974: 14–23; Holst-Warhaft, 1992: 114; Garland, 1985: 29–30; Stears, 1998: 89–100, esp. 96–97.

45 Cicero, *Leg.* 2.26: 65–66.

46 Lucian, *Luct.* esp. 12, 19, 20. Translation and text by A.E. Harmon (LCL).

47 For example, Josephus's description of the death of Moses recounts how women weep and beat their breasts, before Moses tells them to be quiet and steps away from them: *Ant.* 4.320-26

48 In this speech, the mother is depicted as a 'soldier of God' who is 'more powerful than a man' (*4 Macc.* 16.14). See Moore and Anderson, 1998: 249–73.

49 Holst-Warhaft, 1992: 131–33, 144–49; Archer, 1990: 282–83; Starr Sered, 1994: 124, 202–04.

50 De Boer, 2004: 74.

51 van der Horst, 1998: 73–92.

52 On the nature of rituals, in general, see Bell, 1992.

Chapter 3: Body, Clothing and Identity

1 Margaret R. Miles, 1989; Michael L. Satlow, 1997: 429–54; Larissa Bonfante, 1989: 543–70.

2 Indebted to these current theories of the body, power and social control, Berquist tackles the issue of how ancient Israelites controlled corporeality through the household — 'to study the body is to explore the household that produced physical bodies and that formed the social matrix that constructed the understandings of the body' (2000: ix). Indeed, '. . . the household is one of the social units that is paralleled to the body; in some sense, the household is the body on a larger scale' (2000: 15). He concludes that Israel's chief view of the body is one of wholeness. Given that the *whole body* is the controlling metaphor for bodily behaviors and standards in Israel, Berquist continues with an investigation of sexuality and fertility in the context of the household and how it structures sexuality. Sexuality, he concludes, is one of the main means for 'constructing the boundaries of the household, the bonds between individuals within the household, and the links between separate households within the wider culture' (2000: 71). The body is the most dangerous in moments of ambiguity and permeability, because in such a state breaches in that wholeness are symbolically threatening, with the potential of bringing about undesired social changes (2000: 18–52).

3 Anderson cites and uses the Latin *Vita Adae et Evae*.

4 Anderson is obviously addressing the Latin *Vita Adae et Evae* and not the *GLAE*. It will be instructive for us to pursue how the body discourse of the *GLAE* will help us make sense of the treatment of Eve.

5 Johnson defines dress as that which includes 'a long list of changes to the body which can either be permanent or temporary such as tattoos, straightened teeth, exercise, or permed hair as well as additions to the body like clothing' (1).

6 The priestly establishment in ancient Israel assumed, managed image and negotiated power by virtue of the appearance of their bodies vested in extravagant priestly regalia.

7 How a society 'covered and left its impress upon Adam and Eve's individual and corporate identities through dress signs and symbols was its way of showing where they belonged in the order of things, their position and role in the social pageantry. A forked straddling animal with bandy legs can be converted under divers clothing regimes . . .' (Keenan (ed.), 2001: 5).

8 Ann M. Stout, 1994: 77.

9 Western notions of sexuality and bodies are deeply indebted to this idea, as evidenced in the works of Tertullian and Augustine.

Chapter 4: The Exoneration of Eve in the Key of Honor and Shame

1 The *Apocalypse of Moses* was the foundational text that Levison, 1989, initially used to show that Eve's recollections of the events in the Garden tended to exonerate her while other portions tended to condemn her. However, with subsequent *forschungsberichtliche* analysis of the text forms of the *GLAE*, a far more complex picture emerges. Indeed, both the exoneration and denigration of Eve are more widespread and profound than initially thought (2000a: 275). See also Kvam, Schearing and Ziegler, 1999: 42; and A.M. Sweet, 1992: 24.

2 See Chapter 2 of this volume, Arbel's 'Eve, Funerary Practices, and Adam's Death', for further discussion.

3 Virtue and vice lists were common in antiquity and were frequently deployed rhetorically not only to critique the behavior of members of society but also to encourage certain kinds of conduct (Fitzgerald, 1992: 857–59).

4 See Malina, 1986; Peristiany (ed.), 1966; Peristiany and Pitt-Rivers (eds), 1992; and Pitt-

Rivers, 1979, for discussions of the ubiquitous values of honor and shame that define the Mediterranean world in which the *GLAE* was composed.

5 The jealous person was anxious about some valued good that someone possessed and wanted to keep. The envious person was deeply vexed at the valued good that someone else had, with the desire that the rival lose it (Elliott, 2007).

Part Three: J.R.C. Cousland

1 Though it would be a valuable exercise, space and linguistic competence prevent me from considering the genre(s) of the Armenian, Georgian, and Slavonic versions of the 'Lives.'

2 On genre, see, among others: Aune, 1981, 1988, 2003; Burridge, 1992, Fowler, 1982; Hirsch, 1967; Propp, 1968; and Todorov, 1990.

3 For representative discussions, see: Aune, 1981, 1988, 2003; Conte, 1994: 105–28; de Bruyn, 1993: 79–85; Fowler, 1982; Frye, 1957: 243–337; Garber, 1993: 456–59; Hirsch, 1967; Roest and Vanstiphout (eds), 1999; Schippers, 1999; Scholes, 1977; Strelka (ed.), 1978; and Todorov, 1990.

4 This problem appears to be especially problematic in English. Conte notes, 'If my foreigner's ear does not mislead me, the English word "genre" is itself somewhat vaguer, less assertive, and less triumphant than its German equivalent *Gattung*. The Anglo-American tradition seems to feel a positive (empirical!) reluctance with regard to such weighty, demanding abstractions' (1994: 108).

5 For a detailed response to Rosenmeyer, 2006, see Marincola, 1999.

6 Jane Austen's *Northanger Abbey* provides an amusing example of a laundry-list being misinterpreted in just this way.

7 This analogy seems to go back to the eighteenth century, where Lord Kames observed that 'literary compositions run into each other, precisely like colours: in their strong tints they are easily distinguished; but are susceptible of so much variety, and take on so many different forms, that we can never say where one species ends and another begins' (cited in Fowler, 1982: 37).

8 The Armenian versions, however, appear to have arisen from two distinct hyperarchetypes (Tromp, 2005: 97–98).

9 Unless noted otherwise, I use the Greek translation in Anderson and Stone (eds), 1999.

10 I have also consulted the careful editions that have been prepared in recent years by Petorelli, 1998, 1999a, 1999b, 2002, 2003.

Chapter 5: None of the Above? — The Genre of the *GLAE*

1 *Non vidi*; cf. J.L. Sharpe. 1969. 'Prolegomena to the Establishment of the Critical Text of the *Greek Apocalypse of Moses*.' Unpublished doctoral dissertation. Duke University: 97–98, 113, cited in Merk and Meiser, 2005: 166.

2 This section (III.2 §33B) of the revised Schürer was co-authored by Geza Vermes and Martin Goodman.

3 Levison does not actually employ the term 'apologia' to express the genre: rather, he speaks of Eve's 'exoneration.' This issue will be considered more fully below.

4 See Stone, 1992: 6. Denis *et al.*, 2000: 3.

5 The mention of Moses here may be designed to emulate the incipit of *Jubilees*, which attributes it to Moses to draw on his authority; see Sweet, 1992: 40 #132; Tischendorf, 1866: x.

6 While undeniably useful, the term 'rewritten Bible' is problematic. Aune has pointed out that the designation 'rewritten Bible' presupposes the existence of a canonical or quasi-canonical assemblage of texts, see Aune, 2003: 410–14.

7 For discussions of the category 'rewritten Bible', *see*: Alexander, 1988: 99–121; Aune, 2003: 410–14; Eldridge, 2001; Halpern-Amaru, 1994: 4–7; Harrington, 1986; Hayward, 1990; Koskenniemi and Lindqvist, 2008; Nickelsburg, 1984; Schürer, 1987: 3.1: 308–41.

8 The episodes of *GLAE* are drawn from the overview of Merk and Meiser, 2005: 155–56. See also Levison, 2000b: 34–36.

9 Obviously there are a number of other functions that can be adduced for both Genesis and the *GLAE*. My point here is to show that they have at least one or more in common.

10 There are, however, as Johnson's translation indicates (1985), some allusions to Genesis 2–4 in *GLAE* 39–41; cf. Sweet, 1992: 34.

11 Note that Hayward's account (1990) of Vermes' *corpus* does not include Greek examples of the rewritten Bible; cf. Schürer, 1987: 3.1: 308 with 3.2: 357–786.

12 Eldridge expresses two caveats (2001: 166). The first concerns the relation between retelling and legendary expansion. This relation is by no means uniform, but tends to cluster around certain notable figures and themes. Further, he asks whether some of the so-called 'legendary' features might not (*pace* Alexander) be the product of reflection upon Scripture.

13 Harrington seems to be saying something similar when he concludes that 'it seems better to view rewriting the Bible as a kind of activity or process than to see it as a distinctive literary genre' (Harrington, 1986: 243); Aune cites him with favor (2003: 413).

14 See the related criticisms by Koskenniemi and Lindqvist, 2008: 13–15.

15 She excludes Josephus from this assessment.

16 Closing inverted commas missing in original.

17 For discussion of midrash, see: Alexander, 1990: 452–59; Aune, 2003: 302–05.

18 More elaborate definitions of midrash can be found in Porton (2001, 2003).

19 It is unclear when the modern notion of commentary began to be perceived as a noteworthy genre by the ancients. In the Classical tradition, at least, this does not happen until well into the Common Era. See the fascinating discussion by Sluiter. She observes that, 'as for the "genre" of the commentators' own work, it is perfectly possible for the modern student to define the elements that are constitutive of it, but it hardly plays a role in ancient classifications of genre. Moreover, although the ancient commentators are certainly engaged in a constant effort of self-positioning, the distinctions they draw in order to do so are not primarily conceived in terms of "genre"' (2000: 184–85).

20 A.G. Wright has also advanced a third category — 'narrative midrash' (1966: 456), but this classification has not gained general acceptance.

21 Michael Fishbane offers a helpful encapsulation of Haggadah/Aggadah: 'For the ancient rabbis, who first used this term, *aggadah* was . . . comprehensive in scope, and applied to moral and theological homilies, didactic expositions of historical and folk motifs, expositions and re-interpretations of ethical dicta and religious *theologoumena*, and much more. In brief, the *aggadah* of the ancient rabbis encompasses "all scriptural interpretation which is non-halakhic in character"' (Fishbane, 1985: 281 citing Strack, 1959: 7).

22 See, further, Bertrand, 1985: 110. While de Jonge and Tromp (1997: 48–49; cf. Tromp, 1997: 39–40) attempt to downplay the interpretive features of the *GLAE*, Tromp (2004: 217) later appears more open to them.

23 Porton, 1981, explicitly identifies this type of midrash with rewritten Bible.

24 A recent definition of the genre of apology defines it as 'the defense of a cause or party supposed to be of paramount importance to the speaker. It may include *apologia* in the sense of Plato's *Apology*, the defense of a single person, but is distinguished from polemic and from merely epideictic or occasional orations' (Edwards *et al.*, 1999: 1). The genre of apology was very familiar in the ancient world, from Plato onward, and Jews such as Josephus in his *Vita* made effective use of it. For an extensive treatment of the question, consult Friedländer, 1903.

25 Levison, 1989, 2000a, 2000b.

26 Part of the basis for Levison's argument is the assumption that the monologue 'originated separately, either in oral or written form, from the remainder of the Apocalypse of Moses' (1989: 135; cf. Dochhorn, 2005). It has also had notable impact because some scholars consider the 'monologue' to be an interpolation within the *GLAE* as a whole (Eldridge, 2001: 142). Not only is Eve's narrative thought to break the tenor of the *GLAE*'s narrative,

but it also has a paraenetic character that is absent in the rest of the work (Levison, 1989).

27 Kvam *et al.*, 1999: 43. Their book offers a valuable compendium of primary sources on Eve and Adam.

28 For a different assessment, see Dochhorn, 2005: 304.

29 Levison has marshaled a notable array of supporting evidence in the form of 'sympathetic features' in the *GLAE*. In his first article, he suggests that four features help to create this sympathy.

1. One is the first-person point of view of Eve in her testament.
2. The second is Satan's impersonation of a heavenly angel. His ploy was so effective, that it was entirely natural for Eve to have been mistaken; hers was not a culpable act.
3. The third feature is that Eve selflessly gives the fruit to Adam before she knows that it is evil.
4. Finally, with respect to the first transgression, it was Satan who deceived Adam; Eve did not (Levison, 1989: 139–40).

In his later assessments, Levison makes a number of additional observations:

5. He argues that 'the serpent entered Adam's portion first, before it entered her portion, and utilized a male animal, the serpent, to deceive her' (Levison, 2000a: 40). This argument is rather puzzling, but it is likely that Levison means that *Satan* (not the serpent) entered Adam's portion first (cf. Levison, 1989: 140).
6. 'Eve evokes the hearers' empathy . . . by revealing the inner tension that ultimately resulted in her disastrous decision' (Levison, 2000a: 41).
7. Eve is duped by Satan, and gives the fruit to Adam before being aware of its deleterious effects: the 'oath the enemy had extracted from Eve . . . is one that she made while she still believed the fruit was full of glory' (Levison, 2000a: 41).
8. 'Adam excluded Eve from sin altogether when he took full responsibility for the primeval transgression by confessing, "I alone have sinned"' (Levison, 2000a: 41).
9. The frequency with which emphasis is placed on Eve's role as parent: 'It is not Adam who produced his own progeny, but Eve is credited.'
10. Adam relates that it is not Eve, 'through whom I die,' but transgression, 'through which I die' (7.1).
11. Adam still refers to Eve as 'my rib' and 'the image of God' after the second transgression.
12. Satan is a credible deceiver in the second transgression, 'leaving the reader to ask, Who could resist such an angelic imposter?'
13. Finally, 'Eve herself saw visions which she invited Seth as well to see' (Levison, 2000b: 274–75).

30 Obviously, determining what Levison's strongest points are is a highly subjective process. While I do not have space to address all thirteen of them, in my view the next most weighty points of exoneration are (5) and (8). In the former, Levison argues that Satan used the snake, a male animal from Adam's allotment in Eden, to deceive Eve (Levison, 2000a: 40), suggesting that Adam is somehow derelict in guarding his allotment. This episode, however, is better explained otherwise. Since 'snake' in both Hebrew and Greek is grammatically masculine, it is logical that snakes should reside in Adam's allotment and be under his jurisdiction, along with all the other male creatures (15.3). The author would surely be unlikely to introduce a different animal when the snake was already sanctioned by long tradition.

Point (8) is Adam's confession that he alone had sinned. Why does Adam make this statement? — for the simple reason that he is in the position of responsibility. Eve is under his dominion (25.4), and so the consequences of her actions ultimately become his concern. It is for the same reason that God communicates with the angels after the first deception and says 'Come with me into the garden and hear the judgment by which I shall judge Adam' (22.1). He says nothing about judging Eve, but of course she is judged as well. Adam is simply the representative and responsible human, and this is where the issue of his responsibility emerges. Adam's willingness to shoulder the blame actually puts him in a positive light.

31 Literary apocalypses were common in the intertestamental period and for some while afterward, although the actual designation 'apocalypse' was itself a later feature (Collins, 1998: 3). For particulars, see Collins, 1998.

32 For a detailed discussion of the apocalypse genre, see Collins, 1998: 1–42; for it history, see Sacchi, 1997.

33 The details from 38.4 onward are presumably the heavenly events shown to Seth; cf. 38.4.

34 Piñero, 1993, and Patton, 1994, comment on many of these features.

35 The doubt arises from Collins' uncertainty as to whether one of the classified works contains a feature or not. He marks it with an 'x' but follows it with a question mark.

36 For a dissenting view, see Sweet, 1992: 41–42.

37 Bertrand adopts a similar view (1987: 50–51), and considers the apocalyptic account (*GLAE* 31–43) as one of the two primary parts of the work. The *GLAE* as a whole 'n'est que partiellement une apocalypse' (1985: 109).

38 Of the features characteristic of apocalyptic accounts listed in Collins' 'apocalyptic grid' (1998: 7), only about half are to be found in the *GLAE*. Particularly notable in their absence are 'cosmic transformation,' 'eschatological upheavals' and 'judgment/destruction of the world.'

39 See, also, Aune, 1981: 17.

40 On the *bios*, see: Aune, 1988: 204–06; Burridge, 1992; Dihle, 1991; Momigliano, 1993.

41 Hollander and de Jonge in their commentary on the *Testaments of the Twelve Patriarchs* prefer to refer to the 'biographical elements' (1985: 33–35).

42 On testaments, see Aune, 2003; Collins, 1986; Eldridge, 2001; Kolenkow, 1986; Von Nordheim, 1980.

43 For an even more detailed anatomy of these components, consult Van Nordheim, 1980: 229–32.

44 While confession as a literary genre does not really come into its own until Augustine's *Confessions*, the confessional mode is well established in both biblical and Classical writings.

45 Eldridge (2001: 153) notes that there do appear to be 'paraenetic intentions behind parts of Eve's speech.'

46 It is worth noting that Eldridge and I come to the same result though we use different templates. Eldridge assesses the *GLAE* on the basis of the extensive testamentary criteria advanced by Von Nordheim (1980: I.234–36), while I rely on Aune (2003) and Kolenkow (1986).

47 He also cites *T. Zeb.* 1.2–5.1.

48 Aune regards the term 'mixed genres' as 'infelicitous' since it seems to imply that the new genres are merely derivative (1981: 46).

Chapter 6: The Latin *Vita* — A 'Gospel' of Adam and Eve?

1 The Armenian, Georgic, and Slavonic versions cannot be treated here for reasons of space and linguistic competence. The Latin text used here is Lechner-Schmidt, 1990: 233–39, with the verse enumerations and translation edited by Anderson and Stone (1999).

2 The episodes of *GLAE* are based on Merk and Meiser (2005). The italic passages in the *GLAE* show those episodes that are missing (corresponding to the passages in bold in the *LLAE*). The italic episodes in the *LLAE* indicate those that do not follow the sequence of the *GLAE*. A version including the Georgian, Armenian, and Slavonic is presented in de Jonge and Tromp (1997: 26–27).

3 Two Greek MSS (R and M) do contain the 'penitence narrative,' cf. Stone, 1992: 14.

4 Anderson (1998: 10) regards Eve's confession as a doublet of this briefer account by Adam.

5 Eve is to tell their children about their Fall after Adam's death (44.2).

6 It is unlikely, but just possible that Syncellus' reference to a 'Life of Adam' may have been to

the *Vita* (Schürer, 1987: 3.2: 757 n. 3; cf. Meyer, 1879: 187–88). It is not clear from Meyer's remarks whether he himself coined the title *Vita* or merely elected to appropriate it.

7 On the topic of gospel genre, see: Aune, 2003: 204–06; Dihle, 1991; Koester, 1990: 24–31; Vorster, 1992: 2.1077–79.

8 K.L. Schmidt, 1923: 76–79.

9 Though see my reservations about Matthew as a simple *bios*, in Cousland, 2002: 25–27.

10 Technically speaking, the occultation of the sun in the Gospels at Jesus' death cannot be described as an eclipse.

11 Pettorelli, 2004, accounts for the absence of this episode in the *GLAE* by the editor's unwillingness to include it.

12 De Jonge and Tromp argue that the placement of Adam's reception of food closes off the entire food episode (1997: 22), but they do not address the problem of the self-instituted fast.

13 For textual variants on the 40 days, see Nagel, 1974: 2.193–95. Both Moses (*Exod.* 34.28; *Deut.* 9.9) and Elijah (*1 Kgs* 19.8) undertake 40-day fasts: Moses when he is receiving the ten commandments on Sinai, and Elijah when he journeys to Mount Horeb, after being sustained with bread and water by the Lord's angel. Of the two, the Elijah narrative has closer affinities with the *Vita*, as it also brings in the themes of the wilderness and angelic sustenance. When it is compared with the temptation accounts in the Gospel, however, the latter take precedence: the Gospel accounts have both these features. In addition, Elijah does not embark on a deliberate fast, nor does he undergo temptation over the 40 days. The 40 days of fasting, therefore, do show very strong affinities with the Gospels.

14 See, among others: Aune, 2003: 479; Ellis, 1988: 713–16; Fishbane, 1985: 350–79; Goppelt, 1982; McNeil, 1990: 713–14.

15 For critiques of Sharpe, see de Jonge, 2003c: 238–39; Sweet, 1992: 147–48. For a recent extensive listing of works treating Paul's views of the first and second Adam, see Jewett, 2007: 378 n. 98; for Jewett's own analysis, cf. 370–89.

16 I am not arguing that Paul was acquainted with the Adam and Eve literature, merely that he was familiar with these traditions. On aspects of this question, see de Jonge, 2003.

17 As will be shown below, the process is commonplace elsewhere. The *Cave of Treasures* freely invents typological episodes in Adam's life to make them correspond with the more notable antitypes in Jesus' own life.

18 Nickelsburg, 2005: 332; cf. Merk and Meiser, 2005: 767–68. It is not clear whether Nickelsburg is speaking of the *Vita* at this point, or versions of the *GLAE*.

19 See also de Jonge and Tromp, 1997: 75.

20 This conclusion of Davila's has been independently echoed by Nickelsburg, 2005: 332: 'Finally, second- and early-third-century Christian writings that treat the sin and the fate of the first parents sometimes do so without reference to Christ, while employing some striking parallels with these Adam and Eve texts.'

21 Lightfoot, 2007: 419, offers a fascinating discussion of *ex eventu* prophecy about Christ.

22 Allert, 2002; Koester, 1990: 361–402.

23 For a useful stemma of the evolving Diatessaronic traditions, see Petersen, 1997: 86.

24 Interestingly, Tjitze Baarda argues that the savings in money and the convenience would not have been that significant; the *Diatessaron*'s chief advantage seems to have been that it was regarded as both truthful and harmonious (Baarda, 1994: 37–41).

25 Though in this passage, the serpent's hostility may simply be that of the Devil.

26 See Cousland, 2000: 507–10, where I argue that the expression 'her flesh was as grass' means that Eve was 'blue with cold.'

27 Bauckham (1994: 10) remarks of this circumstance: 'In creation God established human dominion over the animals, which should have been peaceful and harmonious, but was subsequently disrupted by violence.'

28 'The name echoes the word "life," however it is to be explained' (Westermann, 1984: 268).

29 Ri makes notice of this in the pseudo-Clementine *Recognitions*: "'l'inculpation d'Ève et la disculpation d'Adam . . . sont basées entièrement sur la doctrine gnostique de la syzygie'" (2000: 167).

30 It is tempting to associate the *Vita* with Syriac Christianity, but safer to say that the *Vita* may have exerted a later influence on Syrian Christianity.

31 Ephrem the Syrian (fl. 306–73) was a prolific Syrian hymn writer and exegete who resided in Edessa. Most of his works were presented in the form of verse, and they exerted great influence on subsequent liturgy and hymnography. The above translation is cited from Brock, 1992: 33.

32 The *Cave of Treasures* is an ancient Syriac work that provides an overview of the millennia from Adam to Christ. Though its dating and editing pose some difficulties, Serge Ruzer observes that 'the fourth century has often been seen as a time of compilation of an earlier version of the text; Ri in his new edition of CT [*Cave of Treasures*] proposes the first half of the third century. In any case it is quite probable that much earlier traditions also found their way into CT. A later (final?) redaction in the beginning of the sixth century by an East-Syrian scholar is usually assumed' (Ruzer, 2001: 252).

BIBLIOGRAPHY

Abegg, Martin, Jr (ed.). 1996. *The Dead Sea Scrolls*. San Francisco: Harper.

Ahlberg, Gudrun. 1971. *Prothesis and Ekphora in Greek Geometric Art*. Göteborg: Elanders Boktryckeri Aktiebolag.

Ahmed, S., and J. Stacey (eds). 2001. *Thinking Through the Skin*. London: Routledge.

Alexander, Philip S. 1983. '3 (Hebrew Apocalypse of) Enoch' in Charlesworth (ed.), 1983, *OTP* 1: 223–315.

_____. 1988. 'Retelling the Old Testament' in D.A. Carson and H.G.M. Williamson (eds), *It Is Written: Scripture Citing Scripture*. Cambridge: Cambridge University Press: 99–121.

_____. 1990. 'Midrash' in Coggins and Houlden, 1990: 452–59.

Alexandre, Monique. 1988. *Le Commencement du Livre Genèse I–V. La version grecque de la Septante et sa reception*. Christianisme Antique 3. Paris: Beauchesne.

Alexiou, Margaret. 1971. 'The Lament of Jephtha's Daughter: Themes, Traditions, Originality.' *Studi Medievali* 12: 819–63.

_____. 1974. *The Ritual Lament in Greek Tradition*. Cambridge: Cambridge University Press.

Allen, A. 1955. *The Story of Clothes*. London: Faber and Faber.

Allert, Craig D. 2002. *Revelation, Truth, Canon and Interpretation: Studies in Justin Martyr's Dialogue with Trypho*. VCS 64. Leiden/Boston/Köln: Brill.

Ambrose. 1961. 'Paradise.' Translated by John J. Savage, in *Hexameron, Paradise, and Cain and Abel*. The Fathers of the Church Series. Vol. 42. Washington, DC: Fathers of the Church Inc.

Anderson, Gary A. 1989. 'Celibacy or Consummation in the Garden? Reflections on Early Jewish and Christian Interpretation of the Garden of Eden.' *HTR* 82: 121–48.

_____. 1998. 'Adam and Eve in the *Life of Adam and Eve*' in Michael E. Stone and Theodore Bergren (eds), *Biblical Figures outside the Bible*. Harrisburg: TPI: 7–32.

_____. 2000a. 'The Exaltation of Adam and the Fall of Satan' in Anderson *et al.*, 2000: 83–110.

_____. 2000b. 'Ezekiel 28, the Fall of Satan, and the Adam Books' in Anderson *et al.*, 2000: 133–47.

_____. 2000c. 'The Original Form of the *Life of Adam and Eve*: A Proposal' in Anderson *et al.*, 2000: 215–31.

_____. 2000d. 'The Penitence Narrative in the *Life of Adam and Eve*' in Anderson *et al.*, 2000: 23–52.

_____. 2000e. 'The Punishment of Adam and Eve in the *Life of Adam and Eve*' in Anderson *et al.*, 2000: 57–81.

_____. 2001. *The Genesis of Perfection: Adam and Eve in Jewish and Christian Imagination.* Louisville: Westminster John Knox.

Anderson, Gary A., and M.E. Stone (eds). 1999. *A Synopsis of the Books of Adam and Eve.* 2nd edn. SBLEJL 17. Atlanta: Scholars Press.

Anderson, Gary A., Michael E. Stone, and Johannes Tromp (eds). 2000. *Literature on Adam and Eve: Collected Essays.* SVTP 15. Leiden/Boston/Köln: Brill.

Arbel, Vita Daphna. 2003. *Beholders of Divine Secrets: Mysticism and Myth in the Hekhalot and Merkavah Literature.* Albany: SUNY.

Archer, Léonie. 1990. *Her Price Is Beyond Rubies: The Jewish Woman in Graeco-Roman Palestine.* Sheffield: Sheffield Academic Press.

Archer, L.J., S. Fischler, and M. Wyke (eds). 1995. *Women in Ancient Societies: An Illusion of the Night.* New York: Routledge.

Arthur, L.B. (ed.). 2000. *Undressing Religion: Commitment and Conversion from a Cross-Cultural Perspective.* Oxford/New York: Berg.

Aune, David E. 1981. 'The Problem of the Genre of the Gospels: A Critique of C.H. Talbert's *What Is a Gospel?*' in R.T. France and David Wenham (eds), *Gospel Perspectives.* Vol. 2. Sheffield: JSOT: 9–60.

_____. 1987. *The New Testament in Its Literary Environment.* LEC 8. Philadelphia: Westminster.

_____. 1988. 'Greco-Roman Biography' in David E. Aune (ed.), *Greco-Roman Literature and the New Testament: Selected Forms and Genres.* Atlanta: Scholars Press: 107–26.

_____. 2003. *The Westminster Dictionary of New Testament and Early Christian Literature and Rhetoric.* Louisville/London: Westminster John Knox.

Baarda, Tjitze. 1994. *Essays on the Diatessaron.* CBET 11. Kampen: Kok Pharos.

Baer, Richard A. 1970. *Philo's Use of the Categories Male and Female.* Leiden: Brill.

Baker, C.M. 1998. 'Ordering the House: On the Domestication of Jewish Bodies' in Wyke, 1998: 203–29.

Bakhtin, Mikhail. 1981. *The Dialogic Imagination.* Austin: University of Texas Press.

Bal, Mieke. 1987. *Lethal Love: Feminist Literary Readings of Biblical Love Stories.* Bloomington: Indiana University Press.

Bar-Ilan, Meir. 1998. *Some Jewish Women in Antiquity.* Atlanta: Scholars Press.

Barber, E.W. 1995. *Women's Work: The First 20,000 Years: Women, Cloth, and Society in Early Times.* New York: W.W. Norton.

Barr, James. 1992. *The Garden of Eden and the Hope of Immortality.* Minneapolis: Fortress Press.

Barton, Carlin. 1999. 'The Roman Blush: The Delicate Matter of Self-Control' in James L. Porter (ed.), *Constructions of the Classical Body.* Ann Arbor: University of Michigan Press: 212–34.

_____. 2002. 'Being in the Eyes: Shame and Sight in Ancient Rome' in David Fredrick (ed.), *The Roman Gaze: Vision, Power, and the Body.* Baltimore/London: Johns Hopkins University Press: 216–30.

Baskin, Judith. 2002. *Midrashic Women: Formations of the Feminine in Rabbinic Literature.* Hanover/London: Brandeis University Press.

Batterberry, M., and A. Batterberry. 1977. *Mirror, Mirror: A Social History of Fashion.* New York: Holt, Rinehart and Winston.

Bauckham, Richard. 1994. 'Jesus and the Wild Animals (Mark 1:13): A Christological Image for an Ecological Age' in Joel B. Green and Max

Turner (eds), *Jesus of Nazareth Lord and Christ: Essays on the Historical Jesus and New Testament Christology.* Grand Rapids: Eerdmans/Carlisle: Paternoster.

Baumgarten, Joseph M. 1988. 'The Qumran Sabbath Shirot and Rabbinic Merkabah Traditions.' *RevQ*; 119–213.

Bechtel, L.M. 1991. 'Shame as a Sanction of Social Control in Biblical Israel: Judicial, Political and Social Shaming.' *JSOT* 49: 47–76.

Beebee, Thomas O. 1994. *The Ideology of Genre.* University Park, PA: Pennsylvania State University Press.

Bell, Catherine. 1992. *Ritual Theory, Ritual Practice.* New York: Oxford University Press.

Berlinerblau, Jacques. 1996. *The Vow and the 'Popular Religious Groups' of Ancient Israel: A Philological and Sociological Inquiry.* JSOT Sup 210. Sheffield: Sheffield Academic Press.

Berquist, J.L. 1998. 'Controlling Daughters' Bodies in Sirach' in Wyke, 1998: 80–106.

_____. 2000. *Controlling Corporeality: The Body and the Household in Ancient Israel.* New Brunswick, NJ: Rutgers University Press.

Bertman, S. 1961. 'Tasselled Garments in the Ancient Mediterranean.' *BA* 24: 119–28.

Bertrand, Daniel A. 1985. 'Le Destin "Post Mortem" des protoplastes selon la *Vie grecque d'Adam et Ève*' in *La littérature intertestamentaire.* Colloque de Strasbourg (17–19 octobre 1983). Paris: Presses Universitaires de France: 109–18.

_____. 1987. *La vie grecque d'Adam et Ève: Introduction, texte, traduction et commentaire.* Recherches Intertestamentaires 1. Paris: Maisonneuve.

Bird, Phyllis. 1981. '"Male and Female He Created Them": Gen. 1:27b in the Context of the Priestly Account of Creation.' *HTR* 74: 129–51.

_____. 1997. *Missing Persons and Mistaken Identities: Women and Gender in Ancient Israel.* Minneapolis: Fortress Press.

Blacking, J. (ed.). 1977. *The Anthropology of the Body.* London: Academic Press.

Blanchot, Maurice. 1959. *Le Livre à venir.* Paris: Gallimard.

Blenkinsopp, Joseph. 2004. *Treasures Old and New: Essays in the Theology of the Pentateuch.* Grand Rapids/Cambridge:

Bloch-Smith, Elizabeth. 1992. *Judahite Burial Practices and Beliefs about the Dead.* Sheffield: Sheffield Academic Press.

Bloom, Harold, and David Rosenberg. 1990. *The Book of J.* New York: Vintage.

Bonfante, L. 1989. 'Nudity as a Costume in Classical Art.' *AJA* 93: 543–70.

Bourdieu, P. 1984. *Distinction: A Social Critique of the Judgement of Taste.* London: Routledge.

Boyarin, Daniel. 1993. *Carnal Israel: Reading Sex in Talmudic Culture.* Berkeley: University of California Press.

Brayford, Susan A. 1999. 'To Shame or Not to Shame: Sexuality in the Mediterranean Diaspora.' *Semeia* 87: 163–76.

Bremmer, Jan. 2008. 'Pandora or the Creation of a Greek Eve' in J. Bremmer (ed.), *Greek Religion and Culture, the Bible and the Ancient Near East.* Jerusalem Studies in Religion and Culture 8. Leiden/Boston: Brill: 19–34.

Brenner, Athalya, and Fokkelien van Dijk-hemmes. 1993. *On Gendering Texts: Female and Male Voices in the Hebrew Bible.* Leiden/New York/Köln: Brill.

Breward, C. 1995. *The Culture of Fashion: A New History of Fashionable Dress*. New York: Manchester University Press.

Brock, Sebastian. 1992. *The Luminous Eye: The Spiritual World Vision of Saint Ephrem the Syrian*. Kalamazoo: Cistercian Publications.

Brook, B. 1999. *Feminist Perspectives on the Body*. London: Longman.

Brooke, George J. 2005. 'Between Authority and Canon: The Significance of Reworking the Bible for Understanding the Canonical Process' in E. Chazon *et al.* (eds), *Reworking the Bible: Apocryphal and Related Texts at Qumran*. Studies of the Texts of the Desert of Judah 58. Leiden/Boston: Brill: 85–104.

Brown, Peter. 1981. *The Cult of the Saints: Its Rise and Function in Latin Christianity*. Chicago: University of Chicago Press.

_____. 1988. *The Body and Society: Men, Women, and Sexual Renunciation in Early Christianity*. New York: Columbia University Press.

Brydon, A., and S. Niessen (eds). 1998. *Consuming Fashion: Adorning the Transnational Body*. Oxford/New York: Berg.

Budge, Sir E.A. Wallis. 1927. *The Book of the Cave of Treasures*. London: Religious Tract Society.

Burkert, Walter. 1979. *Structure and History in Greek Mythology and Ritual*. Berkeley: University of California Press.

_____. 1985. *Greek Religion*. Cambridge, MA: Harvard University Press.

Burridge, Richard A. 1992. *What Are the Gospels? A Comparison with Graeco-Roman Biography*. SNTSMS 70. Cambridge: Cambridge University Press.

Burrus, Virginia. 1987. *Chastity as Autonomy: Women in the Stories of the Apocryphal Acts*. Lewiston, NY: Edwin Mellen Press.

Burton, J.W. 1999. *Culture and the Human Body*. Illinois: Waveland Press.

Butler, Judith. 1990. *Gender Trouble: Feminism and the Subversion of Identity*. London/New York: Routledge.

Butler, Samuel. 1922. *The Authoress of the Odyssey*. London: Cape.

Buttrick, G.A. (ed.). 1962. *The Interpreter's Dictionary of the Bible*. 5 vols. Nashville.

Cameron, Ron, and Merrill P. Miller (eds). 2004. *Redescribing Christian Origins*. Atlanta: Society of Biblical Literature.

Camp, Claudia V. 1985. *Wisdom and the Feminine in the Book of Proverbs*. Bible and Literature 11. Sheffield: Almond.

_____. 1991. 'Understanding a Patriarchy: Women in Second-Century Jerusalem through the Eyes of Ben Sira' in Levine (ed.), 1991: 1–39.

Carmichael, Calum M. 1992. 'The Paradise Myth: Interpreting without Jewish and Christian Spectacles' in Morris and Sawyer (eds), 1991: 47–63.

Carson, A. 1990. 'Putting Her in Her Place: Woman, Dirt, and Desire' in D.M. Halperin, J.J. Winkler, and F.I. Zeitlin (eds), *Before Sexuality: The Construction of Erotic Experience in the Ancient Greek World*. Princeton: Princeton University Press: 135–69.

_____. 1999. 'Dirt and Desire: The Phenomenology of Female Pollution in Antiquity' in J.I. Porter (ed.), *Constructions of the Classical Body*. Ann Arbor: University of Michigan Press: 77–100.

Cartledge, Tony. 1992. *Vows in the Hebrew Bible and the Ancient Near East.* JSOT Sup 147. Sheffield: Sheffield Academic Press.

Cassirer, Ernst. 1955. *The Philosophy of Symbolic Forms. Volume 2: Mythical Thought.* New Haven/London: Yale.

Castelli, Elizabeth A. 1994. 'Heteroglossia, Hermeneutics, and History: A Review Essay of Recent Feminist Studies of Early Christianity.' *Journal of Feminist Studies in Religion* 10: 73–98.

Charlesworth, James H. 2003. 'The Interpretation of the Tanak in the Jewish Apocrypha and Pseudepigrapha' in Hauser and Watson (eds), 2003: 253–82.

Charlesworth, James H. (ed.). 1983. *Old Testament Pseudepigrapha.* 2 vols. Garden City, NY: Doubleday.

Chazon, Esther Glickler. 1997. 'The Creation and Fall of Adam in the Dead Sea Scrolls' in Judith Frishman and Lucas van Rompay (eds), *The Book of Genesis in Jewish and Oriental Christian Interpretation: A Collection of Essays.* Leuven: Peeters: 14–17.

Chesnutt, Randall D. 1991. 'Revelatory Experiences Attributed to Biblical Women in Early Jewish Literature' in Levine (ed.), 1991: 107–25.

Childs, B.S. 1962. 'Adam.' in G.A. Buttrick (ed.), 1962, *IDB* 1: 43.

Chrysostom. 1961, 1985. 'Homilies on Genesis.' Translated by R.C. Hill in *Homilies on Genesis 1\17.* The Fathers of the Church Series. Vol. 74. Washington, DC: Fathers of the Church Inc.

Clark, Elizabeth (ed.). 1983. *Women in the Early Church.* Message of the Fathers of the Church 13. Wilmington: Michael Glazier.

————. 1996. *St Augustine on Marriage and Sexuality.* Washington, DC: Catholic University of America Press.

Clark, Katerina, and Michael Holquist. 1984. *Mikhail Bakhtin.* Cambridge, MA: The Belknap Press.

Clifton, Lucille. 1991. *Quilting: Poems 1987–1990.* Rochester, NY: BOA Editions.

Coggins, R.J., and J.L. Houlden (eds). 1990. *A Dictionary of Biblical Interpretation.* London: SCM Press / Philadelphia: TPI.

Collins, John J. 1979. 'Introduction: The Morphology of a Genre.' *Semeia* 14: 359–70.

————. 1984. 'Testaments' in Stone (ed.), 1984: 325–55.

————. 1986. 'The Testamentary Literature in Recent Scholarship' in R.A. Kraft and G.W.E. Nickelsburg (eds), *Early Judaism and Its Modern Interpreters.* Atlanta: Scholars Press: 268–85.

————. 1998. *The Apocalyptic Imagination.* 2nd edn. Grand Rapids.

Conte, Gian Biagio. 1994. *Genres and Readers.* Baltimore/London: Johns Hopkins University Press.

Corbeill, Anthony. 2004. *Nature Embodied: Gesture in Ancient Rome.* Princeton: Princeton University Press.

Cordell, J.M., and R. Schwarz (eds). 1979. *The Fabrics of Culture: The Anthropology of Clothing and Adornment.* New York: Mouton Publishers.

Corley, Kathleen E. 1993. *Private Women, Public Meals: Social Conflict in the Synoptic Tradition.* Peabody, MA: Hendrickson.

————. 2002. *Women and the Historical Jesus: Feminist Myths of Christian Origins.* Santa Rosa, CA: Polebridge.

_____. 2003. 'The Anointing of Jesus in the Synoptic Tradition: An Argument for Authenticity.' *Journal for the Study of the Historical Jesus* 1: 61–72.

Courcelle, Pierre. 1968. *Recherches sur les Confessions de Saint Augustin.* Paris: Éditions E. de Boccard.

Cousland, J.R.C. 2000. '"Her Flesh Was as Grass": *Vita Adam et Evae* 10.1.' *Biblica* 81: 507–10.

_____. 2002. *The Crowds in the Gospel of Matthew.* NovT Sup 102. Leiden/ Boston/Köln: Brill.

Cox, Patricia. 1983. *Biography in Late Antiquity.* Berkeley/Los Angeles/London: University of California Press.

Crane, D. 2000. *Fashion and Its Social Agendas: Class, Gender, and Identity in Clothing.* Chicago: University of Chicago Press.

Culham, P. 1986. 'Again, What Meaning Lies in Colour?' *ZPE* 64: 235–45.

Czarnecka-Anastassiades, Bozhena M. 2007. '"Death and the Maiden": *Vanitas* and *Voluptas*, Transience and the Erotic in Hans Baldung Grien.' 4th Global Conference on Persons and Sexuality: Narrative, Aesthetic and Creative Representations. *The Erotic: Exploring Critical Issues.* November 16–18, 2007, Salzburg, Austria. Accessed February 11, 2008. PDF available at http://www. inter-disciplinary.net/ci/erotic/er3/ANASTASSIADES_paper.pdf

Dale, L., and S. Ryan (eds). 1998. *The Body in the Library.* Amsterdam: Rodopi.

D'Ambra, Eve. 2000. 'Nudity and Adornment in Female Portrait Sculpture of the Second Century AD' in Diana E.E. Kleiner and Susan B. Matheson (eds), *I Claudia II. Women in Roman Art and Society.* Austin: University of Texas Press: 101–14.

Davies, Margaret. 1990. 'Genre' in Coggins and Houlden (eds), 1990: 256–58.

Davila, James R. 2000. 'The Dead Sea Scrolls and Merkavah Mysticism' in Timothy H. Lim (ed.), *The Dead Sea Scrolls in Their Historical Context.* Edinburgh: T. & T. Clark: 249–64.

_____. 2000a. *Liturgical Works.* Eerdmans Commentaries on the Dead Sea Scrolls 6. Grand Rapids, MI: Eerdmans.

_____. 2005. *The Provenance of the Pseudepigrapha: Jewish, Christian, or Other?* JSJSup 105. Leiden/Boston: Brill.

Davis, F. 1992. *Fashion, Culture and Identity.* Chicago: University of Chicago Press.

Day, Peggy L. 1989. 'From the Child is Born of Woman: The Story of Jephthah's Daughter' in Day (ed.), 1989: 58–74.

Day, Peggy L. (ed.). 1989. *Gender and Difference in Ancient Israel.* Minneapolis: Fortress Press.

De Boer, Esther. 2004. *The Gospel of Mary: Beyond a Gnostic and a Biblical Mary Magdalene.* London and New York: T. & T. Clark.

De Bruyn, Frans. 1993. 'Genre Criticism' in Irena Makaryk (ed.), *Encyclopedia of Contemporary Literary Theory.* Toronto: University of Toronto: 79–85.

De Ward, Eileen F. 1972a. 'Mourning Customs in 1, 2 Samuel.' *JJS* 23: 1–27.

_____. 1972b. 'Mourning Customs in 1, 2 Samuel II.' *JJS* 23: 145–66.

Debrohun, J.B. 2001. 'Power Dressing in Ancient Greece and Rome.' *HT* 51: 18–25.

Denis, A.-M. 1982. 'Les genres littéraires dans les pseudépigraphes d'Ancien Testament.' *JSJ* 13: 1–5.

Denis, A.-M. *et al.* 2000. Introduction à la literature religieuse Judéo-Hellénistique. 2 vols. Turnhout: Brepols.

Di Bella, Maria Pia. 1992. 'Name, Blood and Miracles: The Claims to Renown in Traditional Sicily' in Peristiany and Pitt-Rivers (eds), 1992: 151–65.

Di Lella, Alexander A. 1991. 'Women in the Wisdom of Ben Sira and the Book of Judith' in J.A. Emerton (ed.), *Congress Volume*. Paris. 1962. Leiden: Brill: 39–52.

Dihle, Albrecht. 1991. 'The Gospels and Greek Biography' in Stuhlmacher (ed.), 1991: 361–86.

Dimant, Devorah. 1988. 'Use and Interpretation of Mikra in the Apocrypha and Pseudepigrapha' in Mulder (ed.), 1988: 379–419.

Dimant, Devorah, and John Strugnell. 1990. 'The Merkabah Vision in Second Ezekiel (4Q385 4).' *RevQ* 55: 331–48.

Dochhorn, Jan. 2005. *Die Apokalypse des Mose. Text, Übersetzung, Kommentar*. TSAJ 106. Tübingen: Mohr.

Douglas, M. 1973. *Natural Symbols*. Harmondsworth: Pelican Books.

————. 1975. *Implicit Meanings: Essays in Anthropology*. London: Routledge.

————. 1978. *Purity and Danger*. London: Routledge & Kegan Paul.

Dowd, Garin, Lesley Stevenson, and Jeremy Strong (eds). 2006. *Genre Matters: Essays in Theory and Criticism*. Bristol/Portland: Intellect.

Downing, Gerald F. 1990. 'Apology, Apologetics' in Coggins and Houlden (eds), 1990: 452–59.

Dunn, J.D.G. 1998. *The Theology of Paul the Apostle*. Grand Rapids/Cambridge: Eerdmans.

Edwards, Mark, Martin Goodman, Simon Price, and Christopher Rowland. 1999. 'Apologetics in the Roman Empire' in Mark Edwards, Martin Goodman, and Simon Price (eds), *Apologetics in the Roman Empire: Pagans, Jews, and Christians*. Oxford: University Press: 1–13.

Eicher, J. (ed.). 1995. *Dress and Ethnicity*. Oxford: Berg.

Eldridge, Michael D. 2001. *Dying Adam with His Multiethnic Family: Understanding the Greek Life of Adam and Eve*. SVTP 16. Leiden/Boston/Köln: Brill.

Elior, Rachel. 2004. *The Three Temples: On the Emergence of Jewish Mysticism*. Translated by D. Louvish. Oxford/Portland, OR: Littman Library of Jewish Civilization.

Elliott, John H. 2007. 'Envy, Jealousy and Zeal in the Bible: Sorting Out the Social Differences and Theological Implications — No Envy for YHWH' in Norman K. Gottwald and Robert Coote (eds), *To Break Every Yoke: Essays in Honor of Marvin L. Chaney*. Sheffield: Sheffield Phoenix.

Ellis, E. Earle. 1988. 'Biblical Interpretation in the New Testament Church' in Mulder (ed.), 1988: 691–725.

Entwistle, J., and E. Wilson (eds). 2000. *Body Dressing*. Oxford/New York: Berg.

————. 2000a. 'Fashion and the Fleshy Body: Dress as Embodied Practice.' *Fashion Theory: Journal of Dress, Body and Culture* 4: 120–40.

————. 2000b. *The Fashioned Body: Fashion, Dress, and Modern Social Theory*. Cambridge, UK: Polity Press.

Eskola, Timo. 2001. *Messiah and the Throne: Jewish Merkabah Mysticism and Early Christian Exaltation Discourse*. WUNT 2/142. Tübingen: Mohr Siebeck.

Esler, P.F. 2001. 'Palestinian Judaism in the First Century' in D. Cohn-Sherbok and J.M. Court (eds), *Religious Diversity in the Graeco-Roman World: A Survey of Recent Scholarship*. Sheffield: Sheffield Academic Press: 21–46.

Featherstone, M., M. Hepworth, and B.S. Turner (eds). 1991. *The Body: Social Process and Cultural Theory*. London: Sage Publications.

Feldman, Emanuel. 1977. *Biblical and Post-Biblical Defilement and Mourning: Law as Theology*. New York: Yeshiva University Press, KTAV.

Fentress-Williams, Judy. 2007. 'Location, Location, Location: Tamar in the Joseph Cycle' in Roland Boer (ed.), *Bakhtin and Genre Theory in Biblical Studies*. Atlanta: Society of Biblical Literature: 59–68.

Ferguson, Everett, 2009. *Baptism in the Early Church: History, Theology and Liturgy in the First Five Centuries*. Grand Rapids/Cambridge: Eerdmans.

Fine, Steven. 2005. *Art and Judaism in the Greco-Roman World — Toward a New Jewish Archaeology*. Cambridge: Cambridge University Press.

Fishbane, Michael. 1985. *Biblical Interpretation in Ancient Israel*. Oxford: Clarendon Press.

Fitzgerald, John T. 1992. 'Virtue/Vice Lists.' *ABD* 6: 857–59.

Fonrobert, Charlotte Elisheva. 2000. *Menstrual Purity: Rabbinic and Christian Reconstructions of Biblical Gender*. Stanford: Stanford University Press.

Fowler, Alastair. 1982. *Kinds of Literature: An Introduction to the Theory of Genres and Modes*. Cambridge: Harvard University Press.

Fox, Michael V. 1997. 'Ideas of Wisdom in Proverbs 1–9.' *JBL* 116: 613–33.

Fraade, Steven D. 2000. 'Midrashim' in L. Schiffman and James C. VanderKam (eds), *Encyclopedia of the Dead Sea Scrolls*. 2 vols. Oxford: Oxford University Press: 1.549–52.

Friedländer, Moriz. 1903. *Geschichte der jüdischen Apologetik als Vorgeschichte des Christentums*. Amsterdam: Philo.

Frye, Northrop. 1957. *Anatomy of Criticism*. Princeton: Princeton University Press.

_____. 1982. *The Great Code: The Bible and Literature*. London: Routledge & Kegan Paul.

Frye, Northrop, S. Baker, and G. Perkins. 1985. *The Harper Handbook to Literature*. New York: Harper & Row.

Frymer-Kensky, Tikvah. 1992. *In the Wake of the Goddesses*. New York: Fawcett.

Fuchs, C. 1900. 'Das Leben Adams und Evas' in E. Kautsch, *Die Pseudepigraphen*. 2 vols. Tübingen: Mohr: 2.506–28. Repr. Olms 1962.

Fuchs, Esther. 2008. 'Reclaiming the Hebrew Bible for Women: The Neoliberal Turn in Contemporary Feminist Scholarship.' *Journal of Feminist Studies in Religion* 24: 45–65.

Gaines, J., and C. Herzog (eds). 1990. *Fabrications: Costume and the Female Body*. New York: Routledge.

Game, A. 1991. *Undoing the Social: Towards a Deconstructive Sociology*. Buckingham: Open University.

Garber, Frederick. 1993. 'Genre' in A. Preminger, and T.V.F. Brogan (eds), *The New Princeton Encyclopedia of Poetry and Poetics*. Princeton: Princeton University Press: 456–59.

Garland, Robert. 1985. *The Greek Way of Death*. Ithaca, NY: Cornell University Press.

_____. 1989. 'The Well-Ordered Corpse: An Investigation into the Motives behind Greek Funerary Legislation.' *Bulletin of the Institute Classical Studies* 36: 1–15.

Glazener, Nancy. 2002. 'Dialogic Subversion: Bakhtin, the Novel and Gertrude Stein' in Ken Hirschkop and David Shepherd (eds), *Bakhtin and Cultural Theory*. Manchester/New York: Manchester University Press.

Glucklich, A. 2001. *Sacred Pain: Hurting the Body for the Sake of the Soul.* New York: Oxford University Press.

Goff, Barbara. 2004. *Citizen Bacchae: Women's Ritual Practice in Ancient Greece.* Berkeley: University of California Press.

Goffman, E. 1959. *The Presentation of Self in Everyday Life.* Garden City, NY: Doubleday.

_____. 1965. 'Identity Kits' in M.A. Roach and J.B. Eicher (eds), *Dress, Adornment, and the Social Order.* New York: John Wiley & Sons: 246–47.

Goitein, Shelomo Dov. 1988. 'Women as Creators of Biblical Genres.' *Prooftexts* 10: 1–33.

Goldstein, L. (ed.). 1990. *The Female Body: Figures, Styles, Speculations.* Ann Arbor: University of Michigan Press.

Goppelt, Leonhard. 1982. *Typos.* Grand Rapids: Eerdmans.

Greiner, Susan L. 1999. 'Did Eve Fall or Was She Pushed?' *BRev*: 16–23, 50–1.

Griffiths, Frederick T. 1981. 'Home before Lunch: The Emancipated Woman in Theocritus' in H.P. Foley (ed.), *Reflections of Women in Antiquity.* New York: Gordon and Breach: 247–73.

Gruenwald, Ithamar. 1980. *Apocalyptic and Merkavah Mysticism.* AGJU 14. Leiden: E.J. Brill.

Guelich, Robert. 1991. 'The Gospel Genre' in Stuhlmacher (ed.), 1991: 173–208.

Gullberg, E., and P. Åström. 1970. *The Thread of Ariadne: A Study of Ancient Greek Dress.* Göteborg: Paul Åströms Förlag.

Haines-Eitzen, Kim. 1998. '"Girls Trained in Beautiful Writing": Female Scribes in Roman Antiquity and Early Christianity.' *JECS* 6: 629–46.

Halperin, David J. 1988. *The Faces of the Chariot: Early Jewish Responses to Ezekiel's Vision.* TSAJ 16. Tübingen: J.C.B. Mohr.

_____. 1988. 'Ascension or Invasion: Implications of the Heavenly Journey in Ancient Judaism.' *Religion* 18: 47–67.

Halpern Amaru, Betsy. 1994. *Rewriting the Bible: Land and Covenant in Postbiblical Jewish Literature.* Valley Forge: TPI.

Hancock, P., and E. Jagger (eds). 1998. *The Body, Culture and Society.* Buckingham/Philadelphia: Open University Press.

Hanson, Richard S. 1972. *The Serpent Was Wiser: A New Look at Genesis 1–11.* Minneapolis: Augsburg.

Harrington, Daniel. 1986. 'The Bible Rewritten' in Robert A. Kraft and G.E.W. Nickelsburg (eds), *Early Judaism and Its Modern Interpreters.* Atlanta: Scholars Press: 239–47.

Harris, C., and M. Johnston (eds). 1974. *Figleafing through History: The Dynamics of Dress.* New York: Atheneum.

Hasan-Rokem, Galit. 2000. *Web of Life: Folklore and Midrash in Rabbinic Literature.* Stanford, CA: Stanford University Press.

_____. 2003. *Tales of the Neighborhood: Jewish Narrative Dialogues in Late Antiquity.* The Taubman Lectures in Jewish Studies 4. Berkeley/Los Angeles/London: University of California Press.

Hauser, A.J., and Duane F. Watson (eds). 2003. *A History of Biblical Interpretation. Volume 1: The Ancient Period.* Grand Rapids: Eerdmans.

Havelock, Christine Mitchell. 1981. 'Mourners on Greek Vases: Remarks on the Social History of Women' in Stephen L. Hyatt (ed.), *The Greek Vase.* Latham, NY: Hudson–Mohawk Association of Colleges and Universities: 101–18.

Hayward, C.T.R. 1990. 'Rewritten Bible' in Coggins and Houlden (eds), 1990: 595–98.

Hendrickson, H. 1995. *Clothing and Difference: Embodied Identities in Colonial and Post-Colonial Africa.* Durham/London: Duke University Press.

Hengel, Martin. 2000. *The Four Gospels and the One Gospel of Jesus Christ.* Harrisburg, PA: TPI.

Henry, E. 2000. 'The Social Significance of Nudity in Early China.' *Fashion Theory: The Journal of Dress, Body and Culture* 3: 85–105.

Hertz, R. 1960. *Death and the Right Hand.* Translated by R. Needham. London: Cohen & West.

Heyob, Sharon Kelly. 1975. *The Cult of Isis among Women in the Graeco-Roman World.* Leiden: Brill.

Hieatt, Kent A. 1980. 'Eve as Reason in a Tradition of Allegorical Interpretation of the Fall.' *Journal of the Warburg and Courtauld Institutes* 43: 221–26.

_____. 1983. 'Hans Baldung Grien's Ottawa Eve and Its Context.' *The Art Bulletin* 65: 290–304.

Higgins, J.M. 1976. 'The Myth of Eve: The Temptress.' *JAAR* 44: 639–47.

Himmelfarb, Martha. 1992. *Ascent to Heaven in Jewish and Christian Apocalypses.* New York: Oxford University Press.

Hirsch, E.D. 1967. *Validity in Interpretation.* New Haven: Yale University Press.

Hollander, A. 1978. *Seeing through Clothes.* New York: Viking Press.

Hollander, H.W., and M. De Jonge. 1985. *The Testaments of the Twelve Patriarchs: A Commentary.* Leiden: E.J. Brill.

Holst-Warhaft, Gail. 1992. *Dangerous Voices: Women's Laments and Greek Literature.* London: Routledge.

Horn, M.J. 1968. *The Second Skin: An Interdisciplinary Study of Clothing.* Boston: Houghton Mifflin.

Houten, Christiana de Groot van. 1994. 'Will the Real Eve Please Stand?' in Lovering, 1994: 301–11.

Ilan, Tal. 1997. *Mine and Yours Are Hers: Retrieving Women's History from Rabbinic Literature.* Leiden/Boston/Köln: Brill.

Jeremias, Joachim. 1964. 'Adam.' *TDNT* 1.141–3.

Jewett, Robert. 2007. *Romans.* Hermeneia, Minneapolis: Fortress Press.

Johnson, K.K.P., and S.J. Lennon (eds). 1998. *Appearance and Power.* Oxford/New York: Berg.

Johnson, M.D. 1985. 'Life of Adam and Eve' in Charlesworth, 1983, *OTP* 2: 249–95.

de Jonge, Marinus. 2003a. *Pseudepigrapha of the Old Testament as Part of Christian Literature: The Case of the Testaments of Twelve Patriarchs and the Greek Life of Adam.* SVTP 18. Leiden/Boston: Brill.

_____. 2003b. 'The Christian Origin of the *Greek Life of Adam and Eve*' in de Jonge, 2003a: 181–200.

_____. 2003c. '*The Greek Life of Adam and Eve* and the Writings of the New Testament' in de Jonge, 2003a: 228–40.

de Jonge, Marinus, and Johannes Tromp. 1997. *The Life of Adam and Eve and Related Literature.* Guides to Apocrypha and Pseudepigrapha 4. Sheffield: Sheffield Academic Press.

Kaestli, Jean-Daniel. 2005. '*La Vie d'Adam et Ève.* Un echaînement d'intrigues épisodiques au service d'une intrigue unifiante' in C. Focant and A. Wénin (eds), *Analyse Narrative et Bible*. BETL 191. Leuven: University Press: 321–36.

Kaiser, S.B. 1985. *The Social Psychology of Clothing and Personal Adornment*. New York: Macmillan Publishing Company.

Keenan, W.J.F. (ed.). 2001. *Dressed to Impress: Looking the Part*. Oxford/New York: Berg.

Kelly, Henry Ansgar. 2006. *Satan: A Biography*. Cambridge: Cambridge University Press.

Kenaan, Vered Lev. 2008. *Pandora's Senses: The Feminine Character of the Ancient Text*. Madison: University of Wisconsin Press.

Klinck, Anne L. 2008. *Women's Songs in Ancient Greece*. Montreal/Kingston: McGill–Queens University Press.

Knittel, T. 2002. *Das griechische 'Leben Adams und Evas'. Studien zu einer narrativen Anthropologie im frühen Judentum*. TSAJ 88. Tübingen: Mohr Siebeck.

Koester, Helmut. 1990. *Ancient Christian Gospels: Their History and Development*. London: SCM Press / Philadelphia: TPI.

Kolenkow, Anitra B. 1986. 'Testaments' in R.A. Kraft and G.W.E. Nickelsburg, (eds), *Early Judaism and Its Modern Interpreters*. Atlanta: Scholars Press: 259–67.

Koskenniemi, Erkki, and Pekka Lindqvist. 2008. 'Rewritten Bible, Rewritten Stories: Methodological Aspects' in Antti Laato and Jacques van Ruiten (eds), *Rewritten Bible Reconsidered*. Turku: Åbo Akademi University / Winona Lake: Eisenbrauns: 11–39.

Kovacs, David. 1980. 'Shame, Pleasure, and Honor in Phaedra's Great Speech (Euripides, *Hippolytus*).' *AJP* 101: 287–303.

Kraemer, David. 2000. *The Meanings of Death in Rabbinic Judaism*. New York: Routledge.

Kraemer, Ross Shepard. 1991. 'Women's Authorship of Jewish and Christian Literature in the Greco-Roman Period' in Levine (ed.), 1991: 221–42.

———— 1992. *Her Share of the Blessings: Women's Religions among Pagans, Jews, and Christians in the Greco-Roman World*. Oxford/New York: Oxford University Press.

————. 2004. *Women's Religions in the Greco-Roman World*. Oxford: Oxford University Press.

Kramer, Heinrich, and James Sprenger. 1951. *Malleus Maleficarum*. Translated by Montague Summers. London: Pushkin Press.

Kramer, Samuel Noah. 1983. 'The Weeping Goddess: Sumerian Prototypes of the Mater Dolorosa.' *Biblical Archaeologist* 46: 69–80.

Kressel, Gideon M. 1992. 'Shame and Gender.' *Anthropological Quarterly* 65: 34–46.

Kroll, Wilhelm. 1964. *Studien zum Verständnis der römischen Literatur*. Stuttgart: J.B. Metzlersche Verlagsbuchhandlung.

Kurtz, Donna C., and John Boardman. 1971. *Greek Burial Customs*. Ithaca, NY: Cornell University Press.

Kvam, Kristen E., Linda S. Schearing, and Valarie H. Ziegler (eds). 1999. *Eve and Adam: Jewish, Christian and Muslim Readings on Genesis and Gender*. Bloomington/Indianapolis: Indiana University Press.

Lambden, Stephen N. 1990. 'From Fig Leaves to Fingernails: Some Notes on the Garments of Adam and Eve in the Hebrew Bible and Select Early Post Biblical Jewish Writings' in Morris and Sawyer (eds), 1991: 74–90.

Laver, J. 1969. *A Concise History of Costume and Fashion*. New York: H.N. Abrams.

Le Deaut, Roger. 1971. 'Apropos a Definition of Midrash.' *Interpretation* 25: 259–82.

Lechner-Schmidt, Wilfried. 1990. *Wortindex der lateinisch erhaltenen Pseudepigraphen zum Alten Testament*. Texte und Arbeiten zum neutestamentlichen Zeitalter 3. Tübingen: Francke Verlag.

Lefkowitz, Mary R., and Maureen B. Fant. 2005. *Women's Life in Greece and Rome: A Source Book in Translation*. 3rd edn. Baltimore: Johns Hopkins University Press.

Levine, Amy-Jill (ed.). 1991. *'Women Like This': New Perspectives on Jewish Women in the Greco-Roman World*. SBLEJL 1. Atlanta: Scholars Press.

Levison, John R. 1985. 'Is Eve to Blame? A Contextual Analysis of Sirach 25:24.' *CBQ* 47: 617–23.

_____. 1988. *Portraits of Adam in Early Judaism: From Sirach to 2 Baruch*. JSP Sup 1. Sheffield: JSOT Press.

_____. 1989. 'The Exoneration of Eve in the *Apocalypse of Moses* 15–30.' *JSJ* 20: 135–50.

_____. 2000a. 'The Exoneration and Denigration of Eve in the *Greek Life of Adam and Eve*' in Anderson *et al.*, 2000: 251–75.

_____. 2000b. *Texts in Transition: The Greek Life of Adam and Eve*. SBLEJL 16. Atlanta: Society of Biblical Literature.

_____. 2003. 'The Primacy of Pain and Disease in the *Greek Life of Adam and Eve*.' *ZNW* 94: 1–16.

_____. 2004. 'Adam and Eve in Romans 1.18–25 and the *Greek Life of Adam and Eve*.' *NTS* 50: 519–34.

Lightfoot, Jane. 2007. *The Sibylline Oracles*. Oxford: Oxford University Press.

Lingis, A. 1994. *Foreign Bodies*. New York: Routledge.

Llewellyn-Jones, L. (ed.). 2002. *Women's Dress in the Ancient Greek World*. London: Classical Press of Wales.

Lloyd, Genevieve. 1984. *The Man of Reason: 'Male' and 'Female' in Western Philosophy*. Minneapolis: University of Minnesota Press.

Lovering, Eugene. 1994. *Society of Biblical Literature 1994 Seminar Papers*. Atlanta: Scholars Press.

Lurie, A. 1981. *The Language of Clothes*. New York: Random House.

Maheswari, U.C.S. 1995. *Dress and Jewellery of Women*. Madras: New Era Publications.

Malina, Bruce J. 1986. *Christian Origins and Cultural Anthropology*. Atlanta: John Knox Press.

_____. 1993. *The New Testament World: Insights from Cultural Anthropology*. Rev. edn. Louisville: Westminster John Knox.

Malina, Bruce J., and Jerome H. Neyrey. 1991. 'Honour and Shame in Luke-Acts: Pivotal Values in the Mediterranean World' in Neyrey 1991: 25–65.

Marincola, John. 1999. 'Genre, Convention, and Innovation in Greco-Roman Historiography' in C. Shuttleworth Kraus (ed.), *The Limits of Historiography: Genre and Narrative in Ancient Historical Texts*. Leiden/Boston/Köln: Brill: 281–324.

Mattlia, Sharon Lea. 1996. 'Wisdom, Sense Perception, Nature, and Philo's Gender Gradient.' *HTR* 89: 103–29.

McClure, L.K. (ed.). 2000. *Sexuality and Gender in the Ancient World: Readings and Sources*. Malden, MA: Blackwell.

McDowell, C. 1992. *Dressed to Kill: Sex, Power and Clothes*. London: Hutchinson.

McKinlay, Judith. 1996. *Gendering Wisdom the Host: Biblical Invitations to Eat and Drink*. Sheffield: Sheffield Academic Press.

McNeil, Brian. 1990. 'Typology' in Coggins and Houlden (eds), 1990: 713–14.

Meier, H. 2004. 'Kleidung II.' *Reallexikon für Antike und Christentum* 21: 2–59.

Meisch, L.A. 2000. 'Christianity, Cloth and Dress in the Andes' in L.B. Arthur (ed.), *Undressing Religion*. Oxford/New York: Berg: 65–82.

Merk, O., and M. Meiser. 1998. *Das Leben Adams und Evas. Jüdische Schriften aus hellenistisch-römischer Zeit* 2.5. Gütersloh, Gütersloher Verlagshaus.

_____. 2005. *Das Leben Adams und Evas. Jüdische Schriften aus hellenistisch-römischer Zeit* 2.5. Gütersloh, Gütersloher Verlagshaus.

Merkur, Dan. 1989. 'The Visionary Practices of Jewish Apocalyptists' in L. Bryce Boyer and Simon A. Grolnick (eds), *The Psychoanalytic Study of Society*. Hillsdale, NJ: The Analytic Press: 119–48.

Meyer, Wilhelm. 1879. *Vita Adae et Eva*. Munich: Verlag der k. Akademie.

Meyers, Carol. 1988. *Discovering Eve: Ancient Israelite Women in Context*. Oxford: Oxford University Press.

Miles, Margaret R. 1989. *Carnal Knowing: Female Nakedness and Religious Meaning in the Christian West*. Boston: Beacon Press.

Miller, Patricia Cox (ed.). 2005. *Women in Early Christianity: Translation from Greek Texts*. Washington: Catholic University of America Press.

Momigliano, Arnaldo. 1993. *The Development of Greek Biography*. Exp. edn. Cambridge, MA/London: Harvard University Press.

Montserrat, D. (ed.). 1997. *Changing Meanings: Studies on the Human Body in Antiquity*. London: Routledge.

Moore, Stephen D., and Janice Capel Anderson. 1998. 'Taking It Like a Man: Masculinity in 4 Maccabees.' *JBL* 117: 249–73.

Morray-Jones, Christopher R.A. 1992. 'Transformational Mysticism in the Apocalyptic Merkabah Tradition.' *JJS* 43. 1–31.

Morris, Pam (ed.). 1994. *The Bakhtin Reader: Selected Writings of Bakhtin, Medvedev, Voloshinov*. London/New York/Melbourne: Edward Arnold.

Morris, Paul, and Deborah Sawyer (eds). 1991. *A Walk in the Garden: Biblical, Iconographical and Literary Images of Eden*. JSOT 136. Sheffield: Sheffield Academic Press.

Moss, Joshua L. 2004. *Midrash and Legend: Historical Anecdotes in the Tannaitic Midrashim*. Piscataway, NJ: Gorgias.

Mulder, Martin Jan (ed.). 1998. *Mikra*. CRINT 2.1. Assen: Van Gorcum / Philadelphia: Fortress Press.

Murphy, Ronald E. 1995. 'The Personification of Wisdom' in John Day, Robert P. Gordon, and H.G.M. Williamson (eds), *Wisdom in Ancient Israel*. Cambridge: Cambridge University Press: 222–33.

Nagel, M. 1974. *La Vie grecque d'Adam et d'Ève. Apocalypse de Möise*. I–III, Lille.

Nasrallah, L. 2003. *An Ecstasy of Folly: Prophecy and Authority in Early Christianity*. Cambridge, MA: Harvard University Press.

Neusner, Jacob. 1987. *What Is Midrash?* Philadelphia: Fortress Press.

Neusner, Jacob (ed.). 1985. *Genesis Rabbah*. Atlanta: Scholars Press.

Newsom, Carol. 1987. 'Merkabah Exegesis in the Qumran Sabbath Shirot.' *JJS* 38: 11–30.

_____. 1989. 'Woman and the Discourse of Patriarchal Wisdom: A Study of Proverbs 1–9' in Day (ed.), 1989: 142–60.

Neyrey, Jerome H. 1990. *The Social World of Luke-Acts.* Peabody, MA: Hendrickson.

_____. 1993. 'Nudity' in J.J. Pilch and B.J. Malina (eds), *Biblical Social Values and Their Meaning: A Handbook.* Peabody, MA: Hendrickson Publishers: 119–25.

_____. 1996. 'Clean/Unclean, Pure/Polluted, and Holy/Profane: The Idea and the System of Purity' in R. Rohrbaugh (ed.), *The Social Sciences and New Testament Interpretation.* Peabody, MA: Hendrickson: 80–104.

_____. 1998. *Honor and Shame in the Gospel of Matthew.* Louisville, KY: Westminster John Knox.

_____. 1998. '"It Was out of Envy that They Handed Jesus Over" (Mark 15:10): The Anatomy of Envy and the Gospel of Mark.' *JSNT* 69: 15–56.

_____. 2005. 'God, Benefactor and Patron: The Major Cultural Model for Interpreting the Deity in Greco-Roman Antiquity.' *JSNT* 27: 465–92.

Nickelsburg, George. 1984. 'The Bible Rewritten and Expanded' in Stone (ed.), 1984: 89–156.

_____. 2005. *Jewish Literature between the Bible and the Mishnah.* 2nd edn. Minneapolis: Fortress Press.

Niditch, Susan. 1984. *Chaos to Cosmos: Studies in Biblical Patterns of Creation.* Chico, CA: Scholars Press.

Nitzan, Bilhah. 1994. 'Harmonic and Mystical Characteristics in Poetic and Liturgical Writings from Qumran.' *JQR* 85: 163–83.

Nussbaum, Martha. 1994. *The Therapy of Desire: Theory and Practice in Hellenistic Ethics.* Martin Classical Lectures. New Series 2. Princeton: Princeton University Press.

O'Neill, J. 1985. *Five Bodies: The Human Shape of Modern Society.* Ithaca: Cornell University Press.

Padel, Ruth. 1993. 'Women: Model for Possession by Greek Daemons' in Averil Cameron and Amelie Kuhrt (eds), *Images of Women in Antiquity.* 2nd edn. London: Routledge: 3–19.

Pagels, Elaine. 1988. *Adam, Eve, and the Serpent.* New York: Random House.

Pardes, Ilana. 1992. *Countertraditions in the Bible: A Feminist Approach.* Cambridge, MA: Harvard University Press.

Parker, Robert. 1982. *Miasma: Pollution and Purification in Early Greek Religion.* Oxford: Clarendon Press.

Pastner, Carroll McC. 1972. 'A Social Structural and Historical Analysis of Honor, Shame and Purdah.' *AQ* 45: 248–61.

Patton, Corinne L. 1994. 'Adam as the Image of God: An Exploration of the Fall of Satan in the *Life of Adam and Eve*' in Lovering 1994: 294–300.

Peleg, Yifat. 2002. 'Gender and Ossuaries: Ideology and Meaning.' *Bulletin of the American Schools of Oriental Research* 325: 65–73.

Peristiany, J.G. (ed.). 1966. *Honour and Shame.* Chicago: University of Chicago Press.

Peristiany, J.G., and Julian Pitt-Rivers (eds). 1992. *Honour and Grace in Anthropology.* Cambridge: Cambridge University Press.

Petersen, William L. 1992. '*Diatessaron.*' *ABD* 2: 189–90.

_____. 1997. 'From Justin to Pepys: The History of the Harmonized Gospel Tradition.' *Studia Patristica* 30: 71–96.

_____. 2002. 'The Genesis of the Gospels' in A. Denaux (ed.), *New Testament Criticism and Exegesis: Festschrift J. Delobel.* Leuven: Leuven University Press: 33–65.

Pettorelli, J.-P. 1998. '*La Vie latine d'Adam et Ève.*' *Archivum latinitatis medii aevi* 56: 5–104.

_____. 1999a. '*La Vie latine d'Adam et Ève.* Analyse de la tradition manuscrite.' *Apocrypha* 10: 195–296.

_____. 1999b. '*Vie latine d'Adam et Ève.* La recension de Paris, BNF, lat. 3832.' *Archivum latinitatis medii aevi* 57: 5–52.

_____. 2002. 'Deux témoins latins singuliers de *la Vie d'Adam et Ève.* Paris, BNF, Lat. 3832 & Milan, B. Ambrosiana, O 35 Sup.' *JSJ* 33: 1–27.

_____. 2004. 'Essai sur la structure primitive de *la Vie d'Adam et Ève.*' *Apocrypha* 14: 237–56.

Pilch, J.J. 1981. 'Biblical Leprosy and Body Symbolism.' *BTB* 11: 109–13.

_____. 1994. 'A Window into the Biblical World: Cosmetics and Jewellery.' *The Bible Today* 32: 300–05.

Pilch, J.J., and B.J. Malina. 1993. *Biblical Social Values and their Social Meaning. A Handbook.* Peabody, MA: Hendrickson.

Piñero, A. 1993. 'Angels and Demons in the Greek *Life of Adam and Eve.*' *JSJ* 24: 191–214.

Pitt-Rivers, J. 1979. *The Fate of Shechem or the Politics of Sex: Essays in the Anthropology of the Mediterranean.* Cambridge: Cambridge University Press.

Polhemus, T. 1978. *Fashion and Anti-Fashion: An Anthropology of Clothing and Adornment.* London: Thames and Hudson.

Porter, J.I. (ed.). 1999. *Constructions of the Classical Body.* Michigan: University of Michigan Press.

Porton, Gary. 1981. 'Defining Midrash' in J. Neusner (ed.), *The Study of Ancient Judaism I: Mishnah, Midrash, Siddur.* New York: Ktav: 77–85.

_____. 2001. 'Rabbinic Midrash' in J. Neusner (ed.), *Judaism in Late Antiquity.* 3 vols. Boston/Leiden: Brill Academic: 1.217–36.

_____. 2003. 'Rabbinic Midrash' in Hauser and Watson 2003: 198–224.

Propp, Vladimir. 1968. *The Morphology of the Folktale.* London/Austin: University of Texas.

Prouser, O.H. 1996. 'Suited to the Throne: The Symbolic Use of Clothing in the David and Saul Narratives.' *JSOT* 71: 27–37.

_____. 1998. 'Clothes Maketh the Man.' *BRev* 14: 22–27.

Rabichev, R. 1996. 'Honor and Shame.' *Religion and Theology* 3: 51–63.

_____. 2000. 'The Mediterranean Concepts of Honor and Shame as Seen in the Depiction of Biblical Women.' *University of South Africa Journal* 31: 1–9.

Radley, A. 1990. *The Body and Social Psychology.* New York: Springer-Verlag.

Reed, Walter L. 1993. *Dialogues of the Word: The Bible as Literature According to Bakhtin.* New York: Oxford University Press.

Reinhartz, Adele. 1997. 'Feminist Criticism and Biblical Studies on the Verge of the Twenty-First Century' in A. Brenner and C. Fontaine (eds), *Reading the Bible: Approaches, Methods and Strategies. A Feminist Companion to Reading the Bible.* Sheffield: Sheffield Academic Press: 30–38.

Ri, Andreas Su-Min. 2000. *Commentaire de la* Caverne des Trésors. *Étude sur l'histoire du texte et de ses sources.* Leuven: Peeters.

Roach, M.E., and J.B. Eicher (eds). 1965. *Dress, Adornment and the Social Order*. New York: John Wiley & Sons.

Roach-Higgins, M.E., and J.B. Eicher. 1992. 'Dress and Identity.' *Clothing and Textiles Research Journal* 10: 1–8.

Robinson, Stephen Edward. 1982. *The Testament of Adam*. SBLDS 52. Chico, CA: Scholars Press.

Roest, Bert, and H. Vanstiphout (eds). 1999. *Aspects of Genre and Type in Pre-Modern Literary Cultures*. Groningen: Styx.

Rohde, Erwin. 1925. *Psyche: The Cult of Souls and the Belief in Immortality among the Greeks*. Translated from the 8th edn by W.B. Hillis. London: Routledge & Kegan Paul, 1925; reprinted by Routledge, 2000.

Rooke, Deborah W. (ed.). 2007. *A Question of Sex? Gender and Difference in the Hebrew Bible and Beyond*. Sheffield: Sheffield Phoenix.

Rosencranz, M.L. 1972. *Clothing Concepts: A Social-Psychological Approach*. New York: Macmillan.

Rosenmeyer, Thomas G. 2006. 'Ancient Literary Genres: A Mirage?' in Andrew Laird (ed.), *Oxford Readings in Ancient Literary Criticism*. Oxford: University Press: 421–39.

Ross, Susan A. 1991. Review of *Carnal Knowing: Female Nakedness and Religious Meaning in the Christian West* by Margaret R. Wiles. 1989. Boston: Beacon Press. *Journal of the History of Sexuality* 2: 293–95.

Rowland, Christopher. 1982. *The Open Heaven: A Study of Apocalyptic in Judaism and Early Christianity*. London: SPCK.

Rudofsky, B. 1971. *The Unfashionable Human Body*. Garden City, NY: Doubleday.

Rush, Alfred C. 1941. *Death and Burial in Christian Antiquity*. Washington, DC: Catholic University Press of America.

Ruzer, Serge. 2001. '*The Cave of Treasures* on Swearing by Abel's Blood and Expulsion from Paradise: Two Exegetical Motifs in Context.' *JECS* 9: 251–71.

Sacchi, P. 1997. *Jewish Apocalyptic and Its History*. Sheffield: Sheffield Academic Press.

Safrai, Shmuel. 1987. 'Home and Family' in S. Safrai *et al.* (eds), *The Jewish People in the First Century*. 2 vols. Philadelphia: Fortress Press; Assen/Maastricht: Van Gorcum: 1.728–92.

Sarna, Nahum M. 1989. *Genesis*. JPS Torah Commentary. Philadelphia/New York/Jerusalem: Jewish Publication Society.

Satlow, Michael L. 1997. 'Jewish Constructions of Nakedness in Late Antiquity.' *Journal of Biblical Literature* 116: 429–54.

Sault, N. (ed.). 1994. *Many Mirrors: Body Image and Social Relations*. New Brunswick, NJ: Rutgers University Press.

Schaberg, Jane. 2002. *The Resurrection of Mary Magdalene: Legends, Apocrypha, and the Christian Testament*. New York, NY: Continuum.

Schäfer, Peter. 1992. *The Hidden and Manifest God: Some Themes in Early Jewish Mysticism*. Translated by A. Pomerance. Albany: SUNY.

Schiffman, Lawrence H. 1982. 'Merkavah Speculation at Qumran: The 4Q Serekh Shirot "Olat ha-Shabbat"' in J. Reinharz and D. Swetschinski (eds), *Mystics, Philosophers, and Politicians: Essays in Jewish Intellectual History in Honor of A. Altmann*. Durham, NC: Duke University Press: 15–47.

Schippers, Anda. 1999. 'The Fable Is Dead; Long Live the Fable! Or, Is There Any Life after Genre?' in Roest and Vanstiphout (eds), 1999: 71–78.

Schmidt, K.L. 1923. 'Die Stellung der Evangelien in der allgemeinen Literaturgeschichte' in Hans Schmidt (ed.), *Eucharisterion. Studien zur Religion und Literatur des Alten und Neuen Testaments.* 2 vols. Göttingen: Vandenhoeck & Ruprecht: 2:50–134.

Schneider, C. 1969. *Kulturgeschichte des Hellenismus.* 2 vols. Munich.

Schneider, Jane. 1971. 'Of Vigilance and Virgins: Honor, Shame and Access to Resources in Mediterranean Societies.' *Ethnology* 10: 1–24.

Scholem, Gershom. 1941. *Major Trends in Jewish Mysticism.* Jerusalem: Schocken.

_____. 1960. *Jewish Gnosticism, Merkavah Mysticism and Talmudic Tradition.* New York: Jewish Theological Seminary of America.

Scholes, Robert. 1977. 'An Approach through Genre' in Mark Spilka (ed.), *Towards a Poetics of Fiction.* Bloomington/London: Indiana University Press: 41–51.

Schroeder, Joy A. 1997. 'The Rape of Dinah: Luther's Interpretation of a Biblical Narrative.' *Sixteenth Century Journal* 27: 775–91.

Schürer, Emil. 1973–87. *The History of the Jewish People in the Age of Jesus Christ (175 bc–ad 135).* Rev. and ed., G. Vermes, F. Millar, and M. Black. 4 vols. Edinburgh: T. & T. Clark.

Schüssler-Fiorenza, Elisabeth. 1985. *Bread Not Stone: The Challenge of Feminist Biblical Interpretation.* Boston: Beacon Press.

Schüssler-Fiorenza, Elisabeth (ed.). 1976. *Aspects of Religious Propaganda in Judaism and Early Christianity.* Notre Dame/London: University of Notre Dame Press.

_____. 1993. *Searching the Scriptures: A Feminist Introduction.* New York: Crossroad.

Scott, S., and D. Morgan (eds). 1993. *Body Matters: Essays on the Sociology of the Body.* London: The Falmer Press.

Segal, Alan F. 1980. 'Heavenly Ascent in Hellenistic Judaism, Early Christianity and Their Environment.' *ANRW* II.23.2: 1333–91.

_____. 2004. *Life after Death: A History of the Afterlife in the Religions of the West.* New York: Doubleday.

Shapiro, Alan. 1991. 'The Iconography of Mourning in Athenian Art.' *AJA* 95: 629–56.

Sharpe, John L. III. 1969. 'Prolegomena to the Establishment of the Critical Text of the *Greek Apocalypse of Moses*.' Unpublished doctoral dissertation. Duke University.

_____. 1973. 'The Second Adam in the *Apocalypse of Moses*.' *CBQ* 35: 35–46.

Shilling, C. 1992. *The Body and Social Theory.* London: Sage Publications.

Shuler, Philip. 1982. *A Genre for the Gospels: The Biographical Character of Matthew.* Philadelphia: Fortress Press.

Simms, Ronda R. 1998. 'Mourning and Community at the Athenian Adonia.' *CJ* 93: 121–41.

Sluiter, Ineke. 2000. 'The Dialectics of Genre: Some Aspects of Secondary Literature and Genre in Antiquity' in Mary Depew and Dirk Obbink (eds), *Matrices of Genre: Authors, Canons, and Society.* Cambridge, MA/London: Harvard University Press: 183–203.

Sly, Dorothy. 1990. *Philo's Perception of Women.* Atlanta: Scholars Press.

Smith, Morton. 1981. 'Ascent to the Heavens and the Beginnings of Christianity.' *Eranos Jahrbuch* 50: 403–29.

Smyth, Herbert Weir. 1963. *Greek Melic Poets.* New York: Biblo and Tannen.

Soggin, Alberto J. 1975. *The Old Testament and Oriental Studies.* Biblical Institute Press. BibOr 29.

Sourvinou-Inwood, Christiane. 1995. *'Reading' Greek Death: To the End of the Classical Period.* Oxford: Clarendon Press.

_____. 2004. 'Gendering the Athenian Funeral: Ritual Reality and Tragic Manipulations' in Dimitrios Yatromanolakis (ed.), *Greek Ritual Poetics.* Cambridge, MA/London: Harvard University Press: 160–88.

Stanton, Graham. 1992. 'Matthew: βίβλος, Εὐαγγέλιον or Βίος? ' in F. Van Segbroeck *et al.* (eds), *The Four Gospels.* Vol. 2: 1187–201.

_____. 2004. *Jesus and Gospel.* Cambridge: Cambridge University Press.

Starr Sered, Susan. 1994. *Priestess, Mother, Sacred Sister: Religions Dominated by Women.* New York/London: Oxford University Press.

Staubli, T., and S. Schroer (eds). 1999. *Body Symbolism in the Bible.* Collegeville, MN: The Liturgical Press.

Stauffer, E. 1955. *New Testament Theology.* London: SCM Press.

Stears, Karen. 1998. 'Death Becomes Her: Gender and Athenian Death Ritual' in Sue Blundell and Margaret Williamson (eds), *The Sacred and the Feminine.* London/New York: Routledge: 89–100.

Stegemann, W., B.J. Malina, and G. Theissen (eds), 2002. *Jesus and the Gospels.* Minneapolis: Fortress Press.

Steinberg, Leo. 1975. 'Eve's Idle Hand.' *Art Journal* 35: 130–35.

Sternberg, Meir. 1985. *The Poetics of Biblical Narrative: Ideological Literature and the Drama of Reading.* Bloomington: Indiana University Press.

Stone, Michael E. 1990. *Fourth Ezra: A Commentary on the Book of Fourth Ezra.* Hermeneia, Minneapolis: Fortress Press.

_____. 1992. *A History of the Literature of Adam and Eve.* SBLEJL 3. Atlanta: Scholars Press.

_____. 1993. 'The Fall of Satan and Adam's Penance: Three Notes on the Books of Adam and Eve.' *JTS* 44: 143–56.

_____. 2000. 'The Angelic Prediction in the Primary Adam Books' in Anderson *et al.*, 2000: 111–31.

_____. 2002. *Adam's Contract with Satan: The Legend of the Cheirograph of Adam.* Bloomington/Minneapolis: Indiana University Press.

Stone (ed.), Michael E. 1984. *Jewish Writings in the Second Temple Period.* CRINT 2. Assen: Van Gorcum / Philadelphia: Fortress Press.

Stout, Ann M. 1994. 'Jewelry as a Symbol of Status in the Roman Empire' in Judith Lynn Sebesta and Larissa Bonfante (eds), *The World of Roman Costume.* Madison: University of Wisconsin Press: 77–100.

Strack, H.L. 1959. *Introduction to the Talmud and Midrash.* Philadelphia/New York: Jewish Publication Society/Meridian.

Strelka, Joseph P. (ed.). 1978. *Theories of Literary Genre.* University Park/London: Pennsylvania State University Press.

Stuhlmacher, Peter (ed.). 1991. *The Gospel and the Gospels.* Grand Rapids: Eerdmans.

Swartz, Mark J. 1988. 'Shame, Culture, and Status among the Swahili of Mombasa.' *Ethos* 16: 21–51.

Sweeney, S.T., and I. Hodder (eds). 2002. *Body.* Cambridge: Cambridge University Press.

Sweet, Anne Marie. 1992. 'A Religio-Historical Study of the *Greek Life of Adam and Eve.*' Unpublished doctoral dissertation. University of Notre Dame.

Synnott, A. 1992. *The Body Social: Symbolism, Self and Society.* London/New York: Routledge.

Tabor, James D. 1986. *Things Unutterable: Paul's Ascent to Paradise in Its Greco-Roman, Judaic, and Early Christian Contexts.* Lanham, MD: University Press of America.

Talbert, Charles H. 1977. *What is a Gospel? The Genre of the Canonical Gospels.* Philadelphia: Fortress Press.

Taylor, Joan E. 2003. *Jewish Women Philosophers of First-Century Alexandria: Philo's 'Therapeutae' Reconsidered.* Oxford: Oxford University Press.

Terry, J., and J. Urla (eds). 1995. *Deviant Bodies: Critical Perspectives on Difference in Science and Popular Culture.* Bloomington: Indiana University Press.

Tertullian, 'On the Apparel of Women.' 1890. Translated by S. Thelwall in Alexander Roberts and James Donaldson (eds). *The Ante-Nicene Fathers.* Vol. 4. Buffalo: Christian Literature Publishing Company.

'Theophilus to Autolycus.' 1885. Translated by Marcus Dods, in Alexander Roberts and James Donaldson (eds). *The Ante-Nicene Fathers.* Vol. 2. Buffalo: Christian Literature Publishing Company.

Tischendorf, C. Von. 1866. *Apocalypses Apocryphae Mosis, Esdrae, Pauli, Iohanni.* Leipzig: Mendelssohn. Repr. Olms, 1966.

Todorov, Tzvetan. 1990. *Genres in Discourse.* Cambridge: Cambridge University Press.

Toynbee, J.M.C. 1971. *Death and Burial in the Roman World.* Ithaca, NY: Cornell University Press.

Trebolle Barrera, J. 1998. *The Jewish Bible and the Christian Bible.* Leiden/New York/Köln: Brill.

Trenchard, Warren C. 1982. *Ben Sira's View of Women: A Literary Analysis.* Chico, CA: Scholars Press.

Trible, Phyllis. 1978. *God and the Rhetoric of Sexuality.* Philadelphia: Fortress Press.

Tromp, Johannes. 1997. 'Literary and Exegetical Issues in the Story of Adam's Death and Burial (*GLAE* 31–42)' in J. Frishman and L. van Rompay (eds), *The Book of Genesis in Jewish and Oriental Christian Interpretation: A Collection of Essays.* Leuven: Peeters: 25–41.

————. 2000. 'Cain and Abel in the Greek and Armenian/Georgian Recensions of the *Life of Adam and Eve*' in Anderson *et al.*, 2000: 277–96.

————. 2002. 'The Textual History of the *Life of Adam and Eve* in the Light of a Newly Discovered Text-Form.' *JSJ* 33: 28–41.

————. 2003. 'The Role of Omissions in the History of the Literary Development of the Greek *Life of Adam and Eve.*' *Apocrypha* 14: 257–75.

————. 2004. 'The Story of Our Lives: The *qz*-Text of the *Life of Adam and Eve*, the Apostle Paul, and the Jewish-Christian Oral Tradition concerning Adam and Eve.' *NTS* 50: 205–23.

————. 2005. *The Life of Adam and Eve in Greek. A Critical Edition.* PVTG 6. Leiden/Boston: Brill.

Turner, B.S. 1991. *The Body: Social Process and Cultural Theory.* London: Sage Publications.

————. 1996. *The Body and Society: Explorations in Social Theory.* Thousand Oaks, CA: Sage Publications.

van den Hoek, Annewies. 2000. 'Endowed with Reason or Glued to the Senses: Philo's Thoughts on Adam and Eve' in Gerard P. Luttikhuizen (ed.), *The Creation of Man and Woman: Interpretations of the Biblical Narratives in Jewish and Christian Traditions.* Leiden/Boston/Köln: Brill: 63–75.

van der Horst, Pieter W. 1998. 'Conflicting Images of Women in Ancient Judaism' in Pieter W. van der Horst, *Hellenism–Judaism–Christianity: Essays on Their Interaction.* 2nd edn. Leuven: Peeters: 73–92.

Van der Toorn, Karel. 1994. *From Her Cradle to Her Grave: The Role of Religion in the Life of the Israelite and the Babylonian Woman.* Sheffield: JSOT Press.

van Gennep, A. 1960. *The Rites of Passage.* Chicago: University of Chicago Press.

Vermes, Geza. 1973. *Scripture and Tradition in Judaism: Haggadah.* Studia Post-Biblica 4. 2nd edn. Leiden: Brill.

Vermeule, Emily. 1979. *Aspects of Death in Early Greek Art and Poetry.* Berkeley: University of California Press.

Von Nordheim, Eckhard. 1980, 1985. *Die Lehre der Alten.* 2 vols. Leiden: Brill.

von Rad, Gerhard. 1972. *Genesis: A Commentary.* London: SCM Press.

Vorster, Willem S. 1992. 'Gospel Genre' in *ABD* II: 1077–79.

Wandrey, Irina. 2007. 'Mourning Rituals for Women and for Men' in Tal Ilan, Tamara Or, Dorothea M. Salzer, Christiane Steuer and Irina Wandrey (eds), *A Feminist Commentary on the Babylonian Talmud: Introduction and Studies.* Tübingen: Mohr Siebeck: 269–88.

Weidman, Amanda. 2003. 'Review: Beyond Honor and Shame: Performing Gender in the Mediterranean.' *AQ* 76: 519–30.

Wenham, Gordon J. 1987. *Genesis 1–15.* WBC 1. Waco: Word.

Westermann, Claus. 1984. *Genesis 1–11: A Commentary.* Minneapolis: Augsburg.

Wikan, Unni. 1984. 'Shame and Honour: A Contestable Pair.' *Man* 19: 635–52.

Winston, David. 1979. *The Wisdom of Solomon.* AB 43. Garden City, NY: Doubleday.

Wolfson, Eliot R. 1993. 'Yeridah la-Merkavah: Typology of Ecstasy and Enthronement in Ancient Jewish Mysticism' in R.A. Herrera (ed.), *Mystics of the Book: Themes, Topics, and Typologies.* New York: Peter Lang: 13–44.

———. 1994. *Through a Speculum that Shines: Vision and Imagination in Medieval Jewish Mysticism.* Princeton: Princeton University Press.

Wright, Addison G. 1966. 'The Literary Genre Midrash.' *CBQ* 28: 105–38.

Wyke, M. 1994. 'Women in the Mirror: The Rhetoric of Adornment in the Roman World' in Archer *et al.,* 1994: 134–51.

———. 1997. *Parchments of Gender: Deciphering the Bodies of Antiquity.* Oxford: Clarendon Press.

———. 1998. *Gender and the Body in the Ancient Mediterranean World.* Oxford: Blackwell Publishers.

Young, Serenity. 1993. *An Anthology of Sacred Texts by and about Women.* New York: Crossroad.

Zeitlin, Froma I. 1999. 'Reflections on Erotic Desire in Archaic and Classical Greek' in Porter (ed.), 1999: 50–73.

Zlotnick, Dov. 1966. *The Tractate 'Mourning.'* New Haven/London: Yale University Press.

ANCIENT SOURCES INDEX

SUBJECT INDEX

AUTHOR INDEX

187

Lightning Source UK Ltd.
Milton Keynes UK
UKOW04n0252190118

316444UK00010B/338/P